The Royal Navy, Seapower and Strategy between the Wars

The Royal Navy, Seapower and Strategy between the Wars

Christopher M. Bell

Stanford University Press
Stanford, California

Stanford University Press
Stanford, California

© Christopher M. Bell, 2000

First published 2000 by Macmillan Press Ltd, Houndmills, Basingstoke,
Hampshire RG21 6XS

First published in the U.S.A. by Stanford University Press, 2000

Printed in Great Britain

Cloth ISBN 0–8047–3978–1

Library of Congress Card Number: 99–69170

This book is printed on acid-free paper.

To my parents

Contents

List of Maps

List of Tables

Acknowledgements

I have incurred many debts in the course of completing this book. In particular, I wish to thank John Ferris, who first suggested this subject and offered wise counsel and encouragement at every stage of its progress. Holger Herwig and Andrew Lambert deserve special thanks as well for their valuable advice and generous assistance over the years. I must also express my gratitude to Edward S. Miller and John Beeler for their comments on earlier versions of this work, and to Clare Scammell, Orest Babij, Edward Ingram, Pascal Barras, Caroline Alton, and Ronald I. Cohen.

I have benefited from the courtesy and helpfulness of the staffs of the Public Record Office, the National Maritime Museum, the Churchill College Archives Centre, the Sea Cadet Corps Headquarters, the Wiltshire County Records Office, and the Sir Basil Liddell Hart Archives Centre. I am indebted to these institutions for permission to examine and quote from papers in their possession. Documents in the Public Record Office and all other material under crown copyright are cited by permission of the Controller of Her Majesty's Stationery Office.

My greatest debt is to my wife, Rae, whose unfailing support over many years of research and study made this possible.

List of Abbreviations

ACNS	Assistant Chief of the Naval Staff
ADB	American–Dutch–British
ADM	Admiralty
AGNA	Anglo-German Naval Agreement
ASW	anti-submarine warfare
ATB	Advisory Committee on Trade Questions in Time of War
BAD	British Admiralty Delegation, Washington
BOT	Board of Trade
CAS	Chief of Air Staff
CID	Committee of Imperial Defence
CIGS	Chief of the Imperial General Staff
C-in-C	Commander-in-Chief
CNS	Chief of the Naval Staff
COS	Chiefs of Staff Committee
CP	Cabinet Paper
DCNS	Deputy Chief of the Naval Staff
DNC	Director of Naval Construction
DNI	Director of Naval Intelligence
DNO	Director of Naval Ordnance
D of C	Director of Contracts
D of P	Director of Plans
D of T	Director of Training
DOT	Department of Overseas Trade
DPP	Defence Plans (Policy) Sub-Committee
DPR	Defence Plans (Requirements) Sub-Committee
DPR (DR)	Sub-Committee on Defence Policy and Requirements: Defence Requirements Enquiry
DRC	Defence Requirements Committee
DTSD	Director of Training and Staff Duties
E in C	Engineer in Chief
FAA	Fleet Air Arm
FC	Finance Committee
FO	Foreign Office
FPC	Foreign Policy Committee
HMG	His Majesty's Government
HMS	His Majesty's Ship

IIC	Industrial Intelligence Centre
IJN	Imperial Japanese Navy
JPC	Joint Planning Committee
MNBDO	Mobile Naval Base Defence Organisation
NID	Naval Intelligence Division
NPC	Naval Personnel Committee
NSC	Sub-Committee on the Question of the Capital Ship in the Navy
PD	Plans Division
RAF	Royal Air Force
RN	Royal Navy
SAC	Strategic Appreciation Committee
USN	United States Navy
VCNS	Vice-Chief of the Naval Staff
WO	War Office

Introduction

The importance of the sea remained an article of faith in Great Britain during the interwar period, not only to members of the naval profession, but also to the decision-making elites and general public. Ramsay MacDonald, Britain's first Labour Prime Minister, was expressing a widely held conviction when he stated that the 'way of Great Britain is on the sea...The stock of its people came dashing across the sea; its defence and its highroads have been the sea; its flag *is* a flag of the sea. Our Navy is no mere superfluity to us. It *is* us.'[1] His successor, Stanley Baldwin, claimed that 'There are facts which surely no sane person can dispute: They are that our Navy is essential to our existence, to the maintenance of our trade routes, to the protection of the ships which bring our daily food, and to the security of our Empire.'[2] Winston Churchill claimed that 'Great Britain, since the most remote time, had always been supreme at sea. The life of the nation, its culture, its prosperity, had rested on that basis.'[3] Views such as these cut across class and party lines during the years between the two world wars. The British people readily acknowledged that Britain's empire, trade, and status as a great power had all been derived from the sea, and they expected politicians to protect the state's maritime interests. Decision-makers shared these sentiments and reacted firmly when Britain's maritime position appeared to be threatened from abroad. Even Robert Cecil, the architect of the League of Nations and a leading advocate of disarmament, insisted in 1919 that 'if I were British Minister of the Navy and I saw that British naval safety was being threatened even by America, I should have to recommend to my fellow country men to spend their last shilling in bringing our fleet up to the point which I was advised was necessary for safety.'[4]

Despite this apparent unanimity, maritime supremacy passed from Great Britain to the United States during the course of the Second World War. Traditional interpretations of the decline of British seapower have focused on economic factors and the strategic decision-making process.[5] According to the conventional view, after the First World War Britain's economy was no longer capable of sustaining the armed forces needed to protect its sprawling empire, and could not compete with the superior financial and industrial resources of the United States. This decline was exacerbated by poor strategic decisions. Britain's statesmen, it is argued, were mired in liberal values and lacked the ruthlessness necessary to hold onto a great empire. They mistakenly trusted in arms limitation agreements and poured money into costly social programs at the expense of the armed services. Naval leaders of the interwar period have also been criticized for their part in this process. Most importantly, it is claimed that these men failed to recognize that advances in military aviation had degraded the importance of seapower; they built vessels poorly suited to Britain's strategic requirements; they neglected the threat from Nazi Germany and concentrated on the lesser danger from Japan; and they developed fundamentally flawed strategies to meet these perils.

For a generation of scholars, the history of Britain's interwar navy has been dominated by Stephen Roskill's *Naval Policy Between the Wars*.[6] The scope and seeming authority of this work have tended to stifle serious study of British naval history during this period. Recently, however, historians have begun to challenge orthodox views on this subject. New scholarship has suggested that the decline of Britain's power in general, and of its seapower in particular, have been greatly exaggerated.[7] Revisionist studies of the interwar navy now point towards an officer corps more far-sighted and professionally competent than conventional accounts would suggest.[8] Yet the image of a reactionary, intellectually deficient service remains pervasive. The assumption underlying most criticisms is that the British naval officer corps fundamentally misunderstood the nature, meaning, and utility of seapower.

The term 'seapower' was coined by Alfred Thayer Mahan in the late nineteenth century, and is open to a range of interpretations.[9] Like most of his successors, Mahan regarded this concept as encompassing the combination of naval superiority, maritime commerce, and overseas colonies which produced national wealth and world-power status. Admiral Sir Herbert Richmond defined it as 'that form of national strength which enables its possessor to send his armies and commerce across those stretches of sea and ocean which lie between his country or the country of his allies, and those territories to which he needs access in war; and to prevent his enemy from doing the same.'[10] This definition has gained wide acceptance, but theorists and historians still question what advantages states gain from the possession of seapower, and how that form of national strength is most effectively applied to further the ends of policy. This study does not seek to answer these questions; rather, it examines how British naval leaders of the interwar period answered them.

The ideas of naval decision-makers about seapower have seldom been treated as a significant and coherent subject. Historians have often considered the views of writers like Mahan, Richmond, and Sir Julian Corbett on these issues, and they have even attempted to trace the influence of these individuals on the formulation of policy. But they have not systematically analyzed the thoughts of the decision-making elites who directed naval policy on a day-by-day basis, or how these ideas affected their actions. As a result, our understanding of those actions is flawed. The navy's decisions are often made to appear inexplicable or misguided by those who treat the service as a 'rational actor,' whose actions can be explained and judged entirely by their outcome.[11] The navy's aims and calculations only begin to make sense, however, when the basic assumptions underlying them are taken into account. This book identifies and analyzes the central body of ideas which guided naval policy-makers during the interwar period, and explores how these ideas influenced Britain's naval and strategic policies. This methodology has recently been used to illuminate the actions of Britain's policy-making elites on a range of other issues.[12] Here it will be applied principally to the naval profession, a group which is often thought to have held no important ideas of its own, but which did in fact possess distinct views about the nature and application of seapower.

The first chapter of this study focuses on the Royal Navy as a bureaucratic institution and considers its efforts to secure funds for warship construction and other vital instruments of seapower. Even though the importance of seapower was generally accepted by Britain's decision-making elites, there was no agreement on what seapower was, how it worked, or what was required to maintain it. As a result, naval leaders often found themselves isolated on crucial issues like the size of navy Britain needed, and the role of seapower in British grand strategy. Politicians and Treasury officials seldom accepted the navy's estimation of its strategic requirements, and the Admiralty's ability to obtain money depended on how far its strategic views were shared by the rest of Whitehall.

The ongoing struggle over the size of naval estimates was dominated by the question of naval 'standards,' a subject whose meaning and importance have frequently been misunderstood. Historians have often mistakenly conflated the 'one-power standard' with the navy's appreciation of its strategic requirements or with the real nature of British seapower. They have seldom noted or appreciated the significance of the different definitions of this standard which were promulgated during this period, and they have not fully understood the importance of the navy's struggle to secure a 'new standard' of naval strength during the 1930s. Naval standards were, in fact, little more than a bureaucratic bargaining tool, and only by viewing them from this perspective is it possible to understand how the navy attempted to secure the resources it needed.

Chapters 2–6 deal with perceptions of the utility and application of seapower in wartime. They consider the navy's views on what seapower could accomplish against Britain's enemies, how it should be employed to achieve these ends, and the relationship of the navy to the other fighting services. They also analyze how closely the navy's ideas on these subjects corresponded to those of Mahan and Corbett, whose theoretical concepts have dominated recent discussions of naval strategy and seapower.[13] The influence of Mahan on the interwar navy is widely taken for granted, and his ideas are credited with forging a service obsessed with fleet actions, big-gunned battleships, and decisive sea battles. Corbett's impact, on the other hand, is regarded as negligible, because his theoretical writings are considered too unorthodox and sophisticated for the naval profession. Both assumptions are wrong. Many of Corbett's ideas *were* accepted by the navy during the interwar period, while those of Mahan had far less influence than is usually allowed. However, the navy's ideas of seapower and naval strategy do not fit neatly into either a 'Mahanian' or a 'Corbettian' paradigm. The British naval profession possessed its own distinct views on these questions.

Because these ideas were usually articulated only in vague terms, they must be inferred from a variety of sources, the most valuable being the Admiralty's war plans and strategic appreciations. Even though few of the navy's peacetime plans were ever implemented, these documents represent the only systematic attempt by Britain's naval leadership to come to grips with the questions posed above. In effect, they are the navy's 'best guess' as to what seapower could accomplish in future conflicts, and as such they provide a valuable window into the mind of the naval profession. The navy's war plans have never been systematically examined, however.[14] Historians have often appraised British strategy for a war with Japan, but they have misunderstood the nature of that strategy because of their doubts about its feasibility. Preparations against Nazi Germany, on the other hand, are often judged solely by the navy's performance in the Battle of the Atlantic. Naval plans against Italy are usually viewed only in relation to their effect on grand strategy, while plans against Germany and Japan are frequently removed from their grand strategic context altogether. The application of seapower against other major powers such as the United States is seldom considered at all. These chapters examine the navy's war plans, on a country-by-country basis, in order to build up a picture of what naval decision-makers believed seapower could accomplish against its enemies, and how they attempted to shape British grand strategy to meet the threats posed by potentially hostile powers.

Chapter 7 considers some of the problems involved in maintaining and exploiting seapower in peacetime. It focuses on two recurring issues: how capital ships could be employed as a diplomatic tool in the Far East; and the links between the navy, national prestige, foreign trade, and the naval armaments industry. Finally, this book explores the Admiralty's efforts to shape the British public's ideas about the navy and seapower. Naval officers of this period were inclined to regard anything resembling outright publicity as vulgar and undignified, but their objections were gradually undermined by the realization that public support for naval expenditure could not be taken for granted. In an era of financial stringency, widespread indifference to military matters, and a growing fascination with air power, the navy increasingly felt that it must take an active role in educating the public on the importance of seapower. Chapter 8 examines how the navy became involved with propaganda during the 1920s, the means it employed to reach the British public, the ideas it sought to project, and how its reluctance to play the public card denied it a chance to strengthen the power of its political hand in Whitehall.

Each of these chapters provides a single piece of a larger puzzle. Taken as a whole, they provide an overview of the naval profession's ideas about the navy and seapower during the interwar period. These ideas were often crude and intuitive, but they nevertheless played a crucial role in shaping Britain's naval and strategic policies. Moreover, they were both more sophisticated and coherent than historians have recognized. This book examines how this body of ideas influenced British decision-making during this important period, how well the naval profession and decision-making elites understood the meaning and workings of seapower, and how effectively their policies met Britain's strategic requirements. It also considers whether the Royal Navy's failings during the Second World War can be traced to misconceptions about seapower during the interwar period. The intelligence and foresight of the British naval profession have frequently been questioned, yet the navy's objectives and policies can only be properly evaluated when its underlying ideas about seapower are understood.

1

The Politics of Seapower: the 'One-Power Standard' and British Maritime Security

From the late nineteenth century until the eve of the Second World War, Britain's naval requirements were formally calculated on the basis of officially sanctioned naval 'standards.' These standards specified which power, combination of powers, or number of powers Britain should match in naval strength, and normally resulted from a careful balancing of strategic, diplomatic, and financial considerations. Statesmen considered not only the size of navy needed to defend Britain's vital interests, but also how much the state could afford to spend, and which threats it could realistically expect to face. Insuring against all possible dangers with a massive and sustained naval construction program was prohibitively expensive and would have undermined Britain's economic strength, thereby weakening its overall strategic position. Moreover, the end result of such a program would have borne little relation to Britain's genuine security needs. Conversely, failure to provide against real threats would encourage aggressors and leave Britain dangerously exposed if war did occur. Responsible decision-makers agreed that the navy had to be strong enough to provide security against any reasonably probable foe, but also that expensive preparations against too many powers must be avoided. The responsibility for weighing these considerations and defining the navy's standard of strength rested with Britain's civil authorities. In theory, the Admiralty's role in this process was only an advisory one; in practice, however, the navy often exerted considerable influence over which standard the government adopted and how it was executed.

For most of the period between the two world wars, British naval strength was formally regulated by a 'one-power standard.' Historians have frequently misunderstood how this standard affected naval policy. In the first place, they have usually failed to note that the meaning of the standard varied considerably according to time and circumstances. As Captain Tom Phillips noted in 1937, 'The term "One-Power Naval Standard" is extremely vague and means different things to different people.'[1] Cabinets and cabinet committees modified the formal definition of the standard on a regular basis, while the Admiralty and Treasury engaged in a running battle over how these definitions would be interpreted and applied. Hence, generalizations about the meaning and significance of the standard seldom hold good for the whole of the period when it was in force. Other problems have arisen from the tendency to treat the one-power standard as synonymous with the terms of the Washington Naval Treaty. In fact, the standard had a life of its own. It was adopted before the Washington disarmament conference was held, and it remained in use after quantitative treaty limitations had disappeared. The Washington Treaty and its successors did indeed restrict the strength of the Royal Navy in certain classes of warship, but they did not lay down a *minimum* naval strength for Britain. Hence, the principal role of the one-power standard was to guide decision-makers in their deliberations over how much of the treaty figures Britain needed or could afford to maintain. The impact of quantitative treaty limitations on Britain's naval position and the effect of naval standards on the size and composition of the Royal Navy are almost entirely separate issues.[2]

Historians have also tended to conflate naval standards with actual seapower. They often suggest that the naval standard Britain maintained was synonymous with its real naval strength. Thus, it is argued that the adoption of a one-power standard after the First World War was a sign of Britain's relative decline as a great power – that a *one*-power standard was, by definition, inferior to the earlier *two*-power standard, irrespective of Britain's security requirements or the size of the foreign navies in question. The one-power standard has also been identified as the reason why the navy was under-strength during the 1930s, when Britain faced no less than three potentially hostile powers. Moreover, some historians have implied that the navy accepted this standard because it either miscalculated or misunderstood how great its requirements would be in the event of a war on two or three fronts. These charges are groundless. The one-power standard was imposed on the navy from above, and the Admiralty struggled to meet its strategic requirements as best it could within this framework. During the 1920s, a one-power standard relative to the United States met Britain's real strategic needs as well as the two-power standard had after 1889.

When this was no longer the case, the Admiralty attempted to replace the existing formula with a 'new standard' defined by strategic considerations. Naval decision-makers were well aware of the shortcomings of the one-power standard, and they tried to overcome them by interpreting the standard in ways which would meet Britain's strategic requirements. The naval standards of this period therefore had little to do with Britain's ability to defend its vital interests, but they did play a critical role in the Admiralty's ongoing struggle with the Treasury over the size of the Navy Estimates on a year-to-year basis.

When Lord George Hamilton, the First Lord of the Admiralty in Lord Salisbury's second Cabinet, introduced the Naval Defence Act of 1889, he informed Parliament that the government had 'determined that our new shipbuilding programme should be based upon the fully ascertained requirements of the nation.'

> It is an easy thing to say to the experts, 'Tell us what the requirements of the nation are,' but unless the experts know what is the basis upon which they are to calculate the requirements of the nation, they cannot arrive at a satisfactory conclusion. Therefore Her Majesty's Government directed my advisers to prepare a scheme which should make our naval establishment in 1894 equal to the naval establishments of any two nations.[3]

Between 1889 and 1909, successive British governments formally committed themselves to maintaining the navy at this level of strength, which soon became known as the 'two-power standard.'[4] Calculating the size of the navy in this manner was not a marked departure from earlier practices, but this was the first time that such a formula was promulgated as high policy. It was not long before the two-power standard began to take on an air of inviolability. Governments found it a useful means of quantifying Britain's naval requirements; the navy valued it as a reliable basis for long-term planning; the public viewed it as a reasonable method of placing Britain's maritime security above party politics; and opposition politicians found it a convenient tool for gaining political capital at the government's expense. Once the standard became entrenched in British political life, it became difficult for any government to consider abandoning it without facing a public and political outcry.

The precise meaning of the two-power standard was ambiguous. The goal of politicians in formulating any naval standard was always to ensure 'reasonable security' against foreign threats, but what this actually entailed was open to dispute on a range of points. Given the magnitude of the stakes involved – the survival of the British Empire – many statesmen believed that no risk should be tolerated, however remote it might appear. This view was shared by members of the naval profession, who sometimes pressed it to extreme lengths. Others held that some threats could be accepted without endangering British security, and that efforts to over-insure through large naval construction programs were irresponsible, and might be either diplomatically or financially counterproductive.

Hamilton's statements on the meaning of the two-power standard were deliberately vague and provided little guidance for his successors. The first practical issue to crop up was the ratio of strength needed to achieve equality with the next two naval powers. Did equality mean only numerical equality in warships, or, given the issues at stake and the wide range of duties the navy must perform, was a margin of superiority actually required? Furthermore, should a single ratio be applied to all classes of warships, or did battleships and cruisers require separate treatment? On the latter question a consensus gradually emerged that the standard was only applicable to battleships. Lord Selborne, the First Lord of the Admiralty in Arthur Balfour's Cabinet, informed Parliament in 1903 that

> in respect to cruisers and torpedo craft the [two power] standard has never had a real application, because the strength there must be in proportion to the work the Navy has to perform; and it has never been possible to assess that in proportion to the cruisers and torpedo craft of the next two naval Powers.[5]

But while naval decision-makers always held that 'a larger margin over mere numerical equality is absolutely necessary as regards vessels of this class,'[6] it was only in 1914, after the two-power standard had been superseded, that a definite formula was applied to cruisers. This standard – 100 per cent superiority over Germany alone – was announced in March 1914 by the First Lord of the Admiralty, Winston Churchill, but the Admiralty was, in fact, already working to it when he arrived in 1911.[7]

How to apply the two-power standard to battleships was another matter. Some, such as Lord Goschen, argued that numerical equality in this class would still give Britain superiority in fighting power, in view of

> the immense advantage possessed by a single Power wielding a single fleet with one system of organization, with the same signals, and

with the confidence inspired by constantly working together – in fact, altogether homogenous ... I think that history has shown over and over again that the fleets of two allies have never been considered equal to one homogenous fleet of a single Power, provided the single fleet was relatively as large as the allied fleets.[8]

The view which gradually gained acceptance, however, was that something more than bare numerical equality in this class was necessary. In 1904, Balfour claimed that he had 'certainly always interpreted the two-Power standard as meaning a two-Power standard with something in the nature of a margin.'[9] The following year Selborne informed Parliament that 'the spirit of the two-Power standard is not equality. The object is to win. It is reasonable security of victory in a contest with other Powers.'[10] Another First Lord, Lord Tweedmouth, informed Parliament in 1908 that 'According to what is recorded in the Admiralty, I find that my predecessors have always taken the two-Power standard as meaning the two next strong Powers abroad plus ten per cent.'[11] The Prime Minister confirmed later that year that this formula represented government policy.[12]

In the decade before the First World War politicians also grappled with the question of which powers Britain should measure its strength against. In 1889 the next strongest navies belonged to Britain's two most likely enemies, France and Russia. As long as this held good, politicians were inclined to treat the standard as an immutable formula to be applied against the two next strongest powers irrespective of the current state of their relations with Britain. By 1905, however, the traditional Franco-Russian menace was fast declining. The Russo-Japanese War resulted in Germany replacing Russia as the third strongest naval power, while the danger of war with France receded following the conclusion of the *Entente Cordiale*. In these circumstances, many questioned whether it made sense to base their calculations on the combined strength of France and Germany. Others looked ahead to the day, which could not be far off, when the United States would possess the world's second or third strongest navy. Nevertheless, one school of thought held that the two-power standard should be applied without reference to diplomatic considerations. As leader of the opposition, Balfour criticized suggestions 'that the idea that France and Germany would ever combine against us is so remote that you may put it out of account.'

The idea of imagining that international friendships are of so permanent a character that you may put aside absolutely the idea that your friend of to-day may not be your enemy of to-morrow is not an adequate basis of a national defence. I say you must go beyond the mere probability. If you ask me my opinion upon foreign relations, I should say it is most improbable that we should be at war with France and Germany combined in the next two or three years; yet I say nevertheless, that to put ourselves at the mercy of a coalition of those two powers, even if it be an improbable contingency, is insanity from the point of view of Imperial defence.[13]

This view did not prevail. The Liberal government decided that diplomatic and financial considerations did indeed necessitate a change in the standard governing British naval strength. In 1909 the Admiralty began to base its calculations on the maintenance of a 60 per cent superiority over its single most probable enemy, Germany, in battleships of the dreadnought type.

Britain's pre-1914 naval standards were therefore ambiguous at the best of times. A wide range of interpretations could reasonably be placed on any given standard, while governments could and did alter definitions to accommodate changing financial or diplomatic circumstances. There were, in short, no hard and fast rules and few clear precedents to guide policy-makers. Nevertheless, at the end of the First World War politicians and civil servants remembered the standards which had existed before 1914, and drew upon them freely – and often selectively – for guidance. In 1918 the Admiralty was inclined to view the relatively long-lived two-power standard as having particular legitimacy and hoped that it would be restored at the earliest opportunity. Shortly after the Armistice, the Secretary of the Admiralty, Sir Oswyn Murray, informed the First Lord, Sir Eric Geddes, that the navy would soon require a new standard on which to calculate its requirements in the postwar era.

The question that now will inevitably arise is, what is the future standard to be? The natural course, now that the urgent German menace is removed, would be to revert to the traditional 'two-Power standard', at any rate until the practical results of the discussions on the League of Nations are seen. The fact, however, that the two next strongest Naval Powers will now be the United States and France, the latter our closest Ally, and the former the nation that the Liberal Government of which the present Prime Minister was a prominent member declared we could never contemplate as a Naval rival, is certain to give room for dispute and discussion in the House of

Commons and elsewhere. In this connection it may be mentioned that some of the Unionist supporters of the Coalition – notably Mr. Balfour, Mr. Bonar Law, and Lord Lee of Fareham – were in 1909–10 most strenuous advocates of the 'two-Power standard', whatever the two Powers in question might be.[14]

Geddes was not about to be rushed into a premature attempt to resurrect the two-power standard, particularly if one of the powers in question was the United States. He informed Murray that 'to adopt any such formula as a "Power standard" for the Navy in the six months immediately following the War, while the froth is still upon the pot, would lead us into calculations so far removed from the actual settlement of the situation finally, that we would be hopelessly wide of the mark.'[15] Until the fate of the German High Seas Fleet was settled and the future of the United States' naval program was certain, Geddes maintained that 'a formula on the "Power standard" basis – whether it be the "two-Power standard" or "60% superiority over the next most powerful country," or any other "Power basis" – cannot be framed or adopted.' The First Lord recommended instead, 'as a purely temporary measure, … a 20% cut on man-power on the pre-War numbers.' This would give the Admiralty 'something to work to,' although he conceded 'that merely to say that we are going to have a 20% smaller manning figure than before the War is no justification for the remaining 80%, and it is only as a temporary measure' that such a formula 'can be considered as having any value at all.'[16]

Despite these reservations, this figure did provide a reasonable basis for Admiralty policy over the next six months. During this period, naval decision-makers still hoped eventually to secure a two-power standard relative to the United States and France, the next two strongest naval powers,[17] but they were also conscious of the growing pressure on the fighting services to economize. At the end of the First World War, Britain possessed an overwhelming numerical superiority in warships over any other great power (Table 1.1), and the Admiralty knew it would have difficulty convincing the government that any of its recent allies posed a serious threat to British interests. Knowing that the Cabinet might conceivably impose a naval standard which would result in large-scale *reductions* to the Navy Estimates, naval leaders preferred not to press the issue at this time.

This situation changed abruptly in mid-1919 when the Chancellor of the Exchequer recommended a reduction in the number of capital ships with full crews to a strength below that maintained by the

Table 1.1   Naval strength of the major powers at the end of the First World War

	Great Britain	United States	France	Germany	Japan	Italy
Battleships	61	39	20	40	13	14
Battle cruisers	9	–	–	5	7	–
Cruisers	30	16	21	3	10	7
Light cruisers	90	19	8	32	16	10
Flotilla leaders	23	–	–	–	–	8
Destroyers	443	131	91	200	67	44
Submarines	147	86	63	162	16	78
Aircraft carriers and seaplane tenders	4	–	–	–	–	–

Source: Roskill, *Naval Policy*, vol. I, p. 71.

United States Navy (USN). In June 1919 the Admiralty planned to keep 21 capital ships in full commission; the Treasury, however, wanted this figure decreased to 15 'practically immediately,' and recommended that a 'much larger reduction' be made in 1920/21. In a memorandum to the Cabinet, the Chancellor denied that any power or combination of powers posed a serious or immediate threat to British interests, and maintained that Britain 'would not be endangered' if a high proportion of its capital ships were held in reserve.[18] The Admiralty, which expected the United States to keep 18 dreadnoughts and 11 pre-dreadnoughts in full commission, denounced this proposal, which it believed would 'be regarded generally as the handing over of sea-supremacy by the British Empire to the United States of America.'[19] Leading naval decision-makers believed that Britain's status as a great power ultimately rested upon its maritime supremacy, and they were not prepared to stand quietly by and see Britain sink to the position of the world's second naval power.

The Treasury's recommendations served to focus the Admiralty's attention on the American challenge to Britain's maritime supremacy. In 1916 the United States had authorized construction of eight capital ships, and in 1918 the Wilson administration proposed to lay down another 16. The Admiralty was alarmed not just by the size of these programs, but also by the fighting power of these new vessels compared to their British counterparts, all but one of which was of pre-Jutland design. A belief that the United States was attempting to build up 'a Mercantile Marine with the idea of competing with Great Britain in the world-carrying trade' also contributed to the perception of an American maritime challenge.[20] Most naval decision-makers regarded the prospect of war with the United States as remote, but they also believed that naval inferiority to the US would leave Britain vulnerable to American pressure, and few wished to entrust Britain's vital interests to the goodwill of another power, however friendly it might be. In more immediate terms, the loss of maritime supremacy was expected to undermine British prestige, weaken the bonds between Britain and its Dominions, and hinder the recovery of Britain's international trade. Faced with this threat, the navy hastily abandoned the goal of a two-power standard relative to the US and another power, and began to concentrate on the immediate problem of ensuring its superiority over the USN alone. The new First Lord, Walter Long, informed the Cabinet in August 1919 that: 'In the opinion of the Board of Admiralty, the only Navy for which we need have regard, and in respect of which we desire a decision of the Government, is the Navy of the United States of America.' Japan 'may be put aside for the present,' he maintained, 'whether as an individual opponent or as a partner in any probable combination against us.'[21]

The Cabinet's response to Long's request, though swift, was little to the Admiralty's liking: the navy was told to revert to its prewar standard of 160 per cent relative to the next strongest naval power excluding the United States.[22] The government, alarmed by the size of the navy's postwar estimates and eager to prevent the Admiralty from inflating its demands through comparison with the USN, revived this standard as a short-term expedient to frustrate the Admiralty's most extravagant demands.[23] Britain's naval leaders remained determined, however, not to fall behind the USN in any important aspect of naval strength, and over the next several months the Admiralty sought to overturn the Cabinet's ruling. Its first move was to challenge the claim made by Lloyd George, the Prime Minister, that 'before the War...the United States did not enter into our comparisons of Naval strength.' In a memorandum for the Cabinet's Finance Committee, the First Lord charged that this statement was

> not strictly accurate. All that was ever laid down by any Government was that in applying the 'Two-Power Standard' the United States, owing to their distance from Europe, should not be counted as one of the two principal Powers against whose possible *combination* we were providing.[24]

This sort of tortuous legalism was to mark much of the subsequent debate over the meaning of Britain's naval standards. The Admiralty also attempted to link Britain's maritime supremacy with its national security. This was a difficult line of approach, and one which might easily backfire. To be successful, the Admiralty had to emphasize the negative results which would flow from inferiority to the USN while not appearing to overestimate the possibility of an Anglo-American war.

By October 1919, naval decision-makers grudgingly conceded that a naval standard based on parity with the USN would, in the last resort, be acceptable. The Admiralty advised the Cabinet that Britain could only achieve this through a naval accommodation with the United States or a building program which would 'ensure that we are at least equal in material strength to the United States navy as at present budgeted for.'[25] In February 1920, as the Admiralty prepared its estimates for 1920/21, the First Lord approached the Cabinet for fresh guidance on the question of the USN. He insisted that failure to reach a naval agreement with the United States would make it 'necessary definitely to lay down that a one power standard against the strongest naval power is the minimum standard compatible with our vast sea requirements, and that the building programme in all types of vessels must be such that this one power standard is fully maintained.'[26] The Cabinet agreed and gave permission for Long to make the following statement to the House of Commons:

> I believe it is a fact that the Naval policies of all past Governments, whichever party they represented, have, at least, included the common principle, that our Navy should not be inferior in strength to the Navy of any other Power, and to this principle the present Government firmly adheres … That is the foundation of the Naval Policy of His Majesty's Government.[27]

This announcement was in fact a substantial victory for the Admiralty. Against formidable opposition it had secured a naval standard relative to the United States, a power it freely admitted Britain was unlikely ever to face in war; it obtained the only standard which might conceivably allow it to resume construction of capital ships in the near future; and it received a public commitment to this standard, which no future cabinet could renounce without risking political and public protest. Buoyed by this turn of events, the Naval Staff soon began to calculate its requirements for the maintenance of the new standard. A memorandum circulated to the Board of Admiralty in June

1920 concluded that Britain must lay down four new capital ships in 1921 and five more in subsequent years if it was to maintain numerical equality with the USN in the summer of 1925. 'No less drastic action will meet our needs as regards Capital Ships,' the Assistant Chief of the Naval Staff (ACNS) wrote, 'since we have now our last reasonable chance to keep up with the United States. If we fall further behind the U.S. will be able to *retain* their supremacy, as it will be practically impossible for us to catch them up against their will *once their building slips are clear of the 1916 Programme Ships*.'[28] Admiral of the Fleet Earl Beatty, the First Sea Lord, subsequently revised this estimate to four capital ships in 1921 and four more in 1922, figures which he insisted were 'the minimum for safety,' even though, he claimed, this program would leave 'a period (1923–25) when we shall actually have fallen below the "One-Power Standard" and be somewhat inferior in fighting strength to the United States.'[29]

It fell to the First Lord to introduce a note of reality into the Admiralty's calculations. While agreeing that the Naval Staff's proposals might be considered the 'legitimate outcome' of the one-power standard, he warned the Board that it could still expect 'considerable difficulty' in securing the agreement of the Cabinet in the present economic climate.[30] The extent of these difficulties became apparent in December 1920, when the Admiralty put forward its sketch estimates for 1921/22. Its demands drove home the full implications of Long's public announcement of a one-power standard. Hoping to reassert control over the size of naval estimates, the Prime Minister initiated an inquiry by the Committee of Imperial Defence (CID) into the whole question of naval preparations against the US. Long complained that this amounted to the Board of Admiralty being 'put upon their trial';[31] it was not the Board in the dock, however, but the one-power standard.

When the CID met on 14 December to discuss this issue, Lloyd George was clearly anxious to avoid competitive shipbuilding against the United States, and to this end favored abandoning the USN altogether as a point of reference. The government had ruled out war with the United States before 1914, he argued, and it could do so again without jeopardizing Britain's vital interests. American naval construction would ideally be curtailed through diplomatic means. Alternatively, Britain might rely on its alliance with Japan to counter any genuine naval threat which emerged.[32] An accommodation with the United States would clearly best serve Britain's interests, and the CID gave this proposal its unanimous support. But of the alternatives presented to the Committee – competitive building or reliance on the Anglo-Japanese Alliance – opinion clearly ran in favor of the former. Churchill, the Prime Minister's most vocal critic on this occasion, asserted that 'no more fatal policy could be contemplated than that of basing our naval policy on a possible combination with Japan against the United States.'[33] As events turned out, Churchill represented the dominant view within the Cabinet.

With the CID unwilling to scrap the one-power standard, Lloyd George considered setting up a subcommittee under the chairmanship of Balfour to 'examine into the broad question of the enemies against whom we ought to prepare.'[34] This idea was quickly shot down by the First Lord, who left his chief in no doubt about the depth of the Admiralty's opposition to the abandonment of the one-power standard. 'The one question upon which we have concentrated ourselves at the Admiralty,' Long wrote, 'is whether or no we are to retain supremacy of the sea which we have held for so many years.' He admitted that it might be 'necessary as a matter of high policy for the Government deliberately to abandon this supremacy,' but if this were so, then it would have to 'say so plainly.'

> I, at least, ... cannot be convinced that we are unable to maintain our supremacy, and I could not, in any circumstances, be responsible for a policy which deliberately brought the United Kingdom to the Second or Third place. Therefore I feel that all questions about what we can afford, what alliances we can enter into, etc. are really subsidiary to the main question – are we, or are we not, to retain the supremacy of the sea.[35]

Faced with the possibility of wholesale resignations, Lloyd George abandoned his proposal. When the CID reassembled the following week, the only subcommittee appointed was a technical one to examine the future of the capital ship.[36] Known after its chairman, Bonar Law, this committee met the Prime Minister's immediate needs by deferring expenditure on new construction and providing time to reach a naval agreement with the United States. From the Admiralty's perspective this decision was only a temporary setback. As long as the one-power standard was not formally renounced, the Admiralty's building program was kept alive, and when the Bonar Law Committee's report endorsed the navy's views on battleships, the case for commencing new construction was actually strengthened. In the end, the four capital ships the Board wanted in 1921 were sanctioned by the Cabinet. However, with a naval arms limitation conference now in preparation, ministers regarded these vessels as bargaining counters for the forthcoming negotiations.

The survival of the one-power standard was ensured in the summer of 1921, when it was publicly endorsed by that year's Imperial Conference. In the short term, this also worked to the Admiralty's advantage, adding weight to its claims for new capital ship construction and further increasing the difficulties the government would encounter if it tried to abandon the standard. It was not long, however, before the Washington Conference effectively negated the Admiralty's earlier victories. The Washington naval treaty, concluded in February 1922, established a 5 : 3 : 1.75 ratio for the total tonnage of capital ships and aircraft carriers between the United States and Great Britain, Japan, and France and Italy. The maximum tonnage allowed to each power in these classes was also laid down, and qualitative limits were imposed on battleships, aircraft carriers, and cruisers. Furthermore, the replacement of older battleships was to be abandoned for a period of ten years, despite the Admiralty's insistence that this would have a disastrous impact on the country's naval shipbuilding industry. The four capital ships authorized by the Cabinet the previous year were cancelled, but Britain was allowed to construct two new battleships of 35 000 tons to counterbalance recent construction by the US and Japan.

The Washington naval treaty was precisely the sort of agreement the government was eager to conclude: it prevented a building race between the United States and Great Britain, and established parity between these powers in capital ships, the only class of warship undoubtedly governed by naval standards. It also set out the number of capital ships to be maintained by both powers. Hence, once Britain laid down the two capital ships permitted by the treaty, the one-power standard no longer provided the Admiralty with a lever to prise new battleships out of a reluctant government. But because Britain was still publicly committed to this standard, the navy had little choice but to make the best out of it. To do so, it had to win the interdepartmental battle over how the standard would be interpreted. Would it apply only to capital ships, or should it cover other classes as well? Did equality mean numerical equality in warships or parity in fighting power? Should requirements be calculated on the basis of equality in home, neutral, or enemy waters? All of the departments concerned with naval matters realized that the answers to these questions would have a significant impact on the Admiralty's ability to secure its future programs.

The Admiralty's most effective and powerful departmental critic throughout the interwar period was the Treasury, whose opposition to naval programs was not always motivated solely by financial considerations. Treasury officials shared few of the navy's basic assumptions on strategic issues, and they consistently presented politicians with coherent strategic alternatives. In particular, they took a highly pragmatic view of what constituted Britain's vital interests. The fighting services always maintained that Britain's overseas possessions must all be defended to the utmost of their ability, as the loss of any part of the Empire would undermine British prestige and encourage expansionist powers to challenge Britain's other interests. When the Chiefs of Staff Committee (COS) considered the future of Hong Kong in 1937, for example, the Chief of the Imperial General Staff (CIGS) remarked that 'its loss would constitute a grave blow to our prestige. He felt strongly that this should be a case of "what we have, we hold." A voluntary abandonment of important imperial possessions would be the beginning of the end of the British Empire.'[37] Treasury officials, on the other hand, looked upon defense expenditure as being like an insurance premium. If the premium became disproportionately high, it must be reduced, even if it put some possessions at possible risk. Sir Warren Fisher, the Permanent Under-Secretary of the Treasury, instructed the Prime Minister in 1925 that it was

> common ground between your officials, Civilian and Naval, that an insurance premium has to be paid against the risk of forcible interference with the British Empire by Foreign Powers. The size of that premium is, or should be, conditioned by two principal factors viz.: the degree, character and proximity of the risk, and its correlation with the other risks to which a complex civilisation like ours is subject. Your Naval officials, quite naturally, have regard to the one risk only and as they see it from their point of view; your Civilian officials have to take into account every aspect of national existence, and this involves comparative considerations.[38]

The Treasury also believed that Britain's foreign relations were best managed through 'liberal' means. It consistently rejected the idea that large armed forces and instant readiness for war were needed to keep friendly or distant powers from challenging Britain's interests. Only in the event of a clear threat to truly vital interests did it consider heavy defense expenditure to be justified.

Treasury officials were seldom prepared to push their arguments as far as 'liberal internationalists' such as Ramsay MacDonald, who regarded armaments as an impediment to world peace and were committed to the cause of international disarmament. This group dominated British strategic policy between 1929 and 1931, with disastrous consequences for the navy. Throughout most of this period, the government was in the hands of less idealistic politicians, many of whom shared the Treasury's broad outlook on strategic issues. Influential statesmen like Lloyd George, Winston Churchill, and Neville Chamberlain regarded the navy as an essentially defensive force, whose purpose was to defend British interests in home waters and other areas where Britain had special interests. In 1920 Lloyd George suggested that these included 'the North Sea, the Mediterranean, the Indian Seas, &c.' It was not necessary, he insisted, for Britain to maintain 'complete supremacy in all seas.'[39] Because such views were common outside of the fighting services, the Treasury could usually count on political support for its attacks on Admiralty programs. Treasury officials therefore objected to the use of naval standards, believing that they strengthened the Admiralty's ability to maintain a larger navy than was necessary. A more sensible approach, they argued, would be for the government to keep its hands free to determine naval requirements after weighing for itself strategic, financial, and diplomatic considerations. As one Treasury memorandum remarked:

> The past history of Naval standards shows that each was discarded as soon as it became inconvenient and the true criterion surely is that the Fleet is to be of *such a strength as will protect the vital national interests*. Not all the objects which are desirable are vital, just as not all the risks which are theoretically possible have the remotest probability.[40]

Prior to the Washington Conference, the precise meaning of the one-power standard had been of little concern to either the Admiralty or the Treasury except in so far as it defined Britain's capital ship requirements. The First Lord's parliamentary statements did nothing to clarify this question, while the 1921 Imperial Conference stated only that 'the minimum standard of naval ship construction necessary for the maintenance of the position of the British Empire among the nations of the world is an equality in fighting strength with any other Naval Power.'[41] The Admiralty took this to mean 'that the Navy should be maintained at sufficient strength to ensure the safety of the British Empire and its sea communications as against any other Naval Power.'[42] In practical terms, this meant that the navy must be at least equal in fighting strength to the USN *in American waters*. Whether an Anglo-American war was a realistic contingency was irrelevant to the Admiralty's definition, which required only that Britain be capable of fighting the USN with a reasonable expectation of prevailing against it. To fulfil this standard, the Admiralty demanded a clear margin of numerical superiority, as anything less would force the British fleet to adopt 'a defensive system of strategy, which would leave the [empire's] sea communications at the mercy of the enemy and would invite defeat. Such a strategy has never been contemplated by any Board of Admiralty and never will be.'[43]

The weak spot in the Admiralty's case was that it would probably never be called upon to fight the United States. If the navy would never need to defeat the USN, the only reason to maintain it on this basis was for the sake of prestige, a requirement which could be met at a lower level of strength than the Admiralty was proposing. The Treasury used this opening to challenge the Admiralty's new definition of the one-power standard. If the US did not actually threaten Britain's maritime security, then a navy capable of defeating the USN in its own waters was a luxury Britain could not necessarily afford. In 1922, Sir George Barstow, the Controller of Supply Services at the Treasury, claimed that acceptance of the Admiralty's definition would only make the government 'slaves to a formula. The practical question,' he argued,' is whether the safety of the British Empire and its sea communications are secured against the U.S.A.'

> If they can be regarded as secure with a smaller fleet of Capital Ships than the present fleet, the only object of maintaining a larger fleet is to impress the world at large. Now the principle of equality is conceded by the Washington Agreement as to tonnage of capital ships. The world at large will pay much more attention to this admitted equality than to details of ships in commission, and as the British fleet is much more widely distributed than the U.S.A. and its record is well known, the apprehension that our reputation as the leading naval power will go appears to me to be baseless.[44]

Barstow also denied that it was necessary to maintain strict equality with the USN in numbers. '[I]s the British Empire secure against the U.S.A. if we maintain a smaller fleet in full commission?', he asked. 'The answer is I believe that Great Britain is absolutely secure by its distance … that Canada could not be secured by any Fleet however large: and that the West Indies could not be secured on the One Power standard owing to their geographical position.' In light of these considerations, Barstow hoped that the government would reject the Admiralty's arguments. The adoption of 'a practical as distinct from a window-dressing interpretation of the One Power formula would,' he maintained, 'enable further reductions to be safely made.'[45]

In 1922 politicians agreed that the prospect of an Anglo-American war was sufficiently remote that there was no compelling reason for the navy to calculate its requirements on the basis of a forward strategy in American waters. It was politically inexpedient, though, to abandon any pretense of equality with the USN, especially as the government had only recently conceded parity at the Washington Conference. The obvious solution was to maintain parity, but to do so at the lowest possible level. With this end in view, a Cabinet committee under Churchill outlined a compromise between the positions of the Admiralty and the Treasury in 1922. It was not necessary, the committee decided, that 'the British and United States Navies should be exactly matched in every particular, or that a fair allowance should not be made in estimating personnel for the great reserves which these Islands possess in their seafaring population.'

But we consider that, not only in our own judgment but in that of foreign nations, the standard at which the British Navy is maintained should not be definitely inferior to that of the United States. Any such condition of inferiority would undoubtedly affect our whole position and influence in the world, and indicate to our Dominions that a new centre had been created for the Anglo-Saxon world. We have felt that the Cabinet, and indeed Parliament, would expect us to regard the maintenance of the one-Power standard as an imperative condition.[46]

Thus the one-power standard required only that the navy remain approximately equal on paper to the USN in overall strength. Deficiencies in one area could be counterbalanced by superiority in others, but the navy must not be reduced to a strength where it would be *perceived* as inferior to the USN. The navy would thus be denied the ships which were necessary only to allow it to defeat an American fleet in its own waters, while the Treasury was forced to accept that a certain amount of 'window dressing' was necessary.

With the one-power standard's application to the USN settled by political intervention, debate soon shifted to other areas. The navy's ability to secure its most important programs continued to depend upon the outcome of this discourse. During the first half of the 1920s, the Admiralty probably gained more than it lost through the existence of the one-power standard, not because the standard embodied the navy's genuine strategic needs, but because it strengthened its overall bargaining position. Opposition to the Admiralty's programs on financial or strategic grounds was frequently countered by invoking the one-power standard. As Barstow complained, the Admiralty was

disposed to answer all appeals for reduced naval estimates by reference to the One Power standard. So long as that stands as a canon of naval policy, they say, so long must we, as responsible for the Fleet, require that expenditure must be kept up to a certain level. Otherwise which shall fall below the standard of the U.S.A.[47]

The Admiralty believed that financial considerations should be subordinated so far as possible to the preservation of Britain's maritime security, and Beatty argued that the one-power standard must take precedence over the 'ten-year principle' whenever the two came into conflict.[48] The Treasury held precisely the opposite view, but the existence of a government-sanctioned naval standard gave the Admiralty an important bargaining counter. If the government sought to cut programs the navy considered vital to the maintenance of the standard, the Board was able to insist on a public declaration that the standard was being abandoned. No government could take such a step lightly or contemplate with equanimity the resignation of the Board on these grounds – a possibility which was often hinted at.

After the Washington Conference, the Admiralty realized that any attempt to justify its programs by reference to the US would be closely scrutinized by the Treasury, and it only resorted to this expedient when it appeared that Britain might indeed fall behind the USN in some essential element of naval strength. Increasingly, however, the Admiralty shifted the focus of the one-power standard away from the US and onto Japan. In part, this was a natural response to the Admiralty's growing concern over the perceived threat from Japan to Britain's interests in the Far East, but it was also a deliberate maneuver to deflect Treasury criticism by placing the navy's most expensive programs under the protective umbrella of the one-power standard. To be successful, however, it was necessary to convince the rest of Whitehall that Japan posed a serious threat to British interests. Leading naval officers believed that they were 'as well qualified to give an opinion on the possibility of a conflict in the Far East ... as anyone in the Foreign Office,'[49] but their pronouncements on diplomatic affairs usually carried little weight outside the Admiralty. In the uncertain international climate prevailing in the years immediately following the First World War, the navy's warnings about Japan tended to get a sympathetic hearing. By the mid-1920s, however, opinion in Whitehall had clearly turned against the navy view. When the Foreign Secretary, Austen Chamberlain, informed the CID in 1925 that he regarded 'the prospect of war in the Far East as very remote,'[50] naval leaders realized that it would be futile, and probably counterproductive, to argue this point. In any event, most officers did not dispute the Foreign Office's assessment of Japan's *short-term* intentions. Where they disagreed was over the warning period they could expect if Japan changed its mind, the degree of damage that would be suffered if the Foreign Office (FO) were wrong, and the necessity for insuring against this eventuality.

When the navy's warnings about Japan's long-range intentions were rejected, the Admiralty instinctively fell back on the argument that its preparations for an eastern war were a prudent and necessary measure of insurance. As long as there was any realistic prospect of war with Japan, the Admiralty considered itself duty-bound to prepare for it. If Britain could not defend its vital interests in the Far East, the British Empire would 'exist in the Far East on sufferance of another Power,' a position which Beatty and his naval colleagues regarded as intolerable.[51] The Admiralty therefore rejected the Treasury's contention that the immediacy of the potential threat must be taken into account when framing defense policy. The international scene was not static, it argued, and threats could emerge without warning. Thus William Bridgeman, First Lord of the Admiralty in Baldwin's second Cabinet, declared that he rather disliked

> the idea of setting up the principle that it is for the Government to decide when there is going to be another war and then for the services to have to prepare for it. Governments have not been particularly successful in forecasting wars in the past, and I do not think we should approach it from that point of view at all. I think the only way we can approach it is from the point of view of ensuring ourselves against any reasonable risks wherever they may be in the world.[52]

Privately, naval officers went even further. Captain Dudley Pound, for example, wrote in 1924 that 'all *possible* wars should be taken into account and each Service, as far as finance permits, should prepare for the one which demands the greatest effort.'[53]

Linking the one-power standard to Japan was complicated by the fact that the Washington naval treaty not only regulated Britain's strength in capital ships, but also ensured its superiority over Japan in this class in a 5:3 ratio. To overcome this difficulty, the Admiralty broadened its definition of the one-power standard to encompass not only warships but all aspects of the navy's fighting strength. It insisted that the navy required more than just numerical equality with the Imperial Japanese Navy (IJN) on paper – it also needed all of the other resources necessary to fight a war in the Far East to a successful conclusion. In practical terms, this meant a clear margin of naval superiority over Japan after making allowances for a deterrent force in home waters, as well as docking and repair facilities at Singapore and an ample reserve of oil fuel. If the Admiralty were refused these things, it insisted that the navy would not possess equality in fighting strength with Japan in eastern waters. Hence, these programs were essential for the maintenance of a one-power standard relative to Japan.

Treasury officials disputed the Admiralty's argument on a number of points. Most importantly, they did not believe that Japan would deliberately embark on war with Britain. And even if an Anglo-Japanese war did occur, they were confident that Japan could not threaten Britain's vital interests. 'It seems almost impossible to imagine that Japan would in the near future attack the British Empire,' Barstow wrote in 1921.

> Even if seized with more than Prussian megalomania and obliviousness of the lessons of the last war she felt disposed to attack Great Britain, her ally and best friend, she would almost inevitably bring in the United States of America against her also. The distance from Japan to Australia is so great that her prospect of success in an invasion would be infinitesimal. Even a raid on Sydney would be extremely hazardous. Her finances although strikingly well managed during the Great War are in no condition to support a long and exhausting war, nor are her internal resources such as would enable her to sustain it.[54]

The Treasury admitted that the loss of colonies and economic interests in east Asia would be a serious blow, but it did not believe that this would be fatal to Britain itself; and since the cost of defending these interests was unacceptably high, it was prepared to see them written off if necessary.

Treasury officials were also skeptical of the navy's ability to defend these interests even if the Admiralty's requests were met. Barstow in particular questioned whether Britain could expect to wage war successfully against Japan. To secure victory it would be necessary, he asserted, 'to seize a forward base; and having defeated her Fleet, to blockade her shores, & probably land forces to defeat her land armies. The latter are known to be well disciplined & brave; what sort of forces should we have to use in order to force Japan to sue for peace?'[55] These comments suggest that Barstow appreciated better than many naval officers the serious difficulties a Far Eastern war would pose. For Britain to maintain superior naval forces in the Far East over a lengthy period would 'be practically impossible by the mere fact of distance,' he argued, 'unless we ruin ourselves in the process of building more ships.'[56] The Treasury view, therefore, was that the possibility of an Anglo-Japanese war was so remote that the Admiralty should take comfort in Japan's distance from Britain and its Dominions, abandon plans for projecting British power into Japanese waters, and apply the one-power standard to Japan on the same basis as the United States, with naval strength compared only on paper. Britain would thus be spared entirely the expense of the Singapore Naval Base, and the navy's oil fuel reserve and new construction requirements could be substantially reduced.

The debate over the application of the standard to Japan came to a head in early 1925 when Winston Churchill, the Chancellor of the Exchequer, attacked the Admiralty's cruiser program in his bid to secure substantial economies from the fighting services. Churchill pressed the Treasury's case with vigor, challenging the Admiralty's conclusions about the probability of war with Japan and the wisdom of spending large sums to meet such a contingency.[57] The timing of the Treasury's onslaught found the Admiralty at a distinct disadvantage. The Foreign Office backed the Treasury's contention that war with Japan was unlikely, and the Cabinet as a whole was in favor of large spending cuts. The Admiralty, with its programs clearly vulnerable on financial grounds, was quick to argue its case on the need to maintain the one- power standard relative to Japan. Beatty claimed that if the Admiralty reduced its cruiser program, it would be unable to fulfil the 'one-Power policy and the policy of preserving the territory of the British Empire and safeguarding the means of communications, which has been reiterated again and again.'[58]

The application of the one-power standard to cruisers was not a straightforward matter. The Admiralty asserted that Britain could not measure its requirements in this class in the same manner as it did battleships because the navy needed cruisers both for work with the fleet and for the protection of trade. The former requirement could be measured in relative terms, according to the number of cruisers maintained by the enemy, but the Admiralty maintained that the latter need must be calculated in absolute terms, based on amount of trade and the length of the sea lanes which required protection. The details of this argument were easily challenged, but the contention that Britain's need for cruisers was exceptionally large was never disputed. Moreover, it had been endorsed in the House of Commons on numerous occasions before 1914.[59] Thus Beatty maintained that the navy's cruiser program was not only fully justified 'on the basis of the one power standard with the United States and the 5 to 3 ratio with Japan,' but also that this was 'a matter and a question which can be decided only by the Admiralty.'[60]

The government rejected this line of argument, and it was only the threat of resignations that allowed the Admiralty to lay down new cruisers in 1925. In the long term, however, the navy's position was substantially weakened by the outcome of this debate over naval policy. Most importantly, Churchill obtained a Cabinet ruling that the Admiralty did not need 'to make preparations for placing at Singapore for a decisive battle in the Pacific a British battle fleet, with cruisers, flotillas, and all ancillary vessels superior in strength, or at least equal, to the sea-going Navy of Japan.'[61] This declaration effectively extended the 'ten-year rule' to cover a war with Japan until 1935. The long-term impact of this decision on naval estimates was not immediately apparent, however, and in 1925 the Admiralty looked ready to emerge from its battle with the Treasury in a better position than it might have expected given its opponents' strength. In the first place, it had successfully propagated the idea that the one-power standard should take into account Japanese naval strength. This was accomplished largely by default, as the Treasury was not inclined to dispute the idea that the standard was theoretically applicable to Japan. The real issue at stake in 1925 was the basis of comparison with the IJN. A 1 : 1 ratio in capital ships and aircraft carriers relative to the USN was the only formula that had ever been formally sanctioned. But the Admiralty believed that the navy needed a margin of superiority over Japan in Far Eastern waters if it was to protect Britain's vital interests in this region, and naval decision-makers assumed that this requirement would be met by a 5 : 3 ratio against Japan. The alternative was a 1 : 1 ratio relative to Japan based on a paper comparison of forces. Hence the acceptance of the Washington ratio relative to Japan as a part of the one-power standard was potentially a significant gain for the Admiralty.

The Admiralty also staved off attacks on the Singapore Naval Base and the oil fuel program by having them enshrined as an integral part of the one-power standard. In view of the prevailing opinion in Whitehall regarding the possibility of war against Japan, and the

Treasury's (but not Churchill's) preference for scrapping these programs altogether, this was also a significant accomplishment. On balance, therefore, the new rendering of the one-power standard advanced by the CID at this time represented a genuine compromise between the views of the Admiralty and the Treasury. The Cabinet accepted that the Japanese threat was sufficiently remote that it did not necessitate immediate naval preparations, but also that the Admiralty's long-term projects could continue as a means of insuring against this danger in the more distant future. The CID's definition, which was endorsed by the Cabinet in May,[62] stated that the

> requirements of a one-Power standard are satisfied if our fleet, wherever situated, is equal to the fleet of any other nation, wherever situated, provided that arrangements are made from time to time in different parts of the world, according as the international situation requires, to enable the local naval forces to maintain the situation against vital and irreparable damage pending the arrival of the main fleet, and to give the main fleet on arrival sufficient mobility.[63]

Thus the navy was to calculate its requirements in all classes of warship on the assumption that it would not need to send a fleet to Singapore in the near future, but it was permitted to continue its long-term preparations to ensure that it could eventually maintain a fleet in the Far East.

This compromise was acceptable to Churchill, who had no desire to cancel the Singapore base and oil fuel programs outright. Where he hoped to achieve economies, in 1925 and subsequently, was by reducing the navy's new construction programs. If war with Japan was unlikely, he argued that 'there would fall to the ground the whole expense of building and victualling ships, the submarines and destroyers and depot ships which are required to carry the main British Fleet into Far Eastern waters.'[64] He failed to achieve this goal in 1925, however, because the Admiralty's vigorous defense of its construction program and threats of resignations effectively blunted the Treasury's attacks. To avert a cabinet crisis, the Prime Minister had to produce a compromise which allowed for a steady cruiser program. The Admiralty's victory weakened its position in the long run, however, and left it vulnerable to renewed attacks at a later date.[65] One result of the struggle over the 1925 Navy Estimates was that the 'ten-year rule' became established as the basis of Britain's strategic policy.[66] In subsequent years the Treasury exploited the government's desire for economy to retard spending on the Singapore Naval Base and the oil fuel program, while utilizing the CID's definition of the one-power standard as a means to limit expenditure on naval construction. The Chancellor's ability to cut the Admiralty's estimates ultimately depended on maintaining the backing and sympathy of the Cabinet, but as long as the government supported the Treasury's broad objectives, the existence of the one-power standard did not noticeably strengthen the Admiralty's bargaining position.

When the Treasury returned to the attack in 1927, the Admiralty's political strength was waning, that of the Treasury was on the rise, and the possibility of war with Japan appeared even more remote than it had two years earlier. As a result, Churchill easily reduced the cruiser program that had been settled in 1925 and slowed the accumulation of fuel reserves. The Admiralty attempted to circumvent the extension of the ten-year rule by interpreting it to mean that it must be prepared for a major war in the Far East by mid-1935.[67] This was undoubtedly contrary to the spirit of the Cabinet's decision, and Churchill succeeded in removing this loophole in 1928 by establishing the principle that the rule would advance automatically from day to day.[68] However, this did not induce the Admiralty to abandon the practice of calculating its requirements of personnel, materiel and stores on the basis of a Far Eastern war, an action justified by Sir Oswyn Murray, the Permanent Secretary of the Admiralty, on the grounds 'that the "Ten years ruling" is neither an absolute promise of peace for 10 years nor an abrogation of the principle that the Fleet must be ready for an ordinary emergency at any time.'[69]

During the period dominated by the ten-year rule, the Admiralty's policies and war plans continued to be based on the assumption that the navy must prepare itself for a major war in the Far East. It was inadvisable to advertise this fact outside the Admiralty, however, and packaging the navy's policies for external consumption became a matter of real concern. In 1928 Vice-Admiral William Fisher, the Deputy Chief of the Naval Staff (DCNS), suggested that 'the time may soon arrive when it may be found convenient and politic' to adopt a formula for the basis of Navy Estimates which would be 'of more general application' than the requirements of a major war with Japan. As an alternative, he suggested 'that attention should be directed to the requirements for security of communications to the Far East and for mobility of the Main Fleet on arrival there.'[70] This would have been in harmony with the new definition of the one-power standard, and programs based on this formula would have been less vulnerable to attack by the Treasury.

Admiral Madden, Beatty's successor as First Sea Lord, agreed with this suggestion in principle, but he did not think the time had yet come for such a change. In practice, the Admiralty was already becoming adept at defending its policies in terms that did not explicitly refer to the possibility of an imminent war with Japan, a trend which continued until Japanese aggression in Manchuria in 1931 and at Shanghai in 1932 appeared to vindicate its earlier warnings.[71]

Throughout the mid-1920s, the Royal Navy still possessed the world's largest and most modern fleet, and led the world in new construction. The enforcement of the ten-year rule after 1925 denied the navy some of the vessels it would require for the successful prosecution of a two-front war. In 1927 Baldwin's government dropped two of the three cruisers in that year's new construction program. When Labour returned to power in 1929, both of the cruisers approved for the 1928 program were promptly canceled, and only one was included for 1929. However, despite all of this, and the elimination of British superiority in naval aviation, even in 1929 the Royal Navy was the strongest navy on earth, more powerful than the USN and with a comfortable margin of superiority over the IJN and any one European navy. The greatest blow to the navy was the combination of the great depression and the 1930 London Naval Conference, where the Labour government prolonged the Washington capital ship building holiday until 1936, agreed to scrap many of the navy's old capital ships, and accepted limitations on British cruiser strength. These measures were taken against the Admiralty's strenuous objections by a government committed to the goal of international disarmament. The strategic consequences for Britain were disastrous. The new capital ships needed to revive the British shipbuilding industry failed to materialize, and that industry declined catastrophically in capacity. Britain's existing margin of naval superiority was slashed, and meanwhile, increased naval building in Europe steadily undermined Britain's strength relative to its rivals on the continent. So serious was the decline of British seapower by the early 1930s that naval leaders lost confidence in their ability automatically to despatch a superior fleet to the Far East while retaining a substantial deterrent force in European waters. However, as long as Britain's strength in capital ships and cruisers was regulated by treaty, the Admiralty was unable to press for the replacement of the one-power standard, even though it no longer bore any relation to the country's real strategic requirements. The Admiralty began to lobby for a new standard only when the possibility arose that quantitative limitations would disappear.

In January 1934 the First Sea Lord, Sir Ernle Chatfield, floated the idea of a revived two-power standard, measured against Japan and the strongest European naval power, to the Defence Requirements Committee (DRC), which had been set up by the Cabinet to consider how the armed services' worst deficiencies might be remedied. The only dissenting voice on the DRC belonged to Warren Fisher, who realized the heavy expenditure which would be involved. Fisher did not oppose a new standard on strategic grounds, however, and conceded that the existing standard was 'inelastic' and might not provide the 'necessary degree of security.'[72] Chatfield's next move was to put the navy's case before the Cabinet committee on the forthcoming naval conference. He informed this body in March 1934 that for

> full security our naval defence policy should be such as to enable us to provide in the Far East a force of sufficient strength to ensure security for the Empire and its essential interests against Japanese encroachment or attack, to provide also protection for our merchant ships on all the sea routes, and at the same time to have sufficient forces in European waters and the Atlantic to give us security against the strongest European naval power. This policy has been described as a 'Two Power Standard'.[73]

If the government decided that this was 'an impossible financial task' Chatfield maintained that it would then be necessary to 'accept the fact that the Admiralty cannot guarantee the security of our vital sea communications against attack by sea.' In these circumstances, Britain 'must either trust to a naval combination with some other power to give us security at sea against such aggression, or we must keep the balance of our forces remaining in Europe sufficiently strong to prove an *effective deterrent* to any interference, namely, a "One-Power Standard."' Of these two options, Chatfield claimed that the first 'does not afford a basis for a standard of relative naval strength to be established by treaty,' nor could the government, 'in the absence of our Main Fleet, confide the entire protection of this country and its vital sea communications to a foreign navy.' But if the government continued to rely on a one-power standard, the navy 'cannot simultaneously fight Japan and the strongest European naval Power.'[74]

With a naval conference in preparation, Chatfield probably did not count on an immediate decision on a new standard. His objective in circulating this memorandum appears to have been twofold: to prepare the ground for a full-fledged attack on the one-power standard after the demise of quantitative limitations, and, in the meantime, to create a link between the one-power standard and the navy's current strategic needs. In pursuit of this latter objective, Chatfield declared that the minimum requirements for security under the existing one-power standard were that Britain could despatch to the Far East

> *a fleet sufficient to provide 'cover' against the Japanese Fleet; we should have sufficient additional forces behind this shield for the protection of our territories and mercantile marine against Japanese attack; at the same time we should be able to retain in European waters a force sufficient to act as a deterrent and to prevent the strongest European naval Power from obtaining control of our vital home terminal areas while we can make the necessary redispositions.*[75]

In 1925 the fleets of Europe had been so weak that the Admiralty had not needed an explicit recognition of its requirements in a two-front war, and the CID had made no reference to these needs in framing its definition of the one-power standard. The Admiralty's claim to a deterrent force in home waters was therefore a notable addition to the standard's accepted definition. Just as important, however, is the fact that this interpretation differed little from the Admiralty's proposed definition for a new standard, both being based on the necessity of despatching a fleet to the Far East while retaining forces in European waters. The Admiralty may have been hoping to secure its new standard 'by the back door,' for if its new interpretation of the one-power standard gained currency, the only point remaining for debate would be the difference between a 'deterrent' force and one capable of providing 'full security' for British interests. A naval victory in such a debate would have created a *de facto* two-power standard. In any event, this definition of the one-power standard was eventually accepted throughout Whitehall as the approved definition – a victory by default, which the navy slipped past the notice of the Treasury and of many historians.[76]

The Admiralty formally launched its campaign for a full two-power standard before the reconstituted DRC in October 1935. Chatfield presented the Committee with a clear picture of the naval situation. At present, the RN possessed a comfortable margin of superiority over the navies of Germany and Japan. As Germany was constructing its fleet virtually from nothing, it would be several years before it could build up to the full strength allowed under the terms of the Anglo-German Naval Agreement (AGNA) of June 1935, by which Germany was entitled to a fleet 35 per cent of the size of Britain's. To maintain the navy's position relative to Germany and Japan, Chatfield maintained that Britain must resume battleship construction in January 1937, when the building holiday expired. He recommended laying down seven new battleships during the years 1937–9, which was the most that British shipbuilding resources would allow. Such a program would do no more than replace Britain's oldest battleships and keep the fleet up to its current strength of 15 capital ships. Hence, the navy's relative position would not be improved. In the event that treaty restrictions continued to limit Britain to a fleet of 15 capital ships after 1936, the Admiralty would be unable to lay down more than one battleship annually after 1939. This would not place Britain at a numerical disadvantage relative to Germany and Japan, but, as Chatfield argued, rough equality with these powers was insufficient, as it would leave the navy dependent 'on our superior fighting efficiency' in the event of a two-front war. Ideally the British fleet required a margin of superiority over these powers, and the Admiralty recommended building up a fleet of 20 capital ships through a larger program of new construction after 1939. This would make it possible to despatch 11 capital ships to the Far East to counter Japan's nine, and to retain nine in home waters to match the seven Germany would eventually possess.[77]

The DRC was alarmed by Germany's long-term intentions and accepted that the navy should ultimately reach a strength which would allow it to face both Germany and Japan simultaneously. The committee's final report endorsed Chatfield's recommendations, and proposed a building program which would maintain the navy at its present strength in capital ships (Table 1.2), and increase it slightly in cruisers. It also advised that if the next naval conference ended without an

Table 1.2 Construction required by the DRC program, 1936–42

	1936/ 37	1937/ 38	1938/ 39	1939/ 40	1940/ 41	1941/ 42	1942/ 43
Battleships	2	3	2	2	1	1	1
Aircraft carriers			(4 between 1936 and 1942)				
Cruisers	5	5	5	5	5	5	5
Destroyers	9	–	9	–	9	–	9
Submarines	3	3	3	3	3	3	3

Source: DRC 37, CAB 16/112.

agreement on quantitative limits, Britain should adopt a new standard of naval strength:

(i) To enable us to place a Fleet in the Far East fully adequate to act on the defensive and to serve as a strong deterrent against any threat to our interests in that part of the globe.

(ii) To maintain in all circumstances in Home Waters a force able to meet the requirements of a war with Germany at the same time.

Included in (i) and (ii) would be the forces necessary in all parts of the world, behind the cover of the main fleets, to protect our territories and merchant ships against sporadic attack.[78]

This recommendation was made entirely on strategic grounds. Its principal value to the Admiralty was that it came from a high level interdepartmental committee and could be represented as having at least semi-official status. To make the proposal more palatable to the government, whose sanction was ultimately required, Chatfield stressed that a new standard would not mean an immediate jump in the size of the Navy Estimates. He told the Committee on Defence Policy and Requirements (DPR(DR)) that Britain's 'battle fleet was of such a strength already as to permit us to compete with Germany and at the same time to send a battle fleet to Singapore, adequate to act on the defensive, but it was in light forces that the navy would be deficient and unable to defend our trade interests in the event of a war in both the Far East and in Europe.' Hence, the new standard 'meant principally an increased cruiser strength.'[79] Chatfield conceded, however, that the 'adoption of the new standard might possibly involve a slight increase in our battleship strength at a later date.'[80] This statement was disingenuous. Short of the disappearance of the Japanese navy, a significant increase in battleship strength was unavoidable; indeed, this was the principal reason why the Admiralty sought the new standard. Its goal was ultimately to restore Britain to a position of overwhelming strength at sea such as it had enjoyed during the 1920s and earlier. But since British shipyards would be fully occupied for the next few years keeping Britain up to its existing strength, the government would not have to face increased expenditure on this class until approximately 1939. The Admiralty hoped to secure approval of the standard long before this date in order to bind future cabinets to increased naval expenditure.

The DPR (DR) Committee was not prepared to make a final decision on the new standard until the Admiralty produced definite figures as to its cost.[81] Naval planners soon realized that Chatfield's forecast had been unduly optimistic, and that if the new standard were approved, 'the cost of the fleet would be practically doubled and ... a permanent annual expenditure of between £90 and £100 million would be entailed.'[82] In these circumstances, the Board of Admiralty decided that it would be expedient 'to avoid any discussion at present of a new standard of strength.'[83] Instead, it attempted to secure the warships it wanted by increasing the building tempo of the construction program outlined in the DRC's final report, which had been approved by the Cabinet in February 1936.[84]

In June 1936 the Admiralty put forward a proposal to begin additional construction during the current year in order to hasten the completion of the vessels recommended by the DRC – a program which became known as the 'DRC Fleet.'[85] This course had certain obvious advantages: it enabled the Admiralty to lay down as many ships in 1936 as would have been permitted if the new standard had been approved; it put off the day when the Admiralty had to reveal the cost of building to a two-power standard; and it would undermine the government's ability to cut back on new construction once the 'DRC Fleet' had been completed. In theory there was little for the Treasury to object to. Expenditure on this program had already been accepted in principle, and the money for these vessels would have to be spent sooner or later. The Admiralty maintained that it was simply proposing to spend the money sooner, but in fact it never had any intention of voluntarily curtailing new construction once the DRC objectives had been met. It intended to go on building at this pace, if allowed, until the navy possessed a comfortable margin of superiority over the combined strength of Japan and Germany.

The Treasury was alerted to the Admiralty's ulterior motives when Admiral Reginald Henderson, the Controller, provided Treasury officials with a memorandum outlining not only the Admiralty's 'accelerated' program for 1936, but also its proposed new construction program for subsequent years.[86] This document clearly revealed that 'what the Admiralty have in mind is to *increase* the programmes in 1937, 1938 and 1939 in very much the same measure as they now propose to increase the 1936 programme.' Treasury officials recognized immediately that expansion on this scale would constitute 'a major variation from the D.R.C. programme,' and would increase naval expenditure for the 1936–9 period by about £50 million.[87] The Admiralty may have been hoping to secure approval for its extended building program at this time, but it appears more likely that Henderson put this proposal forward on his own initiative. In either event, the Treasury objected strongly to any long-term program which would exceed the approved 'DRC standard,' and the Admiralty beat a hasty retreat. Henderson withdrew his memorandum and substituted another containing only the proposal to increase the ships laid down as part of the 1936 program.[88]

This scheme, which was approved in July,[89] was only the first move in the Admiralty's attempt to build up to a *de facto* new standard fleet under the guise of 'acceleration.' Admiralty officials admitted privately that the program to which they were 'working is generally larger than that which was laid down' by the DRC,[90] and the Board decided in November 1936 that

> it was proper for the Naval Staff and Admiralty Departments, in considering plans for war, to take into account the likelihood that the higher standard would ultimately be worked to. That standard, particularly on the personnel side, might also properly influence any decision which it was necessary to take at an early date in relation to new works and buildings of a permanent character.[91]

But because the time did not yet appear ripe to seek a formal endorsement of the new standard, the Board also concluded 'that for political and international reasons it was undesirable to raise this question in connection with the 1937 Programme and Estimates.'[92]

The navy's proposed construction program for 1937 was nearly identical to the 'accelerated' program of the previous year, and the Admiralty attempted to justify it on the same basis. Because this program would not actually raise the navy to a level of strength exceeding the approved DRC program in any single class of vessel, the Treasury was unable to object. Its officials were under no illusions though about what the navy was up to. Sir Eric Bridges, for example, doubted that the Admiralty's latest proposals were 'not in fact something more' than acceleration, 'namely a step – and a pretty long step at that – towards the fleet required for the new standard of naval strength.'[93] The Treasury feared that the Admiralty would be allowed to continue laying down ships at the current pace even if no decision on a new standard was taken. Bridges warned his colleagues that 'we have got to consider what will happen in 1938 and later.'

> Is there, for example, any likelihood that the Admiralty would, in any circumstances that can be foreseen, consent to lay down *no* cruisers, *no* aircraft carriers, *no* destroyers in 1938? Obviously not ... Yet

the laying down of a single further flotilla of destroyers in the years 1938–42, or of more than one aircraft carrier in any of those 5 years, would carry us beyond the D.R.C. scheme for these classes of ships.[94]

The Treasury therefore decided that the time had come for a showdown with the Admiralty. Even though there was an element of risk involved in this course, Treasury officials appear to have been confident that the politicians would reject the two-power standard when they finally saw the full cost.

The First Lord and the Chancellor agreed in January 1937 that the question of the new standard would have to be settled in the near future.[95] The Admiralty reopened its campaign in April with a carefully considered memorandum for the Defence Plans (Policy) Sub-Committee (DPP). The timing of this move was propitious. The government, alarmed by the rapid pace of German rearmament, had just floated a major defense loan to help finance Britain's rearmament. Indeed, the First Lord, Sir Samuel Hoare, had to assure the DPP that he was not attempting simply 'to jump in while the going was good.'[96] The Admiralty could no longer defer discussion on this issue, he maintained, because it would soon have built up to the level of strength authorized by the government; it required a definite figure to work to in order to calculate its future manpower requirements; and it had to allay Dominion concerns at the forthcoming Imperial Conference about Britain's ability to despatch a fleet to the Far East in an emergency.[97] Hoare warned that without the formal approval of a new standard there 'was the danger that [the Dominions] would concentrate on local defence in preference to Imperial Defence.'[98]

The Admiralty's memorandum warned that the need for a new standard had increased in the 16 months since the DRC's final report had been issued; and that if it were rejected the navy would soon be unable to defend Britain's interests against both Germany and Japan simultaneously.

At present the outside observer sees the German Navy rising, he knows that on our existing declared One Power standard we might be able to send a fleet to the Far East before Germany's programme is complete, but after that date he cannot see how we can do so unless our strength is increased.

It is of the greatest importance to re-establish confidence in the basis of our system of Imperial defence, and it is considered that this can only be done if the responsible authorities at home and overseas are informed that the strength of the British navy will be increased as necessary to enable it to fulfil its task. Such action presupposes a decision by His Majesty's Government on a new standard.[99]

Moreover, with the estrangement of Italy during the Abyssinia Crisis, the political calculations on which the DRC based its recommendations might even be obsolete, in which case even a two-power standard would be insufficient to meet Britain's security needs. 'If we must include Italy as well as Germany and Japan among our potential enemies,' the Admiralty warned, 'our naval strength must either be still further increased or we must rely on a naval combination with another power.'[100]

The threat posed by a hostile combination of Germany and Japan was not a difficult proposition to sell; the real problem facing the Admiralty was convincing the government to spend enough on the navy for it to face this threat with confidence. The Admiralty had by this time taken 'acceleration' as far as it could, and had no choice but to reveal the full cost of building and maintaining a 'two-power' navy. The committee was informed that the total strength of the navy would in fact be significantly increased under the new standard, and that new construction would have to continue at its present pace until 1944. Once the expansion of the fleet was completed the Admiralty estimated that its annual 'stabilized' cost would fall between £97 and £104 million. Reductions might be possible, however, if the government were able to reach an accommodation with either Germany or Japan (Table 1.3). Faced by the 'immense implications' of the Admiralty's proposals, the DPP decided

> to postpone the formulation of definite recommendations to the Cabinet until there had been an opportunity for the CID to examine them in greater detail, together with those of the other Services, and thus to present to the Cabinet a complete picture of what the 'stabilised' cost of the Defence Departments would aggregate after the period of expansion and making good the deficiencies has elapsed.[101]

The Admiralty's cards were now all on the table and the Treasury was alarmed by what it saw. In 1935 the DRC had estimated the stabilized cost of its 'one-power' fleet at approximately £65–70 million per annum. The Admiralty now placed this figure at £88 million, and if the

Table 1.3   Total strength of the DRC and new standard fleets

	DRC fleet	New standard fleet			
		Optimum	Reduced	Under-standing with Japan	Agreement with Germany
Capital ships	15	20	20	20	20
Aircraft carriers	8	15[1]	14[1]	13	10
Cruisers	70	100[2]	88[3]	83[4]	68[5]
Destroyer flotillas	16[6]	22[7]	18[8]	16[8]	14½[9]
Submarines	55	82	73	73	55
Estimated total cost	£88 million	£104 million	£97 million	£94 million	£88 million

[1] This figure to include three ships at long notice for which no aircraft would be provided in peace.
[2] 10 of these might be maintained by the Dominions.
[3] Another 10 would be maintained by the Dominions.
[4] Another 7–10 would be maintained by the Dominions.
[5] Another 8 would be maintained by the Dominions.
[6] Including 4 overage flotillas.
[7] 3 of these might be maintained by the Dominions.
[8] Another 3 would be maintained by the Dominions.
[9] Another 1½ would be maintained by the Dominions.

Source: 'Board Memorandum on a New Standard of Naval Strength,' 26 April 1937, ADM 1/9081.

new standard were approved, this might easily rise to £104 million or higher.[102] Treasury officials believed Britain could not afford to spend this amount on the navy without impairing its economic strength and, ultimately, its war-making capacity. Even if the Admiralty's case rested on firm strategic foundations, they argued that the preservation of Britain's economic power must take precedence, and that expenditure on the fighting services would have to be brought into line with what Britain could afford to pay. Thus Bridges maintained that although

the naval experts may be able to prove that on certain hypotheses we ought to have a fleet of a certain size, the answer to them may very well be that we just can't afford to spend £100 millions a year for all time on our navy in peace time; for if this were necessary we should have to reconcile ourselves to having virtually no Air Force and no Army, which is ridiculous.[103]

In the summer of 1937, the Treasury, confronted with growing demands from all three of the fighting services, pressed the government to impose definite financial limitations on rearmament. In a clear exposition of his department's position, Sir Richard Hopkins, the Second Seceretary, claimed that

> in present conditions there is no foreseeable limit to the money which could be spent in providing defence measures of one form or another, for which on technical grounds a good case can be established, against some risks, which may possibly mature; and on the other hand, it is impossible to provide a full measure of security against all possible risks without imposing an intolerable burden on the financial, economic and commercial resources of the country. We must face the fact that we cannot do everything we should like to do; that there is a limit to the amount of money that can be made available for defence measures and that the money available for defence must be allocated to those purposes, which, on a broad review of the whole situation, are regarded as of prime importance. The system under which individual Departments put up great new schemes at odd times, without regard to the aggregate bill, is fast leading to financial chaos.[104]

Hopkins' immediate objective was to re-establish Treasury control over the estimates of the fighting services, which by mid-1937 appeared to be in danger of disappearing entirely.[105] A government-imposed spending cap would give the Treasury a trump card to play against claims by the services that authorized programs and standards had to be adhered to at any cost. In putting this proposal forward, the Treasury effectively conceded that the services' case for rearmament was strategically sound and that the maximum possible amount would have to be spent on defense for the next few years. The Treasury expected to have a major voice in determining what that maximum amount would be, but once that issue was settled, it intended to allow the services a relatively free hand in spending the money allocated to them – a clear indication of how far 'Treasury control' had slumped since 1932.

The new Chancellor, Sir John Simon, put this proposal before the Cabinet in June 1937.[106] Ministers received it favorably and instructed the defense departments to submit fresh estimates of the overall size and cost of their individual rearmament programs. When these forecasts were received in October, the Cabinet referred the whole matter to Sir Thomas Inskip, the Minister for Co-ordination of Defence, 'in consultation with representatives of the Treasury and such others as he may from time to time invite, including political Ministers specially concerned.'[107] Although Inskip was not specifically charged with examining the Admiralty's proposals for a new standard, the composition of the 1938 new construction program came under consideration in late 1937 and he was compelled to address this question pending his review of defense expenditure as a whole. Inskip was not prepared to reach a final decision on this matter, and in an interim report to the Cabinet he asserted that there was no pressing need to do so since any definite ruling could not have a significant impact on the navy's new construction programs for another year. 'For the time being,' he ruled that the Admiralty should 'proceed broadly on the basis of the D.R.C. Fleet without prejudice to the adoption at a later date of the proposed new standard should a decision subsequently be given to this effect. This enables us to defer for the time being a decision on a matter which would have far-reaching consequences.'[108]

This ruling set the stage for further confrontation between the Admiralty and the Treasury. In November, the Admiralty outlined a program of new construction for 1938 virtually identical to the accelerated programs of the previous two years, the main difference being that these latest proposals would begin to put the navy above the totals set out in the DRC report[109] (Table 1.4). Phillips, the Director of Plans, realized that Inskip's report, 'if rigidly interpreted by the Treasury, might be held to preclude any new construction which could not be fully justified on the D.R.C. standard. Since our arguments for justifying our 1938 programme generally on the D.R.C. standard are very thin,' he recommended that 'it might be well to make it clear in

Table 1.4   The Admiralty's proposed new construction program for 1938 and its relationship to the DRC program

	Authorized in 1936 and 1937 programs	Proposed by Admiralty for 1938 program	Admiralty's proposed total for 1936–9	DRC total for 1936–9	DRC total for 1936–44
Battleships	5	3	8	7	12
Aircraft carriers	4	2	6	4	4
Cruisers	14	7	21	15	35
Destroyers	34	8	42	18	36
Submarines	15	7	22	9	21

Source: CP 29 (38), 'New Construction Programme, 1938,' Memorandum by the First Lord of the Admiralty, 11 February 1938, CAB 24/274.

the Cabinet that the Admiralty read this section of the Report in general as authorising them to put forward in 1938 a new construction programme based on the needs of the New Standard.'[110] Phillips' interpretation was not as implausible as it might appear at first glance. Inskip's report could, in fact, be interpreted as suggesting that the Minister had accepted the Admiralty's proposed 1938 construction program, including the vessels which would raise the navy above the approved DRC standard. Moreover, the report recommended that the Admiralty should not prematurely scrap vessels which had only recently been modernized, thereby explicitly sanctioning an increase in battleship strength over the DRC standard.[111] The Admiralty therefore decided to ignore the Treasury's protests and in February 1938 put its entire program before the Cabinet. The First Lord, Alfred Duff Cooper, assured his colleagues that this program did not commit the government to the new standard and was fully justified on strategic grounds by the continuing deterioration of the international situation. 'In these circumstances,' he stated, 'the position of a defence Minister in this country who was unable truthfully to assert that he was taking every step in his power to complete, and to hasten the completion of, his preparations for the worst eventuality would be most unenviable.'[112]

The Admiralty's proposals only served to confirm Treasury opinion 'that the Admiralty have not sincerely and honestly accepted the Cabinet decision that substantially they are to work on the D.R.C. programme unless and until it be decided in a year's time from now that a greater programme can be sanctioned. On the contrary,' Hopkins claimed,

> they are now both preparing a better jumping off ground than the D.R.C. programme and also putting forward a 1938 programme which while paying lip-service to the D.R.C. provision is in essence indefensible except as part of a far larger whole the sanction for which they confidently expect sooner or later to obtain. To those who believe, as I do, both that the aims of the Admiralty are far above the true necessities of the case and that they are far beyond our means, it is obvious that a halt ought to be called.[113]

Applying the brakes was not a simple matter, however, and Treasury officials recognized that the task would become more difficult if a third 'accelerated' program were approved for 1938. If this happened, the Admiralty would have succeeded in laying down approximately 80 per cent of the DRC building program in three years rather than the seven originally intended. Naval decision-makers had recognized when they embarked on this course that they might have to curtail new construction drastically once this point had been reached, but they had gambled that they would be allowed to go on building new ships once existing limits had been realized. Whether this gamble paid off depended ultimately on what the government was more afraid of – being inadequately armed for war with Germany and Japan, or facing a financial crisis two or three years down the road. The Treasury and the Admiralty both realized that when the time finally came for a decision, politicians would be influenced by the public outcry which would result from appearing to abandon naval rearmament, and by the dislocation such a move would cause in the British shipbuilding industry. The Treasury feared and the Admiralty hoped that these considerations would eventually tip the balance in favor of naval expansion.

On the surface, therefore, the struggle over the navy's 1938 construction program was simply one more skirmish in the ongoing war between the Treasury and the Admiralty. Both sides were aware, however, that a decision on the future size of the navy could not be long delayed, and both were consciously preparing their positions for the impending battle. In these circumstances, the composition of the 1938 program took on an exaggerated importance to both sides. Not surprisingly, the Treasury insisted on a 'rigid' interpretation of Inskip's report. Its officials scrutinized the navy's proposed construction program and concluded that if the DRC fleet was not to be exceeded the Admiralty must drop one of its proposed aircraft carriers, a destroyer flotilla, and a submarine, and to be certain that the question of the new standard was in no way prejudiced, the Admiralty should also abandon its other carrier, a cruiser, and three more submarines.[114]

In February 1938 the Cabinet ordered the Admiralty to strike from its program one battleship, an aircraft carrier, a destroyer flotilla, three submarines, and assorted smaller vessels.[115] This decision was immediately overshadowed, however, by the appearance of a further report by Inskip on defense expenditure.[116] This document supported the Treasury's case for rationing the fighting services and recommended that a limit of £1650 million be placed on defense spending for the five-year period 1937–41. The Cabinet accepted this recommendation and on 11 March Inskip wrote to the First Lord suggesting an allocation of £480 million to the Admiralty over the years 1938–41.[117] This proposal was not well received, and the First Lord warned the Minister that acceptance of this figure would put not only the proposed new standard out of reach, but the DRC standard as well.[118] The navy had no intention of accepting this latest turn of events without a fight, and on 4 April the First Lord circulated a departmental minute seeking advice on how to respond to the new rationing scheme.[119] The Director of Plans (D of P) felt that the

> the present moment is not a very opportune one to press our case very strongly. Opinion in Government circles seems to move in waves, and at the moment, as a result of recent events, the particular bogey which has prominence is that of the air menace to this country, and I doubt if at this moment the Cabinet could be brought to look at matters from the Imperial point of view, which is necessary if we are to get a satisfactory decision about the Naval Standard of Strength.[120]

He was confident, however, that the Admiralty would eventually achieve its goal. 'The need for a New Standard is, of course, simply due to the growth of the German Navy,' he asserted, 'and as that Navy grows no Government will really be able to let us fall behind Germany plus Japan in Naval strength. If they try to do so the country will certainly insist that the necessary ships are built.' The best course, in his opinion, was 'to take things as we find them and press for the approval of those measures now which can be fully justified from the point of view of the particular menace which is influencing the Government at the moment, i.e. the air threat from Germany.'[121]

On 5 April the First Lord met with his principal naval advisers to discuss this problem. The D of P's suggestion to approach the government for money to protect naval vessels and installations against German air attack was approved, but not his advice to put off discussion of the new standard. Taking a wider view of the problem, Chatfield stressed that 'the Admiralty had enjoyed considerable advantage in the past in obtaining its annual new construction programme from the fact that it was working to a recognised policy which successive Governments could only disturb with difficulty; at the present time we had lost that advantage.'[122] The most pressing danger facing the Admiralty was that rationing might supplant naval standards as the principal means of determining the size of the navy. In these circumstances the First Lord preferred to launch a full-fledged attack on the new scheme before it had time to become entrenched. In a memorandum drafted for circulation to the Cabinet, he complained that the 'very word "rationing" denotes a situation of extreme scarcity, which does not appear to have arisen.'

The first duty of a Government is to ensure adequate defences of the country. What these adequate defences are is certainly more easily ascertainable than the country's financial resources. The danger of underrating the former seems to me greater than the danger of overrating the latter, since the one may lead to defeat in war and complete destruction, whereas the other can only lead to severe embarrassment, heavy taxation, lowering of the standard of living and reduction of the social services. It seems to me that in this matter we should decide first upon our needs, for after all the continuance of the Empire depends upon its defences, and that we should then inquire as to our means of meeting them. If it is found to be quite impossible to meet them, then it must be necessary to alter either the whole of our social system or the whole of our foreign and imperial policy.[123]

From the Admiralty's perspective, rationing was tolerable only if the sums involved were large enough for the navy to meet its strategic requirements. Naval decision-makers believed that the best, if not the only, way to ensure this was to secure a formal naval standard laying out what these requirements were. With the rationing system already accepted in principle, the Admiralty no longer had anything to lose by pressing for a decision on the new standard. Approval, and hence a complete victory for the navy, was clearly unlikely at this time, but Cabinet endorsement of even the outdated DRC standard would now improve the navy's position. The First Lord therefore pressed for the issue to be placed before the DPP for consideration.

The Treasury had no desire to reopen this discussion, believing that any further debate could only lead to concessions in the Admiralty's favor – an estimate which proved to be correct. The Treasury's position was actually much weaker than it appeared at this time, despite the Cabinet's endorsement of Inskip's report. Officials at both the Treasury and the Admiralty recognized that a ration at the level originally proposed would mean a drastic reduction in the pace of naval rearmament, and that this might result in strong public and political pressure to increase naval expenditure. Inskip therefore advised the Chancellor that he should 'go slow' on the question of rationing.

The House of Commons has rather lost its head at the moment and there is widespread comment, inspired of course by the press and one or two people, that we are not facing up to the situation. You and I know what the answer to this is, but anything we can do to prevent the suspicion from becoming an open charge, I feel ought to be done. It would never do for us to have to make the case in Parliament that some steps, which otherwise we should have to agree were desirable, could not be taken on the ground that we had exhausted our financial resources.[124]

The Admiralty successfully forced the issue, however, by refusing to provide a revised forecast of naval expenditure based on the rationing proposal. When Simon complained about the Admiralty's failure to comply with his requests for information, Duff Cooper replied that 'as it would be impossible within that figure to produce the D.R.C. fleet and as the Board considered the D.R.C. fleet hopelessly inadequate it had seemed to me a waste of time to provide a picture of anything smaller.' He added, however, that he was 'quite willing...to add a paragraph to my memorandum to the effect that the ration would make any further construction during the next three years impossible and would still leave us with £9 m. to find.'[125] The Admiralty's intransigence ensured that a solution could not be worked out at the departmental level.

Once the depth of the Admiralty's opposition to rationing became clear, Treasury officials accepted that the issue must be submitted to the Cabinet for a decision. Although Inskip and the Chancellor were resigned to some increase to the navy's ration, the Admiralty's demands for a fleet based solely on strategic requirements threatened to undermine the whole rationing scheme. Sir Alan Barlow, an Under-Secretary, advised Hopkins that the 'easiest way of settling this very difficult question would be to tell the Navy that they can only have so much money and must cut their coat according to their cloth.'

The objections are, firstly, that it will be difficult to get Ministers to take such a decision and, secondly, that the Sea Lords may say with some force that they cannot plan a Fleet on a money basis only but must have a policy laid down to guide them...The Sea Lords up to now have made no attempt to arrive at a compromise fleet. It is probable that if they were told definitely that the New Standard Fleet is beyond our means and that some lower basis must be adopted, and if Ministers, while accepting their view that for what may be called the two power Standard the Fleet which they suggest is the right one, took the responsibility of saying that it could not be provided, the Sea Lords would apply their minds to producing a satisfactory compromise which could be expressed in terms of policy.

It seems essential, therefore, if progress is to be made that the New Standard Fleet should be ruled out.[126]

The problem facing the Treasury, then, was that it could not enforce the rationing scheme until the government stated *explicitly* that financial considerations must take precedence over naval standards. Once this was done, it would not matter greatly to the Treasury what standard the navy adopted. The Chancellor therefore advised Chamberlain in late June that 'the best course would be ... to have the question what is the size of the Fleet we can afford raised and decided in Cabinet.'[127] The Prime Minister agreed, and Inskip brought the question of naval expenditure before the Cabinet on 20 July.[128] Ministers accepted the Admiralty's contention that a two-power standard was desirable on strategic grounds, but upheld the view that financial considerations must have priority. Thus, it was decided that 'in the present circumstances we cannot commit ourselves to the Standard known as the New Standard Fleet.'

The Admiralty was not pleased with this decision and immediately put forward its own interpretation of the Cabinet's ruling. Duff Cooper wrote to Inskip on 21 July suggesting that 'the Cabinet are not disposed to reject the advice of the Sea Lords on the strength of the naval forces which they consider necessary to carry out the duty laid upon the Board of Admiralty by H.M. Government, and it is now a question of deciding at what rate we should proceed towards our agreed goal, namely the New Standard.'[129] The First Lord also wrote to Maurice Hankey, the Cabinet Secretary, asking that the wording of the Cabinet's conclusion be rephrased, as he felt that 'no decision of any kind' had in fact been 'reached with regard to the New Standard.'[130] This plea was rejected by the Prime Minister,[131] while Inskip informed the First Lord that in his view:

> The Cabinet were not prepared to commit themselves to the standard known as the 'New Standard Fleet' though, of course, this also means that they did not reject it. If it is possible to get away from the two rather misleading phrases 'the D.R.C. Fleet' and the 'New Standard Fleet,' I think the substance of the Cabinet decision was that we were to try and find a middle way between the rigid ration previously allocated to the Navy and the demand put forward in your memoranda.[132]

The only question remaining was the size of the Admiralty ration. Treasury officials accepted that the navy must have something greater than the DRC fleet, but they were determined that it should not be much greater. Inskip had originally proposed a figure of £355 million for the three years 1939–41. The Admiralty calculated that it would require no less than £395 million for the DRC fleet and £443 million for the full new standard. Treasury officials believed the DRC program could be completed for £385 million, and thought that £400 million was a perfectly reasonable figure.[133] After some hard bargaining, a compromise of £410 million was finally agreed, almost exactly between the two original positions.[134]

Because no precise standard of naval strength was laid down by the Cabinet, this settlement allowed the Admiralty to exceed the limits set out in the DRC report and to build up to a strength as near to the new standard as it could manage without exceeding the agreed ration figure. Most importantly, it ensured that the Admiralty's new construction programs would not be drastically curtailed once the vessels authorized in the original DRC program had been laid down. This settlement effectively ended the debate over naval standards, but it did not prevent the Admiralty from taking every opportunity to increase naval spending and supplement its shipbuilding program. During the course of discussions over the 1939 estimates, Treasury officials complained that the Admiralty had

never accepted the Ration decision which had been confirmed by the Cabinet on three separate occasions and never made any serious or honest attempt to apply it … In a word, it really comes to this, that the Admiralty apparently consider that they are not bound to accept any decisions which are distasteful to them, even if these decisions have been given by the Cabinet.[135]

This judgement stemmed from the Admiralty's penchant for proposing additions to its ration.[136] The deteriorating international situation in the year following the Munich settlement ensured that the navy's demands found an increasingly receptive audience. In March 1939, the Committee on the Acceleration of Defence Programmes, chaired by the new Minister for the Co-ordination of Defence, Lord Chatfield, invited the Admiralty to consider measures for the acceleration of existing programs. The Treasury rejected the navy's proposals for increasing the production capacity for heavy guns, on the grounds that any additional capacity created would become 'completely redundant at a comparatively early date'[137] – a claim which was true if capital ship construction dropped off sharply after 1941, as the Treasury hoped it would. The Admiralty was undeterred, however, and continued to press its case. In July the issue was taken to the CID. Lord Stanhope, the First Lord, attempted to exploit Hitler's denunciation of the AGNA in April to press for the inclusion of one additional battleship in the navy's 1940 construction program. More importantly, he advised that with Germany now unfettered by treaty restrictions, Britain must lay down no less than three battleships a year from 1941 onwards if it were not to fall behind Germany and Japan in new capital ship construction.[138] The CID approved measures to begin an extra battleship in 1940, but was not yet prepared to endorse more far-reaching proposals to expand industrial capacity for an increased construction program. The Admiralty was invited to prepare a report to present the full implications of its proposals to the CID by October 1939. If these recommendations had been accepted, the Admiralty would have secured a *de facto* two-power standard in capital ships. At all events, Britain's declaration of war against Germany in September prevented another showdown with the Treasury and ensured that the Admiralty's final bid for a two-power standard would not be realized.[139]

Historians have frequently misunderstood the significance of the Admiralty's campaign for the new standard. Until recently, the accepted view has been that financial considerations imposed serious limitations on naval rearmament during the latter half of the 1930s. If the government had provided more money, it was argued, the navy could have had more ships. Hence, the Admiralty's failure to secure the new standard was a serious defeat which damaged the navy's position in the short term. More recently, Andrew Gordon has demonstrated that naval construction during this period was limited more by production constraints than financial ones.[140] Thus, even if the government had approved the new standard and spent more on naval rearmament, the Admiralty could not have built significantly more ships than it did during this period. Gordon also argues, however, that

> the withholding of approval for the enlarged standard had little influence on new construction output; industrially speaking, the controversy surrounding the New Standard was a matter only 'of academical interest since we shall already be working towards that standard at our best speed and cannot attain it for several years to come.'[141]

This statement is not entirely accurate. The navy did not lobby as hard as it did for the new standard simply to ensure that its needs would be met in the distant future. The Admiralty had every reason to treat the new standard as a matter of immediate and practical concern, for while it could not build more ships than it did, it could have been forced to build considerably fewer if Treasury control had been rigidly applied. Approval of the new standard would have significantly lessened the financial restraints on naval rearmament. As it was, the navy still had to gain approval for its programs on an annual basis, and it possessed no guarantee that it would be allowed to continue building to the limits of Britain's shipbuilding capacity when its estimates next came up for consideration. The only reason that the navy could build as much as it did during the years 1936–8 was that it successfully exploited the DRC standard and the government's concerns over German rearmament to 'accelerate' the existing program. The Treasury objected to this process, but was unable to stop it because the Cabinet refused to renounce the new standard. Thus, even though approval was withheld, the Admiralty benefitted simply by keeping the issue alive.

The most common charge against the one-power standard – that it deprived the navy of its ability to fight in two hemispheres simultaneously – is unfounded. During the 1920s, Britain possessed a *de facto* two-power standard relative to Japan and the strongest European naval power. Its ability to send a fleet to the Far East did indeed decline in the 1930s, but this was the result of quantitative treaty restrictions, the series of decisions taken between 1925 and 1935 which allowed the navy to drop below the strength it was legally entitled to, and the emergence of a third hostile power, Italy. The one-power standard cannot be held responsible for any of these developments – indeed, during the period when the navy was most damaged, 1929–34, the one-power standard lost its influence and the real factor was tightly enforced treaty limits.

Nor can the Admiralty be blamed for accepting a naval standard which could not meet its basic strategic requirements. The one-power standard the navy lobbied for and received in 1920 was fundamentally different from the one-power standard it found itself saddled with after the Washington Conference. In its original form, this standard did nothing more than lay down the optimum size of the RN relative to the USN. Thus if the United States increased the size of its navy, the British government had an obligation either to do the same or abandon the standard. But if the USN were reduced in strength, Britain still had complete freedom to decide whether to follow suit. If reductions were undesirable on strategic grounds, the government could always lay down a new standard. Indeed, this option was available any time that the government decided that the standard ceased to meet Britain's strategic requirements. All of this was changed, however, by the decision to accept a quantitative naval limitation agreement. The Washington Treaty and its successor, the first London Treaty, laid down the size of the RN in both relative and absolute terms, thereby depriving Britain of the ability to increase its naval strength in response to changing strategic circumstances. To make matters worse, when Britain finally abandoned quantitative limitations, it found that its ability to expand the navy quickly was thwarted by financial and industrial restrictions.

As long as the maximum size of the navy was limited by international treaties, the only direction to go was down. The real significance of naval standards lies in their influence on how much of the maximum treaty figure Britain *chose* to maintain. The overall impact of standards on the size of the navy during the interwar period is difficult to assess, but it is probably fair to say that if they had never existed, Britain's naval strength in September 1939 would not have been much different than it actually was. Governments continued to employ the one-power standard after Washington as a convenient means of regulating the size of the Navy Estimates over the long term. If the standard clashed with political, diplomatic, or financial concerns, it was either modified or ignored. On the other hand, the Treasury's ability to control the size of naval estimates during the interwar period has been considerably exaggerated by historians such as Roskill.[142] When the international climate appeared threatening, ministers were usually willing to overrule the Treasury and lay down ships that the Admiralty wanted. The existence of the one-power standard did not, for example, prevent the navy from building to the limits of Britain's industrial capacity during the years 1936–9. Conversely, if the government felt that the advantages of disarmament or the need for retrenchment outweighed strategic considerations, then no appeal to the sanctity of the current standard could save the Admiralty's programs. Thus Ramsay MacDonald canceled the Singapore Naval Base, accepted parity with the United States in cruisers, and slashed Britain's margin in battleships – but never considered it necessary to renounce or even modify the one-power standard. Over the long term, the size of the Royal Navy was determined by the Cabinet's views on Britain's financial, diplomatic, and strategic needs, and not by any abstract formula. At times, such as in 1921, the one-power standard could, by its mere existence, compel the government to take actions it had little enthusiasm for, but any administration willing to accept the political risks could overrule the Admiralty and ignore its demands.

On a year-to-year basis, however, naval standards did often have an impact on the precise size of the navy's estimates. As long as the government believed that the current definition of the standard met its needs, the Admiralty and the Treasury were generally left to settle the annual Navy Estimates between them. In these circumstances, the existence of a naval standard, the way it was worded, and how it was interpreted could give one side of the debate leverage against the other. This often had an important bearing on the outcome of the interdepartmental discussions on Navy Estimates for any given year. But because this factor favored the Treasury nearly as often as the Admiralty, naval standards did not by themselves have a significant long-term impact on the size and well-being of the Royal Navy.

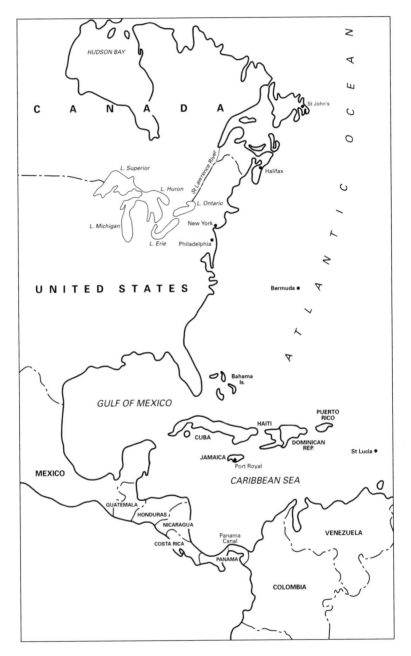

Map 2.1 The Atlantic Theater

2
'Main Fleet to Bermuda': Naval Strategy for an Anglo-American War

The consequences of war with the United States were potentially so great that British decision-makers could not afford to dismiss the prospect out of hand. No less a figure than Winston Churchill, the architect of the Anglo-American 'special relationship' and, after 1963, an honorary US citizen, could write in 1927 that it was 'quite right in the interests of peace to go on talking about war with the United States being "unthinkable". Everyone knows that this is not true.'[1] The likelihood of war was so remote, however, that the British navy, unlike its American counterpart, did not prepare formal plans for such a contingency at any time during the first half of the twentieth century. Asquith's Liberal government had ruled in 1909 that the Admiralty should not treat the USN as a potential opponent; and Lloyd George's Cabinet reaffirmed the ruling in August 1919 to prevent the Admiralty from using US naval construction to justify a large building program of its own. These concerns were justified: at the end of the First World War, the USN was in fact beginning to play a prominent role in the Admiralty's calculations. Official memoranda on future naval requirements prepared following the Armistice contained explicit references to the possibility of an Anglo-American war[2] and, in June 1919, the Plans Division recommended that an officer be assigned to draw up plans for one.[3]

The Cabinet's decree of 1919 virtually ended talk of war with the United States within naval circles. The Admiralty continued to argue that Britain must match American naval strength for reasons of prestige, but it rarely suggested that an Anglo-American war was a serious possibility and, in the decades following the Washington Conference, it did not prepare specifically for such a conflict. The following discussion of British views on strategy for an Anglo-American conflict is therefore drawn from two principal sources: Admiralty documents prepared in 1918–19, and testimony presented to the Bonar Law Committee in early 1921.[4] This committee's formal charge was the future role of the capital ship in the navy, but the hypothetical case most frequently cited was a war between Britain and the US. The committee's records therefore contain the detailed views of both committee members and expert witnesses, including two future first sea lords, Madden and Chatfield, on this problem.[5] The records reveal the existence of agreement among naval officers about the principal aspects of strategy in a war with the US.

The views of British naval officers, who did not look upon the prospect of an Anglo-American war with any enthusiasm, were shaped by geopolitics as well as by sentiment. Most officers would have agreed with Beatty that the United States was a 'country which is allied to us in blood, in language and in literature and with whom we share the mutual aspiration of maintaining the peace and progress of the world.'[6] In his view, Britain's wisest course would be to pursue the closest possible cooperation with the United States. Beatty asserted:

> From motives of economy alone, but also from the far mightier motive of a union between the English-speaking nations of the World, it seems inevitable that our whole political Naval Policy should be directed towards an Alliance or Entente with the United States, and that the British Empire and the United States should then be able to advance hand in hand in their peaceful avocations, increasing happiness, contentment, and prosperity.[7]

These sentiments were later expressed rather more bluntly by Admiral Sir Barry Domvile, who insisted that anyone 'who is not a congenital idiot must realise that the greatest guarantee for world peace is that lasting friendship should exist between the British Empire and the United States, and every policy having for its object the increased cordiality of their mutual relations should be encouraged.'[8]

The principal obstacle to such an arrangement was that the Americans could not be counted upon to play along. On the contrary, the United States' maritime ambitions during and immediately after the First World War convinced many naval officers that ample room existed for British and American interests to clash in the future.

The DCNS, Vice-Admiral Sir Osmond Brock, believed that the 'late war has removed Germany as a possible enemy, but the other effect of the War has been that the United States has become our rival for the carrying trade of the world.'

> The United States are endeavouring, as we know, to build up a very large mercantile marine, and they therefore to a certain extent do threaten our existence. Since Great Britain has been a naval Power I think I am right in saying that the ultimate cause of all our wars – even though these causes may apparently be covered by dynastic or territorial reasons, or balance of power – has been commercial rivalry. In the Dutch wars, the Spanish, the French, and the last War certainly, the ultimate cause was commercial rivalry, and if the United States perseveres in her aims we shall inevitably, not necessarily go to war with her, but we shall come into conflict with her in various parts of the world. The question therefore arises whether we ought to reconsider the decision … that we cannot fight the United States. I am quite ready to allow that a war with the United States is very improbable, but that it is impossible I cannot allow.[9]

More extreme views were also expressed from time to time. The C-in-C China Station, Vice-Admiral Arthur Leveson, recommended in 1924, for example, that the Plans Division should devote some of its attention to 'a war against AMERICA with JAPAN as our ally. From what I have seen in the Far East, AMERICA is much more mischief-making and aggressive in every way than JAPAN.'[10] Similarly, the C-in-C Mediterranean, Roger Keyes, confided in 1927 to Winston Churchill that

> If we are ever at war, with America neutral, and the American Fleet, present and potential, sets out in convoys to force her trade and maintain the Freedom of the Seas for neutrals, I pray that the Government of the day will have the nerve to deny their claim and will allow the British Fleet to deal with the situation. Nothing in the world could possibly please me more than to be in command of such an undertaking.[11]

Few, if any, British naval officers thought that the United States would deliberately resort to armed force to supplant Britain as the world's pre-eminent maritime power. The greatest danger always appeared to be that the United States might unintentionally maneuver Britain into a position whence it could not retreat, thereby compelling a resort to arms. The most likely scenario envisaged was a clash arising from Britain's attempts to regulate trade during a war with a third power.

How to bring a war with the United States to a successful conclusion presented an intractable problem. An invasion of the United States was ruled out as an operation beyond Britain's capabilities. The alternative of economic pressure, which would include a naval blockade of the United States' coast and the interception of its seaborne trade, was slow acting and probably indecisive against a self-sufficient continental state. The consensus, therefore, was that Britain could hope at best for a stalemate leading to negotiations for peace. According to Brock:

> All we could do would be to make the condition of affairs on both sides of the American coast so unpleasant that the American people would say 'This is not worth it; we have nothing to gain, we do not want colonies, it has never been our policy to obtain colonies; we do not want money from Great Britain; therefore the best thing we can do is to come to some agreement.'[12]

His colleagues agreed that commerce raiding, the bombardment of coastal naval and military installations, and small-scale amphibious assaults might cause enough economic and social upheaval to undermine the Americans' political will to continue the fight.

Because Britain was dependent on seaborne imports, a knockout blow against its trade appeared to be a real danger. But while Britain's goal would be simply to 'hold on' until the Americans tired of the war, a purely defensive strategy of keeping the British fleet in home waters and attacking the US fleet only if it crossed the Atlantic was ruled out. Britain might obtain the tactical advantage in the event of a fleet action, but in the meantime it could expect to lose a large portion of its overseas trade. The importance of protecting that trade, the possibility that the Americans might withhold their fleet, and the desire to improve Britain's negotiating position, all pointed to the need for an offensive campaign. The navy would therefore have to protect British maritime trade and apply pressure on the United States. It was agreed that these goals could best be accomplished by establishing the British fleet in the western hemisphere, for which purpose Bermuda was generally regarded to be the most suitable location.[13] A powerful fleet would be sent across the Atlantic at the earliest possible moment to neutralize the US fleet while British cruisers based in Canada and the West Indies protected imperial trade routes and disrupted the enemy's trade. As the C-in-C Atlantic Fleet, Madden, explained:

> I should send the main fleet to Bermuda. I should hope that you would be able to hold Halifax as a submarine and light cruiser base

on the northern flank of the American defences and to hold Port Royal in Jamaica for a similar purpose on the southern flank and also to hold St. Lucia as a submarine and destroyer base for attacks on the trade passing through the Panama canal. Probably also if the air offensive is sufficiently advanced at the time to use aircraft to attack the Panama canal and also for the protection of the communications between this country and your advanced base at Jamaica.[14]

Such a strategy offered the best hope of neutralizing the US fleet and protecting British merchant vessels. As long as American capital ships did not have easy access to the Atlantic trade routes, it was thought that cruiser forces could provide a reasonable level of protection to British commerce. Trade with Canada, however, would almost certainly be cut off. As Richmond remarked, there was nothing 'in the world to prevent an American army from marching from the state of Maine and commanding the St. Lawrence with heavy guns. So long as they have a population of 110 millions and we have a population of 60 millions, it is not within bounds of possibility to prevent them commanding the St. Lawrence.'[15] Trade with South America would probably be seriously disrupted as well, but the complete loss of both Canadian and South American trade was not regarded as fatal to Britain.

British officers never expressed any doubt as to the outcome of a fleet action if one did occur, and even American officers conceded that Britain's position at sea was a strong one. Throughout the 1920s, American naval opinion still regarded the British fleet as superior in fighting power, even though parity in capital ships had been established by the Washington Treaty.[16] In 1922, for example, the General Board of the USN was told that investigations by the Naval War College at Newport had concluded that once the treaty was implemented, 'the ratio of fighting strength of the British [fleet] is to our own as their 1.4 is to our 1 at ranges of 20,000 yards or less, while at over 20,000 yards their strength is 2.5 to our 1.'[17] In 1930, American planners still believed that the British navy as a whole was 'better balanced' than the American navy, and 'also has greater speed and gun range.' The British were also expected to benefit from their 'many well located, fortified naval bases' and the possession of a 'large and efficient naval reserve.' In terms of fighting strength, Britain would possess an advantage at maximum range, although at 'slightly less ranges,' the advantage would be with the Americans. 'At short ranges' it was thought that the 'main batteries of both fleets are equally effective.'

The only clear US advantage was in ship-borne aircraft, in which the United States possessed 'a great superiority.'[18]

Most British naval officers expected that an Anglo-American war would be a predominantly naval affair in which large-scale land operations would only take place, if they took place at all, in Canada and the Far East. A determined US invasion of Canada would be difficult, if not impossible, to repel. Canadian forces alone would be insufficient for this task,[19] and whether the British government would despatch large-scale reinforcements to Canada was impossible to predict. However, if an expeditionary force were sent, the Admiralty acknowledged that 'the Empire would be committed to an unlimited land war against the U.S.A., with all the advantages of time, distance and supply on side of the U.S.A.'[20] The navy was confident, however, that with a fleet at Bermuda it could tie down the US fleet and maintain an expeditionary forces' communications with Britain. But what a British expeditionary force in North America could hope to accomplish was another matter. Naval opinion hoped, at the very least, to hold Halifax for use as a naval base. Indeed, this was considered to be essential if the navy were to support a land campaign in Canada. As a precaution against failure, however, one Admiralty memorandum recommended that 'the possibility of obtaining a large ice-free anchorage elsewhere should be investigated by the Canadian authorities.'[21]

The Far East, on the other hand, would probably be the scene of only subsidiary operations. The Americans were expected to keep their main naval force in the Atlantic, but the possibility always existed that it could be sent to the Pacific through the Panama Canal. Unless a superior British fleet were then despatched to the Far East, the United States would be in a position to inflict considerable damage on British trade in the region, and possibly capture Hong Kong. With a British fleet in the Far East, however, the balance of advantage would be reversed: Britain could protect its own trade while disrupting US trade with Japan, China and South-East Asia. Thus, 'every effort should be made to deprive the United States of her only naval bases in that area by the capture of the Philippines... [as] the most economical and effective method of trade protection.' Men and materiel for the expedition would be drawn from India and Australia.[22]

British thinking about an Anglo-American war was not limited to the forward strategy outlined above. As the USN was the one opponent which would at least equal, and possibly surpass, the British in capital ship strength, when hostilities broke out the British might find themselves with the weaker fleet. As long as the disparity was small, it was agreed that Britain should still send its main force across the Atlantic, to adopt a fleet-in-being strategy while looking for opportunities to whittle away US superiority. An attempt by the Americans to set up a close blockade of Bermuda, for example, would give the British numerous opportunities to destroy individual ships through air and submarine attacks. According to Madden, as long as Britain

> could afford to let [its fleet] wait long enough, with a bit of good luck if the enemy is stupid enough to invest Bermuda closely with big ships, then I think there is every chance. My point is that the fleet is no use in home waters, you might just as well pay it off. While if stationed at Bermuda it compels the enemy to concentrate and covers to some extent your Atlantic trade, and you then wait for the enemy to make a mistake urged by the impetuous and ill-informed American press.

If the Admiralty were unable to send a fleet of *any* strength to the western hemisphere, and the US fleet crossed the Atlantic first, defeat was the probable outcome. A US offensive was expected to be essentially a mirror image of the Admiralty's 'main fleet to Bermuda' scheme. The US fleet would cross the Atlantic, take up a covering position at a suitable forward base, and detach cruiser forces to sever Britain's maritime communications.[23] The actual location of the enemy base was impossible to foresee. The United States might have a European ally willing to supply one; or it might seize one, perhaps in the Azores or along the coast of Spain. In either case, once the Americans possessed a secure base in the eastern Atlantic, there was no doubt that Britain would be placed in a 'most awkward' position. If the weaker British fleet came out to protect trade, it would be destroyed; if it remained in harbor, British trade would be annihilated. As Richmond declared, 'It would be a very bad situation indeed; I think that we should probably be at her mercy.'[24]

Other officers shared this gloomy prognosis. British naval opinion accepted that the presence of superior American naval forces off the western approaches would compel Britain's capitulation in short order. The enemy could cut off the flow of food and essential raw materials into Britain from overseas, and it was assumed that Britain would be unable to obtain its essential imports from Europe. This belief was not based on quantifiable data, but rather rested on the assumption that Britain's survival depended on its unfettered access to the oceanic trade routes. In fact, so great was Britain's vulnerability to this form of pressure that some admirals argued that the United States could achieve decisive results without ever having to send a fleet across the Atlantic at all, as the United States, unlike Japan, possessed sufficient naval forces and overseas bases to intercept a significant proportion of Britain's merchantmen outside of European waters.[25]

The Admiralty's thinking about an Anglo-American war never advanced beyond this rudimentary beginning, but its ideas were hardly less advanced in 1918–21 than its contemporaneous plans for war with Japan. The latter eventually formed the basis of the Admiralty's early War Memoranda (Eastern), and it is likely that if war plans against the United States had been developed, they would have evolved along the lines described above. Notably, the navy's basic strategies against the United States and Japan – the only two non-European naval powers capable of threatening vital British interests – were remarkably similar in their essentials. Both hinged on the prompt despatch of a substantial battle fleet to a base as near as possible to the enemy's shores; both gave greater prominence to neutralizing the enemy's fleet than to destroying it; and both relied heavily on economic pressure to force the enemy to negotiate. While the British consistently overestimated both their own economic vulnerability and that of Japan, the United States' immunity to this form of attack was never questioned. In the end, this realization was crucial to the navy's calculations. If British seapower alone could not hope to defeat decisively a major non-European naval power, then war with that power would have to be avoided at almost any cost. This proved to be a sound appreciation, and one which was based on a clear understanding of the limitations of seapower.

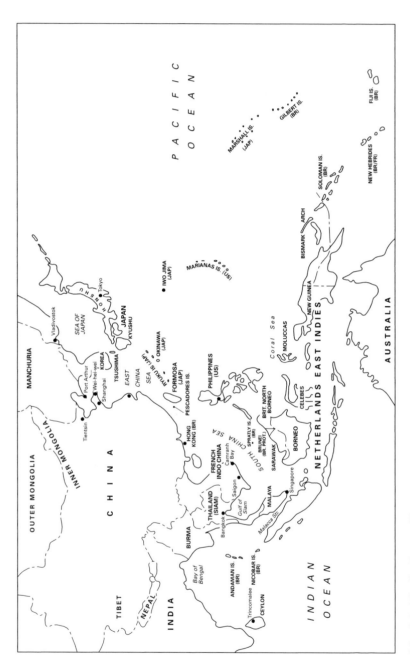

Map 3.1   The Far Eastern Theater

3
Far Eastern War Plans and the Myth of the Singapore Strategy

The 'Singapore Strategy' has been the subject of derision for generations of historians. According to the conventional view, Britain, unable to maintain a large naval presence in the Far East in peacetime, planned to despatch a battle fleet from European waters to Singapore once war with Japan had begun. Before these vessels arrived, British forces already present in the Far East would prevent Singapore from falling into enemy hands. Subsequent operations would be directed exclusively towards securing a fleet action with the Japanese navy.[1] This is little more than a caricature of the Admiralty's real intentions, but a consensus has nevertheless emerged that the idea of sending a fleet to the Far East was unrealistic when it was conceived in the early 1920s; that it became completely impractical during the 1930s; and that the Admiralty stubbornly clung to it long after its flaws should have been obvious. It has also been suggested that devotion to this strategy was responsible for the destruction of the *Prince of Wales* and *Repulse* off the Malayan coast in December 1941.

These claims rest on two basic misconceptions. In the first place, historians have been so preoccupied with whether Britain could ever have sent a fleet to the Far East that they have not carefully studied the strategy it was meant to adopt when it arrived there.[2] The passage of a fleet to Singapore is usually treated as an end in itself – indeed, this movement has become virtually synonymous with British Far Eastern naval strategy. However, the Admiralty's plans were more complex than is usually recognized. Sending a fleet to Singapore was only to be the opening move in a strategy which would project British power against Japan in its own home waters. Rather than being obsessed with

59

sinking the Japanese fleet, the Admiralty envisaged a prolonged war of attrition which would strangle the enemy's economy and compel it to seek terms whether a great sea battle took place or not. Second, it is usually assumed that the Admiralty possessed only a single rigid and unchanging strategy for war with Japan, a sort of naval Schlieffen plan which they could neither abandon nor modify. In fact, naval decision-makers considered the offensive strategy developed in the early 1920s as only one of the options open to them. They knew that their optimum plan was feasible only if the requisite bases were available and Britain's margin of naval superiority was sufficient. These factors were clearly beyond their control, and a less-than-ideal strategy was always a possibility. Consequently, the navy developed plans covering a wide range of contingencies. The nature of these plans has been obscured, however, by the haphazard use of the term 'Singapore Strategy' to cover all of the schemes produced during the interwar period. There were, in fact, several 'Singapore strategies.' Between 1920 and 1941, the Admiralty formulated both offensive and defensive war plans in which the main fleet might operate from Trincomalee, Singapore, Hong Kong, or any number of improvised bases.

This chapter traces the evolution of the navy's Far Eastern war plans between 1919 and 1941, and shows that the Admiralty's strategic planning against Japan, though deficient in many respects, was not as flawed as its critics maintain, and that its most serious shortcomings have gone largely unnoticed.

From the Washington Conference until the mid-1930s, naval war planning was dominated by the problem of defending Britain's eastern empire against Japanese encroachments. No other power appeared to possess to the same degree both the willingness and the ability to threaten the British Empire. The United States was clearly capable of inflicting greater damage, but few decision-makers regarded an Anglo-American war as a realistic possibility. Japan was in a different category altogether. Naval officers were inclined to view the Japanese as an intensely nationalistic, self-sacrificing and militaristic race, dominated by a 'very Prussian minded' military caste.[3] This perception was based in large part on a cynical reading of modern Japanese history. The naval staff believed, for example, that Japan's rise 'from a fourth rate position to the position of a first-class power,' was an ascent which 'has at once demonstrated and confirmed her belief in her mission.' It concluded that

> a set purpose has guided her local outlook in the East and her International policy generally and her armaments and her strategy

have been and are among, if not, the main factors of her unparalleled rapidity of material and political advancement. She has taken risks with courage: both when she embarked on war with China and again later with Russia, the general belief was that Japan would lose ... Today there is a large body of Japanese opinion which believes that victory in war is an efficient cause of improvement in National economy.[4]

British naval officers often expressed a grudging respect for Japan's expansionist ambitions. As one Director of Naval Intelligence (DNI) stated, it was necessary to 'recognize in all fairness that she [Japan] is in her Elizabethan era, and is doing what we ourselves gloried in. Such a recognition should at least remove some bitterness on our part.'[5] However, once Japan began to pursue its aims at Britain's expense, a degree of bitterness was unavoidable. The navy's disillusionment with its ally began during the First World War. Japan's contribution to the Allied war effort was regarded as perfunctory and self-serving. Beatty later claimed that there 'was reason to believe that if the war had taken a definite turn against us, Japan would have thrown over the Allies and associated herself with Germany, and that even during the war Japanese agents were in touch with Indian agitators.'[6] However, it was Japan's readiness to take advantage of her allies' distractions to press its '21 Demands' on China in 1915 that seemed to offer the clearest confirmation of Japan's propensity towards unscrupulous and opportunistic behavior.

Within naval circles Japan was widely credited with working to a long-range program of expansion. The scope of its ambitions was never defined with any precision, but it was generally regarded as falling somewhere between the political and economic domination of China, and hegemony over the entire Far East. What seemed clear though was that Japan's goals could only be achieved at the expense of the Western powers in general, and of Britain and the United States in particular. As Keyes declared, 'as surely as she [Japan] turned China out of Korea, Russia out of Manchuria, Germany out of Tsingtao, she will turn Europeans out of China and, in time, Asia, unless we are sufficiently strong to make it not worth her while to attempt it.'[7] The Admiralty also feared that internal pressures might drive Japan to adopt a more aggressive foreign policy. A typical naval staff assessment warned that in addition to 'the incentive of Japanese racial pride' and Japan's 'full confidence in her National mission and National destiny,'

Japan has other incentives for a policy of expansion; there is a certain restlessness amongst the Japanese: the population of the mainland, having regard especially to the poor quality of much of the soil, is already very overcrowded and is growing rapidly; the growing industrial sections in the large towns for economic and social reasons require outlets: In fact the need of outlets for the population and for increased commerce and markets, especially new sources of self-supply, will probably be amongst the most compelling reasons for Japan to push a policy of penetration expansion and aggression.[8]

It also appeared that war might arise out of Japanese resentment over the Dominions' discriminatory immigration policies. These considerations suggested that Japan could not be trusted to behave itself if opportunities for expansion arose. Even though it might appear pacific at present, Japan was still considered 'essentially autocratic and militaristic by tradition, with a conservative people who are easily rallied to the standard. The possibility, therefore, of a reversion at a favourable moment to a policy of conquest and a recrudescence of the war spirit cannot be overlooked.'[9]

The ability of the United States and Britain to defend their position in the Far East was seen as the principal restraint on Japan. Prior to the Washington Conference, the Admiralty derived some comfort from the belief that Japan was more likely to become embroiled with the United States than Britain. After the Conference, however, the former no longer appeared to be in a position to project its naval power into the western Pacific,[10] and the Admiralty concluded that the RN remained the only effective barrier to Japanese expansion. To meet this threat it would ideally have stationed a fleet in the Far East in peacetime, but financial considerations ruled this out. The alternative was to maintain the ability to despatch a fleet to the Far East in the event of a crisis. As long as Britain possessed sufficient warships and suitable bases, the Admiralty was confident that the threat of force would not need to be carried out. As Keyes stated on one occasion, it would not actually be

> necessary to fight a great war in the Pacific, or 'to put a battle fleet in the Pacific,' but it is necessary that we should be able to send a fleet to the East capable of defeating or neutralising the Japanese fleet should the occasion arise, and this fact being known to the Japanese would at least make them discreet and check their forward policy.[11]

The Admiralty was not prepared to rely solely on a deterrent strategy, however, and insisted that the navy must be able to make good its threats. This was never regarded as an easy task. Historians have often treated isolated racist remarks by naval officers as proof of a general contempt within the navy for all things Japanese, but there is a danger of taking this charge too far.[12] The navy's confidence during the 1920s stemmed principally from its quantitative superiority over the Japanese navy, rather than from any systematic tendency to downgrade its opponents' capabilities. In fact, the Admiralty was not inclined to disparage Japanese efficiency at this time. Throughout the 1920s, British naval attachés in Tokyo still enjoyed good access to Japanese naval establishments, and they generally described the Japanese navy in favorable terms. As one attaché noted, in a characteristically mixed assessment:

> It appears to me that the Japanese Navy is an efficient weapon of war which in the hands of a leader of imagination might yield great results; but that in the absence of such a leader it might be expected to be somewhat stereotyped in its methods and unable to adapt itself to changed conditions or unexpected difficulties.[13]

Thus while British naval planners clearly viewed their own fleet as superior to that of Japan, they also regarded the latter as being qualitatively equal to the other great navies of the 1920s, and they intended to fight it with at least equality in fleet strength, and preferably with more.

For planning purposes, the navy assumed that a numerically equal British fleet would be superior to a Japanese one, but they always believed that Britain should not take the risk of fighting with numerical inferiority. Thus, while the Admiralty did not treat Japan as being in all respects the equal of a first rate European power, neither was it prone to underrate the damage Japan could inflict to British interests in the Far East. The perception of the Japanese as a martial race, the size of the Japanese navy, and its distance from the center of British power made Japan a danger to be taken seriously. As Beatty remarked in 1925, Japan 'can deal us a naval blow, a maritime blow, which we are absolutely powerless to prevent and from which we should never recover.'[14] This was not simply rhetoric. Naval officers believed that without adequate local defenses and the ability to send a fleet to the Pacific, Japan could liquidate Britain's position in the Far East whenever it chose to.

During the 1930s, as reliable data on the IJN became harder to acquire, greater scope existed for British appraisals to be distorted by ethnocentric bias.[15] Historians have often noted the navy's reluctance to appreciate Japan's technical accomplishments and major developments in its tactical thought, most importantly relating to naval aviation.[16] The tendency to underrate Japanese fighting abilities did undoubtedly result in British forces experiencing unpleasant tactical surprises, both in December 1941 and for some time after. But it should not be held responsible for the disasters which the navy suffered off the coasts of Malaya and Indonesia in 1941–2. It is also wrong to suggest that faulty qualitative estimates of the IJN were an important factor contributing to Britain's 'reliance on inadequate military forces in the Far East, which ended in the shocking fate of Force Z.'[17] The British did not choose to rely on inadequate forces in this region in 1941 – this was forced upon them by circumstances and the dictates of grand strategy.

Nor did the inclination to underrate the IJN's capabilities affect British planning for war against Japan during the 1930s in a simple fashion. Here three things should be noted: the Admiralty always wanted its naval forces to be larger than they were; it always wished to have numerical superiority in case of war with the IJN; and it always calculated the numerical balance through simple 'bean counting,' on the assumption that one Japanese warship was worth roughly one British warship of equivalent size. Yet parallel to this view, the underestimation of Japanese fighting qualities did lead many decision-makers to think that the Japanese threat might be more manageable than 'bean-counting' would suggest. For example, the navy's Plans Division wrote in 1937 that:

> In discussing the operations of our fleet subsequent to its arrival at Singapore it has been assumed that the Japanese approximate to our own standard in naval warfare. If, as may well be the case, they prove to be lacking in enterprise, skill, resource or fighting qualities, we should be prepared immediately to exploit our advantages in these respects and increase the boldness of our conceptions accordingly.[18]

This was not, in principle, an unreasonable calculation to make. After all, not all navies are equally effective fighting forces – as Chatfield once noted, Britain would have lost the Battle of Trafalgar based on simple 'bean counting.'[19] The mistake made by the Admiralty was in assuming that the British navy was, man for man and ship for ship, always qualitatively superior to every other navy simply by virtue of being British. This generalization affected British thinking towards all other navies, including those of the United States and Germany. Although Japan's navy was generally rated slightly below these, it was still considered to be at least on par with the Italian navy and probably better – and notably, the RN always aimed to amass as much numerical superiority as possible against even the Italian navy between 1940 and 1943.

Thus, at the formal level, the Admiralty's calculations were not seriously affected by the predisposition to underestimate Japanese efficiency. Admittedly, it always doubted that the Japanese were as good as the British and felt that the Japanese fleet would be characterized by predictable and routine behavior. The Admiralty even attempted to quantify its assumption of superiority in 1939 by arbitrarily rating the IJN's efficiency as 80 per cent of the Royal Navy.[20] This formal estimate was not grossly wrong, however, and too much should not be made of it. The naval staff was at this time thinking solely in terms of a defensive war fought far from Japanese bases and in waters dominated by British land-based aircraft. In such circumstances, planners assumed that they could afford a slight inferiority in capital ships at Japan's selected moment – but only if this could not be avoided. If a superior fleet could be sent, the Admiralty always intended that it would be, and it always calculated that it would have to despatch a force numerically stronger than the Japanese fleet in order to adopt an offensive strategy. There was never any question of holding back battleships out of contempt for Japanese fighting abilities. The Admiralty expected that it would be able to accomplish more with relatively weak forces than it actually proved able to do in 1941–2, but this belief was not the reason that only weak forces were employed.

The navy's plans for a war with Japan were embodied in the series of War Memoranda (Eastern) prepared by the Plans Division for the guidance of the commanders-in-chief (Cs-in-C) of the principal British fleets.[21] These documents were not intended to provide a detailed blueprint for the conduct of a Far Eastern war. As Vice-Admiral Sir Osmond Brock noted in 1919, 'plans drawn up in peace never fail to require many modifications when war arises; the actual circumstances cannot be foreseen, there are so many possible combinations, but a large amount of preparation *can* be made which is applicable to any situation.'[22] Until the mid-1930s, therefore, political considerations were excluded from these documents. No attempt was made to predict the cause of an Anglo-Japanese war, or to forecast which powers, if any, would be allied to either of the main combatants. Drafting plans on the basis of a purely Anglo-Japanese conflict allowed planners to reduce the number of variables to a manageable level. Because these plans were meant to be of immediate practical value to naval commanders in the theater of operations, and because of Britain's numerical superiority at this time, this expedient was considered acceptable. As long as Britain possessed a *de facto* two-power standard in relation to Japan and the strongest European naval power, planners did not foresee any European complications which would alter their basic strategy for war in the Pacific. Britain would either despatch a fleet with a slight superiority over the Japanese, or it would send a fleet with overwhelming superiority. In either case, the basic plan would not require modification. By the late 1930s, however, this assumption was no longer valid. The Admiralty realized this, and planners began to develop contingency plans to account for different alignments of the great powers.

The Admiralty framed all of these plans on the assumption that a Far Eastern war would be a predominantly naval affair. Naval planners expected a maritime economic blockade of Japan to produce victory, and they saw no need to share center stage in the Pacific with the other fighting services. The air force and the army entered into the navy's calculations only insofar as their assistance was necessary to defend the fleet's bases and support naval operations. It was not until 1926 that the First Sea Lord, Admiral Beatty, invited the War Office and Air Ministry to contribute to the Admiralty's war plans; and even then he believed that the other services' plans would only be 'superimposed' on the navy's.[23] And that is essentially what happened. The army and air force accepted a subsidiary role in the Far East without demur. The army manifested no serious desire to prepare an expeditionary force for use in the Far East, and the RAF displayed no interest in equipping itself for a bombing campaign against the Japanese home islands. Because the War Office and the Air Ministry were usually preoccupied with other matters, the Admiralty easily dominated the formulation of the services' combined Far Eastern strategy. The navy often differed with the politicians and the other services over the relative importance of the European and the Far Eastern theaters, and over the scale of resources required for imperial defense generally, but the CID, the COS, and the Joint Planning Committee (JPC) all took their cue from the Admiralty in matters relating solely to the Far East.

The navy's basic strategy for war with Japan emerged shortly after the First World War. Before the Admiralty had even secured approval for the construction of a naval base at Singapore, naval decision-makers envisaged the despatch of a British fleet to a main base in the Far East, whence it would proceed to an advance base and begin exerting pressure on Japan. It was assumed from the outset that the conflict would be, at least from the Japanese perspective, essentially unlimited in nature. The possibility that an Anglo-Japanese war might be fought for limited objectives scarcely entered into naval calculations during this period. Planners were certain that Japan would not embark on war unless they intended to overthrow Britain's entire position in the Far East, and they believed that such an attempt could only be countered by bringing the maximum possible pressure to bear on Japan.

In 1924 the Plans Division concluded that a successful campaign would likely unfold in three distinct phases:

Phase I. The Period before Relief. i.e. the period that will elapse between beginning of hostilities and the arrival of the British main fleet in Far Eastern waters.

Phase II. The Period of Consolidation. After its arrival in Far Eastern Waters, the Main Fleet will require a period of time to consolidate the position before embarking on operations on a larger scale.

During this period (which must not be likened to a period of inaction) British trade will be released in those areas protected by the main fleet, supplies for the fleet will be accumulated and its ancillary services organised. Whether this process of consolidation will take place with the fleet based on Hong Kong or Singapore must depend upon circumstances which cannot be foreseen.

Phase III. The Period of Advance. The final strategic phase wherein the British Fleet will endeavour to isolate the enemy country and bring the maximum pressure to bear on the national life of Japan.[24]

During the 1920s, the Admiralty was chiefly concerned with the first of these phases; indeed, throughout the decade operations following the arrival of the main fleet at Singapore were seldom considered except in the vague terms outlined above.

The first section of the War Memorandum that the Plans Division attempted to flesh out was the passage of a fleet from home waters to Singapore, which was selected in 1921 as the site for Britain's main eastern base. British planners never doubted their ability to despatch a fleet to the Far East. Admiral Brock, for example, rejected the idea that it 'would be an enormous effort, almost beyond our capabilities to send a fleet of battleships to the Far East.'

I need only go back to the Russo-Japanese war in which the most inefficient navy in the world, the Russian, succeeded in sending an armada out to Port Arthur round the Cape accompanied by colliers, light craft and everything else, and if Russia could do it, I think to say that Great Britain could not succeed in sending a portion of her most efficient fleet through the canal down the Red Sea to Singapore, is farce. We could do it off our heads.[25]

The Japanese were not expected to offer any significant opposition to this movement, although it was thought that they might detach small forces for minor operations such as 'interference with the Suez Canal, mining of routes, attacks on oilers and oil tanks etc.'[26] However, the possibility of encountering a major Japanese force west of Singapore appeared unlikely. The problem of the fleet's passage was thus largely a logistical one, and detailed plans covering a variety of alternative routes were completed without difficulty by 1925.[27] This left naval planners free to deal with the more difficult problem of securing Britain's essential bases during the initial period of Japanese dominance.

The Admiralty considered both Singapore and Hong Kong indispensable for the successful prosecution of offensive operations against Japan. Singapore would serve as the navy's principal eastern base. 'Its capture by the Japanese would be disastrous,' planners concluded, 'as we should have to fall back on some distant base from which it would be difficult if not impossible to exert decisive naval pressure on Japan.'[28] But while the docking and repair facilities planned for this site would be essential for a fleet operating in eastern waters, its distance from Japan made it unsuitable for offensive operations. For this purpose, Hong Kong was considered essential. As a 1933 memorandum stated, 'Hong Kong is necessary if we are to be able to bring our sea power to bear for the protection of our interests in China and for effective pressure on our enemy.'

Without it we cannot operate with our main forces in Japanese waters. To bring the war to a satisfactory end, it would probably be essential also to seize and defend an advanced base without which our forces could not effectively interrupt the short sea communications between Japan and China, upon which Japan is dependent for the maintenance of her population and armament industries. If Hong Kong were lost, it is probable that we should be unable either to seize such a base or to protect the communications to it.[29]

Naval planners believed that the loss of both possessions would constitute 'the heaviest possible blow against the British Empire.'[30] Because the Japanese would be aware of this, they were expected to make the capture or neutralization of one or both bases their main objective during Phase I.

The defense of Singapore and Hong Kong at the beginning of a war depended on the army and air force garrisons stationed there in peacetime. Singapore might hope for reinforcements from India, but Hong Kong could not count on any relief prior to the arrival of the main fleet. The navy's principal contribution to the defense of these bases would be the relatively weak naval forces which the Admiralty maintained in the region during peacetime.[31] These detachments were instructed to give priority to the security of these essential bases. All other objectives, including the 'defence of Borneo and of our trade in the South Pacific, Indian Ocean and Arabian Sea, and attack on enemy trade,' were considered secondary.[32] The *'main object of British forces'*, according to the War Memorandum, *'is to attack the enemy's trade and transport routes* while avoiding action with superior forces.' To accomplish this, they were advised to adopt 'a policy of evasion, punctuated by bold offensive action against Japanese communications whenever favourable opportunity offers. Undetected and unlocated ships, even though inferior in strength, threatening Japan's communications, will hamper and possibly sensibly delay an enemy's arrangements'.[33]

The division of forces between Singapore and Hong Kong was often at issue during this period. The Admiralty always maintained that the security of Singapore was paramount, but Hong Kong's greater vulnerability and the desirability of retaining both bases provided a perpetual temptation to increase the resources allocated to the latter. The 1923 War Memorandum laid down that the defense of Singapore 'must not be jeopardised by staking all on the defence of Hong Kong,' and it advised that British forces should be 'so disposed that, whilst constituting the menace to Japanese attacks on Hong Kong, they can fall back if necessary on Singapore, leaving the former to its fate should its retention be hopeless. Should, however, the security of Singapore be beyond doubt, then we should be justified in sacrificing if necessary the whole of our available forces in hampering enemy operations against Hong Kong.'[34] As long as a British fleet could operate from Singapore, the possibility of recapturing Hong Kong would always exist, but the loss of Singapore would inevitably mean the loss of Hong Kong also. Hence, planners insisted that the *'safety of Singapore must…be the keynote of British Strategy* and it is only after provision has been made for its security that the use of Naval forces in the defence of Hong Kong can be justified.'[35]

The naval forces allocated to the protection of Hong Kong hinged on the prevailing views regarding the security of Singapore. During the 1920s, the possibility of the Japanese capturing the latter was not rated very highly, and naval commanders in the region advised the Admiralty to divert resources to the defense of Hong Kong.[36] In 1928, after the government approved the installation of gun defenses at Singapore, the Admiralty concluded that this base would be 'reasonably secure' from Japanese attack by 1933.[37] The Director of Plans recommended that when the defenses were completed, it would be time to alter the War Memorandum so as to give Hong Kong the first claim on Britain's eastern naval forces. However, the First Sea Lord decided that this change could be made immediately,[38] and the C-in-C China Station was informed that he need not 'wait until the defences of Singapore are actually in position before modifying the War Memorandum, but to do this at once; accepting the small risk to Singapore in the meanwhile, should an Eastern war occur, before the first stages of the defences are completed.'[39]

This decision marks the high water mark of the Admiralty's confidence in its basic strategy. With Singapore apparently secure and British naval strength still sufficient to allow a substantial fleet to be despatched to the Pacific, the Admiralty was confident that it could transport its forces to Hong Kong without delay and immediately begin offensive operations. The failure to proceed with Singapore's defenses as planned and the rapid deterioration in the international situation after 1931 undermined this confidence. When Chatfield became First Sea Lord in 1933, he was sufficiently concerned about the situation to have the War Memorandum revised in order to give Singapore first call on British eastern naval forces.[40] It was hoped that this change was only temporary, and that once Singapore's security was assured, the War Memorandum would be altered again. This never occurred though, and Singapore continued to enjoy priority in the allocation of resources until 1941.

Throughout the 1920s, the nature of offensive operations following the relief of Singapore was only outlined in the most general terms. The 1923 War Memorandum stated, for example, that the navy's principal objective was 'to obtain control of maritime communications,' which could 'best be achieved by destruction of the enemy fleet.'

> Should the Japanese Fleet decline decisive action and remain based in its own waters, the war is likely to be protracted, as it will be extremely difficult for us to attack with success the more vital of the

Japanese communications. In the latter case, however, our aim must still be eventually to force an action, and in the meantime, whilst protecting our world-wide sea communications, to

(i) bring economic pressure to bear on Japan by instituting world-wide measures which would have for their object the severance of her sea communications wherever possible. Should this pressure become really effective, it must have the consequence of forcing Japan to take risks with her Main Fleet.

(ii) make it possible for land forces to capture Japanese possessions. This again may force a Fleet action.[41]

A copy of this Memorandum was sent to Richmond, then serving as C-in-C East Indies, who was unimpressed with what he read. In his opinion, the document was too vague about operations in the period after the relief of Singapore and failed to coordinate the activities of all three services.[42] The following year, Richmond informed the Plans Division that its latest War Memorandum,[43] issued in July 1924, was, 'in reality, not a war plan, but a plan of naval movements, irrespective of the use to which the other fighting forces would be put. It visualises war between Great Britain and Japan purely as a struggle at sea.'[44] Richmond was especially critical of the War Memorandum's appreciation of ends and means in a Far Eastern war. The Admiralty's plans for exerting economic pressure on Japan were, in his view, fundamentally flawed, as they depended upon 'reasoning which runs in a vicious circle':

(a) We are going to force Japan to surrender by cutting off her essential supplies.
(b) We cannot cut off her essential supplies until we defeat her fleet.
(c) We cannot defeat her fleet if it will not come out to fight.
(d) We shall force it to come out and fight by cutting off its essential supplies.

which brings us back again to (b) and to (c) and (d) in succession.[45]

More importantly, he questioned the wisdom of relying on economic blockade to achieve Britain's objectives in the first place. 'The plan visualises one method only of fighting the enemy,' he complained, 'Economic Pressure, irrespective of the cause of war.' This was 'not necessarily the most efficient method of forcing Japan to abandon whatever pretensions had brought her into collision with us.'

Our power of exercising economic pressure, and the resulting efforts we are preparing to make, are greatly overestimated in the Memorandum. A war of economic exhaustion is proverbially long, and Japan is peculiarly well situated to hold out against it. Allied to military action, as our economic efforts in past wars have nearly always been, it is an instrument of far reaching effects, but by itself, economic pressure is most unlikely, *pace* experience, to produce surrender.[46]

And even if the Admiralty's expectations for economic pressure were sound, Richmond doubted that it was necessary to crush Japan in order to secure Britain's interests in the region. 'Wars are not always decided by that means,' he warned.[47]

Richmond recommended that the Plans Division turn its attention to the problem of fighting a strictly limited war against Japan. Notably, however, his ideas about this type of conflict did not differ in essentials from the scheme sketched out in the War Memorandum. For all his complaining about the lack of inter-service cooperation in the navy's plans, Richmond himself was also clearly thinking in terms of a predominantly naval campaign in which the air force and army would play only a supporting role. Moreover, both Richmond and the Admiralty envisaged the campaign developing along the same general lines. Both expected the establishment of superior British naval forces in the Far East to contain or destroy the Japanese fleet, and both assumed that the British fleet would operate not only from Singapore, but also from Hong Kong and, ideally, another base further north. Richmond's principal differences with the Admiralty concerned the nature of British operations once the fleet was established in the Far East. Generally speaking, Richmond advocated the employment of a wider range of weapons than the War Memorandum envisaged, and the pursuit of more limited objectives. What he visualized was, in essence, a limited conflict on the model of Britain's maritime wars of the eighteenth century. He admitted, however, that if the Japanese continued fighting rather than accept a negotiated settlement favorable to Britain, it would become necessary to crush Japan after all. His suggestions for achieving this goal were hardly more advanced than those put forward by the Admiralty, however. If an invasion of Japan was not possible, Richmond concluded that there would 'be no alternative to the slow, expensive and not necessarily effective measure of investment,' by which he meant blockade.[48] Thus, Richmond implicitly acknowledged that the Admiralty's basic strategy *for an unlimited* Anglo-Japanese conflict was essentially correct.

Richmond's most important criticism of the Admiralty's war memo-randum concerned Britain's ability to despatch an adequate naval force to the Far East in the event of European complications. His remarks on this subject have, however, frequently been misinterpreted. Historians of British naval strategy often cite the following passage from Richmond's critique:

> To my mind, since our forces are not adequate for a war in the East at the same time as one calling for the use of naval force in Europe, there is a great deal of unreality in a plan for such a condition of affairs: and wholly wrong to convey the impression that our strength is sufficient to enable us to do so. It is better frankly to acknowledge our inability, than to live in a fool's paradise.[49]

Taken out of context, this statement appears to support the charge that the Admiralty's strategy was fundamentally flawed, and that this was apparent in the 1920s to perceptive observers such as Richmond. However, these remarks were meant to support Richmond's call for the preparation of two separate Eastern War Memoranda, one for the despatch of Britain's full naval strength to the Far East and another for the division of the navy between eastern and European waters. 'The difference between a war with Japan and one with Japan and a European power is so great,' Richmond wrote, 'that the two wars can only be considered in separate Memoranda. The very strategy is funda-mentally different – offensive in one case, defensive in the other.'[50] Thus, Richmond was not arguing that the despatch of a fleet to the Far East would be *impossible* if a naval threat existed in Europe, only that the Admiralty's objectives would have to be scaled down if this were the case. He appreciated that an offensive strategy would require not just rough equality with the Japanese fleet, but crushing numerical superiority. For this reason he objected to the Admiralty's plans to retain in European waters forces which would remain inactive while a war was actually being fought in the Far East. Such a deployment, in his opinion, 'offends against the principle of concentration against the enemy's fighting force.'[51] If Britain were engaged in a two-front war, Richmond did not believe a British fleet at Singapore could do more than secure Britain's defensive position in this region. The prob-lem with this, as he remarked to Lord Haldane, is that he had 'never heard of a war won by defence alone.'[52] Richmond realized that Britain's naval strength was insufficient for *offensive* campaigns in two theaters simultaneously, and he recommended that diplomatic means be employed to prevent this situation arising.

Richmond's critique was carefully examined by the Plans Division. Its Director, Rear-Admiral W. A. Egerton, pointed out that most of Richmond's comments actually concerned 'the presumed attitude of the Admiralty to Phase III [the offensive phase] of the War, but the War Memorandum only deals with Phase I [the Period before Relief] and in no way commits anyone to any particular line of conduct in the later phase.' He concurred, however, that offensive operations would 'require study by all three services together.'[53] The Admiralty was, in fact, already aware of this need. Captain Dudley Pound, for example, had informed Richmond the previous year that:

> We are making progress, though slow, towards combined staff work. The chief difficulty that arises is that the soldiers always want to know who our Allies or the enemy's will be. The Chiefs of Staff Sub-Committee of [the] C.I.D. is a great advance but does not go far enough. I put forward a scheme for a Combined Planning Committee but the Soldiers are all for 'ad hoc' committees.[54]

Egerton concluded that the principal value of Richmond's critique was as a treatise to assist the Admiralty in planning the offensive phase of a war 'on correct lines. Its value in this respect will be very great.'[55] The only major point on which the Plans Division disagreed with Richmond was the need for two separate Eastern War Memoranda. 'The fact remains that European complications may exist,' it wrote. 'If they do not all the better and the main fleet can be reinforced. Two war plans for *Phase I* appear unnecessary as it must be common to all cases.'[56]

   The Admiralty's reaction to Richmond's criticisms was thus generally favorable. Within a few months, Egerton was writing to inform him 'that we are in much closer touch with the DMO & I's [Director of Military Operations and Intelligence] people than has hitherto been the case & that we are about to have a small committee of all 3 services to consider Phase II of a certain war you know of.'[57] What became of his committee is uncertain, but the authors of the next War Memorandum, issued in 1931, did address most of Richmond's concerns.[58] This document was the Plans Division's first attempt to map out offensive plans for the period following the relief of Singapore. The first objective it laid down was the transfer of the fleet from Singapore to Hong Kong with the least possible delay. The nature of subsequent operations would then depend entirely on the situation prevailing at Hong Kong when the fleet arrived. At worst, the Japanese might have captured the base, in which case 'the whole trend of the war would be changed,' since the Japanese would 'be fully alive to the immense strategic value of the base and would have nothing to gain by risking a fleet action in a hurry.' If this occurred, the Japanese would probably 'set about making Hong Kong impregnable' and attempt to prevent its recapture. The British fleet might also arrive to find that the Japanese had established a strong force on the Chinese mainland in the vicinity of Hong Kong. Planners feared that such a force might employ artillery and land-based aircraft to make the harbor untenable. 'In this case, the arrival of a British Fleet would not immediately relieve the fortress,' they concluded, 'and it would probably be necessary for the British Fleet to return to Singapore in order to cover the transport of military and air reinforcements.' Operations to remove such a threat were expected to take no more than two or three months.

Ideally, the British fleet would operate from Hong Kong without first having to undertake operations for its relief or recapture. This would occur if the fleet's arrival caused the Japanese to abandon their operations against the base; if a Japanese attack had already failed; or if the enemy had not attempted to capture it at all. The nature of operations after the fleet's establishment at Hong Kong was not considered in detail owing to the many uncertainties which would exist at this stage. In general terms, however, the War Memorandum contemplated 'a progressive campaign from Hong Kong to the Northward.'

This would, in the first place, be directed against Formosa and the Pescadores unless in the meantime the Japanese have seized a base on the coast of China between the Pescadores and Hong Kong. Any success against these is likely to bring the Japanese fleet to the southward whether it be to relieve the pressure by fighting a fleet action or to cover the arrival of military reinforcements. If the Japanese refuse to expose their Main Fleet to the risk of a fleet action we can proceed with our progressive campaign to the northward until they are forced to accept action. This suggestion does not preclude raids against Japanese lines of communication, trade, focal points, harbours, but it does imply that the use of an advanced base to the North of Formosa from which our Main Fleet can carry out extensive operations to the Northward is unjustified while Formosa and the Pescadores remain unmolested.[59]

Planners clearly hoped that a progressive advance would break the 'vicious circle' that Richmond had complained of earlier. It was, in fact, the shortage of advance naval bases, rather than the continued existence of the Japanese fleet, which appeared to pose the greatest obstacle. The nearer British bases were to Japan's home waters, the greater the pressure British forces could bring to bear on Japanese national life, and hence the more inclined the enemy would be to take risks with its fleet. If the Japanese fleet were destroyed, Britain could then begin to inflict decisive pressure immediately; and if the enemy declined battle, the British advance would gradually wear down Japanese strength and ultimately achieve decisive results on its own.

The Admiralty expected pressure on Japan to take a variety of forms. The most direct method, an invasion of the Japanese home islands, was ruled out entirely 'as an operation beyond our powers.' Planners believed, however, that it might be 'necessary to undertake smaller scale operations in order to establish ourselves on Japanese territory.' They also hoped to launch raids on Japanese possessions with the object of effecting 'as much lasting damage as possible by sea and air bombardment and by a raiding party landed for purposes of destruction and demolition.'[60] Most importantly though, the navy would attempt to destroy the enemy's overseas trade.

Japan's vulnerability to economic pressure was taken for granted when the navy's basic strategy was formulated in the early 1920s, and it was only at the end of the decade that the Plans Division began to analyze Japan's economy and patterns of overseas trade. Intelligence on this subject was culled from a wide range of sources. Nearly all of it was taken from the public domain, and most was channeled to the Admiralty from the Board of Trade (BOT) and the Department of Overseas Trade (DOT), supplemented by the press, the British naval attaché in Tokyo, and other similarly placed sources. On the basis of this information, the naval staff affirmed what it had assumed from the outset: that 'the Japanese industrial system is ill-equipped to withstand any great dislocation of trade such as would occur in the course of a war with the British Empire.' This intelligence also suggested that 'Japan lacks most of [the] raw materials necessary for industry and for the manufacture of those articles necessary for waging war.'[61]

Japanese imports of strategic raw materials appeared to be the navy's most promising target. To this end, the Admiralty compiled statistics detailing the sources of Japan's principal imports in peacetime, and estimated where it might turn for these supplies in wartime.[62] Planners calculated that Japan would be forced to rely principally on China and the United States to make up any shortages following the cessation of trade with the British Empire, which accounted for around 27 per cent of its total imports. The effectiveness of British economic pressure would therefore depend on the navy's ability to cut these channels of trade, particularly those carrying certain key materials, including ores and metals, machinery, chemicals, oil, rubber, cotton and wool.[63]

In the course of preparing its 1931 War Memorandum, the Plans Division grappled for the first time with the problem of how to interfere with this trade.[64] It concluded that only 'a constant patrol of surface craft off the focal points on the coast of Japan, particularly the entrances to the Inland sea' could impose an effective blockade of the Japanese home islands. This could not be accomplished, however, until the main Japanese fleet had been destroyed or neutralized. The British fleet would always be at hand to seize such an opportunity, but that could only arise if the enemy wished to do the same. In the meantime, naval planners intended to establish a distant blockade of Japan. By their own calculations, this measure held little prospect of achieving decisive results. Even if the British fleet could operate from a base to the north of Hong Kong, it probably could not significantly hamper Japan's trade with northern China and Korea, and curtailing Japanese imports from the United States would be nearly as difficult. Planners hoped that naval forces operating off the west coast of America and the Panama Canal could intercept some of the trade bound for Japan across the Pacific, but they predicted that the remoteness of British naval bases and the vast areas involved would limit the effectiveness of any such operations.[65]

The objective of the navy's distant blockade, therefore, was to dislocate the Japanese war economy in hopes of compelling the Japanese fleet to accept battle with superior British forces. Once this occurred and the Japanese fleet was destroyed, the navy could cut off the enemy's trade with China and begin to inflict decisive pressure. The Japanese government, recognizing the futility of further resistance, would probably seek terms immediately rather than wait for the blockade to achieve its full effectiveness.

This offensive scheme represents the Admiralty's best case appreciation of how Japan could be forced to accept British terms. In hindsight it was a remarkably optimistic assessment. It required that Hong Kong be relieved or recaptured; that a fleet operate safely from this base; and that military forces be available for combined operations in the area north of Hong Kong, and possibly for the relief or recapture of Hong Kong itself. At the time this plan was drafted, these requirements did not appear unrealistic. As the decade progressed, however, the Admiralty gradually lost confidence that an advance from Hong Kong would be feasible, or that the fleet could operate from this base except under the most ideal circumstances. This development stemmed principally from a reconsideration of Hong Kong's utility as an advance fleet base. Naval planners had always accepted that the colony might be captured before it could be relieved, but they also assumed that Japanese operations against the base would end concurrently with or shortly after the arrival of the main fleet in the area. During the early 1930s, the Admiralty was increasingly concerned that the Japanese might establish ground and air forces on the Chinese mainland capable of maintaining themselves even if their maritime supply lines were cut. It feared that such forces could render Hong Kong unusable by the main fleet for an indefinite period, even if the base itself remained in British hands.[66]

Although this threat was taken seriously, naval opinion continued to hope that Hong Kong might still be usable as a base for the main fleet. The 1937 War Memorandum was drafted on the assumption that the course of an Anglo-Japanese conflict was sufficiently unpredictable that it would be unwise to count on Hong Kong being unavailable in all circumstances. It was conceivable that Japan might not have the resources needed for large-scale operations against Hong Kong if, for example, Britain had a major ally such as the United States. Reducing Hong Kong's defenses would virtually eliminate any chance of holding the colony, but a serious attempt to defend it would leave open the possibility that Britain's position there might be retrieved. The Admiralty always held that Hong Kong should be defended to the utmost until it was certain that it could not be used as a naval base. However, while resources were scarce and Singapore's security was uncertain, little could be done to overcome this problem. To make Hong Kong's harbor safe from artillery and land-based air attack would have required a standard of defense far exceeding anything that had ever before been contemplated; indeed, it would have meant placing Hong Kong's defenses on a level comparable to Singapore's. At no time during the 1930s was this considered a practical option. As Hankey remarked, Britain 'could not afford to maintain two first class bases in the Far East.'[67] However, naval decision-makers always hoped that they could eventually provide a reasonable degree of security for Hong Kong. In the meantime, they endeavored to ensure that this prospect was not precluded by the permanent reduction of the colony's approved scale of defense. The main proponents of such a course were the army and air force, which were never enthusiastic about diverting their resources to the defense of Hong Kong. They accepted this responsibility in the

1920s because the Admiralty insisted that the colony must be held as a base for operations against Japan, but if this requirement dis-appeared, they believed the sensible course was to reduce the defenses to a token level.

The Admiralty delayed such a step during the mid-1930s by asserting that Hong Kong's strategic value was not dependent solely upon its availability as a base for the main fleet. Naval representatives maintained that it might still be usable by submarines and other small craft, and they suggested that defending Hong Kong might compel the Japanese to detach forces to capture or mask it, thereby reducing the scale of attack they could direct against Singapore.[68] These tactics enabled the Admiralty to keep alive until 1938 the principle that Hong Kong's defenses should be maintained at the highest possible level. A major review of this issue was undertaken by the COS at that time, and, with the colony's position being increasingly undermined by Japanese incursions into China, the navy's case was rejected. The Air Ministry and the War Office doubted that even the most lavish spending could render Hong Kong safe for naval vessels in wartime, and they opposed increased expenditure on Hong Kong as long as higher priority needs were not being met.[69] They agreed that the colony must be defended for reasons of prestige, but in 1938, the COS was only prepared to recommend the defense of Hong Kong island, with the limited aim of denying 'the use of the anchorage to an enemy.'[70] This decision was accepted by the Admiralty on financial grounds, but senior naval decision-makers hoped that they might eventually adopt the full scheme of defense.[71]

Besides the possibility that Hong Kong would not be available as a naval base, the Admiralty was also confronted with the prospect that the scale of combined operations during Phase III would be severely curtailed, if not precluded, by a shortage of military and air forces. The 1931 War Memorandum had assumed that the army and air force would supply the additional resources needed to seize an advance base and launch raids against Japanese territories. But when this question came before the JPC and COS in 1934, the War Office and Air Ministry maintained that they could not meet these needs.[72] Admiral Sir Frederic Dreyer, the C-in-C China Station, was subsequently informed by the First Sea Lord that 'Any idea of an expeditionary force … is out of the question, there is none.' The most that Chatfield hoped for at this time was 'that the armed Force from India, which is at present earmarked in an emergency for Singapore, would accompany the Fleet to Hong Kong with aircraft assistance to relieve that place if it had not fallen.'[73] But even the relief or recapture of Hong Kong was complicated by the likelihood that large military forces would be unavailable. Further difficulties were also beginning to arise from Britain's declining ability to despatch a superior fleet to the Far East. In light of these problems, planners accepted that a progressive advance northward from Hong Kong was no longer realistic.

The first attempt to develop an alternate strategy was initiated by Admiral Dreyer during his tenure as C-in-C China Station. Dreyer began to take an active interest in British preparations for Phases II and III of a Far Eastern war in early 1934, at a time when the Plans Division in London was preoccupied with other problems. His first initiative was to set up a 'Harbour Defence Committee' to gather detailed information on harbors north of Singapore and consider the defenses they would require if the navy wished to use them in wartime.[74] At this time, Dreyer was thinking in terms of the relief of Hong Kong followed by a gradual campaign northward. By the end of the year, however, he had concluded that in the event of a single-handed war against Japan, a less ambitious strategy would be required. Dreyer advised the Admiralty that in these circumstances the navy should concentrate on denying 'all access by sea to the Japanese to the south and west of a line joining Malaya–Fiji.'

> By the use of Fleet bases in North Borneo, this line to be pushed up to the northward to include the Dutch East Indies in the area denied to the enemy in the western Pacific, as this is vital to our security. The retention of Hong Kong, which might be effected with the aid of periodical relief expeditions supported by our Main Fleet from North Borneo, would possibly include the South China Sea also in the area denied to the enemy.[75]

This strategy, which Dreyer dubbed 'Plan X,' would ideally be followed up by a more ambitious 'Plan Y' once Britain had acquired allies. The latter scheme would consist 'of what may be described as a stereotyped plan; of Phase 2, establishment at Hong Kong, and Phase 3, period of advance.' This was, in effect, the same strategy outlined in the 1931 War Memorandum, and Dreyer believed that it could not be implemented without undertaking 'stupendous combined operations.'[76]

As C-in-C, Dreyer continued to collect information on harbors north of Hong Kong 'so that when we have recovered from the blighting effect of the "10 years no war" rule...we may be ready to carry out Plan "Y" if the opportunity to do so is afforded us.'[77] But he also advised the Admiralty to concentrate for the present on preparations for Plan X. To this end, he recommended that 'when the permanent defences of Singapore are completed, priority should be given to the provision of storage at Singapore of the defensive equipment necessary for a selected advanced base in British Borneo, so that its establishment can be effected with the minimum of delay after the arrival of the main fleet at Singapore.'[78] Naval planners in London agreed that such a base would probably be useful, but they deferred any action until they had an opportunity to reconsider their plans for Phase II in their entirety.[79]

It was only in late 1937 that the Admiralty issued a new War Memorandum[80] covering the period following the relief of Singapore.[81] Planners no longer believed that an Anglo-Japanese war would necessarily unfold in clearly-defined stages, and the new Memorandum considered several different options once a fleet was established at Singapore. In the event that European complications precluded the despatch of a force at least equal in strength to the Japanese main fleet, planners concluded that British strategy would have to be defensive in its initial stages. They did not rule out the possibility that Hong Kong might serve as the base for an inferior fleet, but they recognized that this was unlikely if there were any substantial Japanese forces in the vicinity. If operations to capture Hong Kong were proceeding when the British fleet arrived, the Plans Division hoped that the navy could relieve or evacuate the garrison, but they advised against using Hong Kong as a fleet base in these circumstances. Even if the harbor were relatively secure, the fleet would always run the risk of attack from shore-based aircraft and superior naval forces. The severity of this threat made it appear that the fleet would be unable to operate not only from Hong Kong, but from *any* advance base.[82]

If Hong Kong had fallen when the fleet arrived, the need for a forward base from which to relieve or evacuate the colony's garrison would disappear. In this event, planners believed that the fleet should not advance beyond Singapore, although it hoped that it could establish an advanced base in Borneo, 'which should simplify the control of the sea communications between Japan and the Netherlands East Indies.'[83] The War Memorandum did not attempt to spell out how an inferior fleet could protect British interests in the Far East, but it was assumed that the Japanese fleet's advantage would steadily diminish as it moved further away from its bases and approached Britain's. Hence, a slightly weaker British force could meet the Japanese fleet on roughly equal terms in the vicinity of Singapore. Inside the zone in which the British fleet could operate with land-based air support, planners believed that an inferior naval force could provide a reasonable degree of protection for British interests.

The Admiralty always assumed that as long as Singapore remained secure, it could eventually reinforce the eastern fleet and switch to an offensive strategy. Ideally though, naval planners hoped to despatch to Singapore a fleet superior or equal in strength immediately hostilities commenced. If this was possible, the 1937 War Memorandum envisaged an offensive strategy which would force the Japanese to accept British terms. If no serious attempt had been made to capture Hong Kong, a superior fleet was to proceed there immediately and attempt to utilize it as a base for offensive operations. If a Japanese attack on the colony was still proceeding, British action would depend on whether the fleet could use the harbor. If it could, the navy's first objective was to rush reinforcements into Hong Kong so that it could continue holding out. The fleet would then operate from Hong Kong and attempt to cut the maritime communications of the forces investing it.

If the fleet could not operate from the harbor, the British objective 'must be to relieve Hong Kong in order if possible to regain its use as a fleet base.' Naval planners recognized that this would be a difficult task. An expeditionary force would not be available, and even if one was, the difficulties involved in such operations, 'at the end of very long communications, against Japanese forces operating comparatively near their home resources,' were so great as to be considered 'strategically unsound at the present time.'[84] As a result, planners believed they would have to rely solely on naval operations to effect the colony's relief. This would be complicated, however, by the need to establish an advanced base from which the fleet could operate. The only British harbors which could be used for this purpose were located in North Borneo, but their distance from Hong Kong made them poorly suited for this purpose. The Plans Division hoped that a harbor belonging to the United States or France might be available, in which case Manila would be the ideal choice. Chinese harbors offered another possibility, but they would need extensive defenses before they could be utilized. This would require the employment of the navy's Mobile Naval Base Defence Organisation (MNBDO), which was expected to be unavailable for 'some considerable time after the arrival of the Main Fleet in the Far East.'[85]

Should Hong Kong fall before the fleet arrived, the Admiralty no longer intended to be drawn into costly and protracted operations for its recapture. During the late 1930s, naval planners ceased to regard this base as essential for the conduct of offensive operations. As long as the British fleet was not outnumbered, they now intended to exert pressure on the enemy from another base to the north of Singapore. This important development resulted from a reassessment of the means available to exert pressure on Japan after the transfer of a fleet to an advance base. With large-scale combined operations no longer a realistic option, economic pressure assumed greater prominence in the Admiralty's calculations. The problem of how to inflict this pressure without an advance base north of Hong Kong, and possibly without Hong Kong itself, was worked out in 1937 during the preparation of the JPC's Far Eastern Appreciation.[86]

Whereas the 1931 War Memorandum assumed that the Japanese fleet must be destroyed before a decisive blockade could be implemented, the JPC now concluded that the navy could inflict decisive economic pressure without first fighting a fleet action. This revised assessment was not the result of new information about the state of the Japanese economy, but rather arose from a new interpretation of old information. Economic intelligence for strategic purposes was by this time being supplied to the service departments by the Industrial Intelligence Centre (IIC). As regards Japan, the IIC's assessments rested on the same sources the naval staff had used during the previous decade, and it drew similar conclusions concerning Japan's vulnerability to economic pressure.[87] A comprehensive report by the IIC on Japan's economic position in late 1936 maintained that decisive results could 'only be attained through the virtual stoppage of trans-Pacific trade in addition to that of Europe and the British Empire, and by a serious interruption of communications with Formosa, China and Korea.'[88] The Joint Planners, however, derived a more optimistic appreciation from the same information. Their Far Eastern Appreciation concluded that Japan could not make up all of its deficiencies in essential raw materials from the Asian mainland. They calculated that after approximately six months of war, Japan must begin 'importing raw materials by the long sea routes at the rate of at least half a million tons a month, if she is not to suffer severe industrial restriction and a consequent cumulative economic embarrassment.'[89]

This conclusion appeared to simplify the problem facing Britain. Even if Japan's communications with China remained relatively secure, which would be the case so long as the Japanese fleet remained afloat, it now appeared that Japan might be starved into submission if its trans-Pacific trade were severed. The JPC hoped to accomplish this through a variety of methods. Most importantly, British patrols in key locations would intercept enemy vessels and contraband runners. Naval forces maintained off the Panama Canal and Cape Horn would 'effect a large measure of interception' of vessels proceeding along these routes, while strong patrols off American ports would intercept trade originating along the west coast of the Americas. The latter would be supplied with information by an intelligence network set up in American ports shortly after the outbreak of war.[90] Besides these purely naval measures, the Joint Planners also recommended that 'Every effort should be made to hamper both the placing and the finance of Japanese orders in the United States.' This would be facilitated by the fact that Britain controlled the original sources of certain important commodities – including manganese, nickel, tin, and rubber – and could restrict exports which might be expected to reach Japan. Planners also recommended that Britain should reduce the neutral tonnage available to the Japanese 'by such methods as refusal of insurance to ships trading with Japan, black lists, chartering shipping, and other measures of which we had experience in the last war.'[91] The JPC calculated that it might take up to two years, and possibly longer, to achieve victory in this manner. How long the Japanese war economy endured would ultimately depend on the reserves Japan had built up before the war began, and the effectiveness of the British blockade. Early results could be expected only if the Japanese fleet were sunk.

Scholars have paid remarkably little attention to the economic basis of British naval planning for a Far Eastern war. Many have simply ignored it;[92] others have acknowledged it without examining its implications.[93] Those few who have considered this topic have generally misunderstood it, and for two reasons.[94] First, because they have not examined British naval planning during the entire interwar period, they mistakenly view the Admiralty's interest in economic warfare during the 1930s as a late development brought on by Britain's declining strategic position. Second, they have wrongly inferred that the Admiralty's optimistic assessments of Japan's vulnerability to economic pressure were belied by contemporary appraisals produced by the very bodies charged by the government with evaluating this question – the CID's Advisory Committee on Trade Questions in Time of War (ATB), and the IIC.[95] These critics maintain that the economic appraisals produced by these organizations during the 1930s correctly stressed the strength of the Japanese economy and Britain's inability to disrupt it to any significant degree without the full cooperation of the United States. If true, then the Admiralty's strategy was not only unworkable, but should have been recognized to be so at the time.

In fact, this charge is wrong because these historians have confused the imposition of a wartime blockade with the enforcement of economic sanctions in peacetime. These are entirely different matters. In the case of sanctions, everyone, including the COS and the Admiralty, considered the voluntary cooperation of the United States to be essential. Economic intelligence made it clear that if all British trade with Japan ceased, the enemy could still acquire the raw materials it needed from the United States, which Britain could not stop. In the case of a wartime blockade, however, Britain could exercise its belligerent rights to interfere legitimately with US–Japanese trade and seize contraband goods. It was this capability which underlay the navy's high expectations for economic pressure. Whether economic blockade could have proven an effective weapon for Britain against Japan is another matter, but the intelligence record of the time certainly does not demonstrate that it was infeasible.

The JPC's appreciation of Japan's vulnerability to a British blockade was later incorporated into the Admiralty's 1937 Eastern War Memorandum. This document envisaged two means to win a war with Japan. The first was the traditional plan of provoking a fleet action so as to open the prospect of cutting Japan's short sea routes. This might produce a rapid decision, but as ever there was no guarantee that the Japanese would accept battle with superior British forces, while the likelihood that a fleet action could occur under conditions favorable to the British declined because of the decreased possibility of operating from Hong Kong or further north. Nevertheless, the possibility still existed and the navy intended to grasp it. The second course was to wait for economic pressure against Japan's 'long sea routes' to disrupt the enemy's war economy and force the Japanese to seek terms. This appeared to be a slower but more certain route. As these strategies were complementary, the Admiralty planned to pursue them both simultaneously.

Although the 1937 War Memorandum outlined both offensive and defensive strategies, the latter was more likely to be implemented at this time. The Admiralty calculated that from summer 1937 to spring 1938, and from summer 1939 to spring 1940, it could despatch a fleet superior to Japan's by one capital ship, but that from spring 1938 to summer 1939, it could only send a force one capital ship weaker.[96] The Admiralty was not at all optimistic about its ability to inflict a crushing defeat on Japan in such circumstances. After the Munich crisis of 1938, for example, Commander T. C. Hampton of the Plans Division unofficially informed representatives from other Whitehall departments that if Hong Kong fell before the arrival of the British fleet, which appeared likely, 'a position of stalemate may develop with neither Fleet able to bring the other to action.' This was 'no new feature in naval warfare,' he maintained. 'In fact, it is rare for two Fleets to be willing and able simultaneously to engage in a Fleet action.' Britain's success would depend, he argued, on 'the weapon which command of the sea gives us namely economic pressure.'[97]

After 1936 the Admiralty also had to deal with the increasing likelihood that Italy would enter a European war on Germany's side. In 1937 a three-front war was dismissed by the COS as a prospect beyond Britain's capacity to meet, and its Far Eastern Appreciation did not consider Britain's strategy should this occur. After the Munich crisis, however, this danger appeared both possible and imminent. The COS acknowledged in its 1939 European Appreciation that the fleet Britain could send to the Far East might in certain circumstances not only be weaker than that of the Japanese, but significantly weaker. In early 1939 the new First Sea Lord, Sir Roger Backhouse, calculated that Britain must retain a force of no less than six capital ships in European waters to contain the German and Italian navies. This would only leave 5–6 capital ships available for despatch to the Far East, and Backhouse asserted that a force of this size 'against a Japanese Fleet of 10 ships plus her full strength in other classes of ships is not adequate in the proper meaning of that word.'[98]

Two schools of thought existed on how to deal with this problem. The first, represented by Backhouse and Admiral Reginald Drax, who was brought to the Admiralty to develop offensive war plans, maintained that in the event of a three-front war the navy should concentrate first on knocking out Italy, the weakest of Britain's enemies, while providing only a covering force for the Far East. This suggestion was unorthodox and controversial. It meant reversing Britain's priorities to favor the Mediterranean over the Far East, which would involve political difficulties with Australia and New Zealand, and it violated the accepted tenet that any fleet sent to Singapore must be capable of meeting the whole of the Japanese fleet in British-dominated waters. The idea of sending a weak force to meet a stronger one was repugnant to the naval mind. Backhouse believed, however, that a fleet-in-being strategy would allow an 'inadequate' fleet of four or five capital ships to protect Britain's vital interests in the Far East.[99] His calculations were later refined by Drax, who suggested that it was only necessary to despatch a 'flying squadron' composed of two fast battleships, two aircraft carriers, four large cruisers, and nine large destroyers.[100]

In an appreciation drafted in March 1939, Drax suggested that such a force could provide reasonable protection to British trade and territory in the Indian Ocean. The Japanese would be unable to concentrate in that area as long as Britain possessed any significant naval forces at Singapore; hence, it was only necessary to despatch a force strong enough to prevent the Japanese from establishing a base in the Indian Ocean, and 'mobile enough to hunt down Japanese raiding forces of inferior strength.' Drax maintained that this same force would also pose a 'threat to Japan itself and her communications with China, provided it was sufficiently mobile to make the Japanese think twice before venturing too far south, leaving their vital interests in the north exposed to attack.' He hoped that this force's ability to raid Japan's maritime communications would deter an invasion of Australia. And should this deterrent fail, he believed that a 'flying squadron' would be able to exploit its superior speed and mobility to disrupt the maritime communication of a Japanese expedition. This would not stop an invasion, but it should delay enemy operations long enough to allow 'the Australians to mobilise their defence of the mainland.'[101]

Drax maintained that his 'flying squadron' could not only defend Britain's eastern interests for a reasonable period, but that it could do so better than a fleet that was larger but still inferior in strength to the Japanese. Such a force would contribute nothing to the security of Singapore, it would be more than was required for the protection of British interests in the Indian Ocean, and it would be of less value in delaying an invasion of Australia. 'A superior fleet would be a definite deterrent,' he acknowledged, but

what chance of success would a slow and inferior British battle fleet of 6–8 battleships operating 3000 miles from its base have against the concentrated strength of the Japanese fleet? The purely mathematical chance of our fleet bringing an action before they ran out of fuel would be no greater than that of a British fleet from Halifax trying to intercept a convoy proceeding from Spain to South America.

Even if the Singapore fleet succeeded in locating the Japanese fleet and convoy on passage, the chances of victory are less than that of defeat.[102]

Drax also proposed that if Italy remained neutral while Britain was engaged in a war against Germany and Japan, the Admiralty should still rely on a 'flying squadron' to defend imperial interests in the Far East. This would allow a small force to be maintained in the eastern Mediterranean to watch the Italians and a larger force to be concentrated in home waters to take the offensive against Germany. 'There is no prospect of taking the offensive in both theatres,' Drax declared, 'for both our enemies are hard nuts to crack: it is no use dividing our forces and finding that we can only defend ourselves in both areas.'[103]

The Backhouse/Drax scheme has been both commended for its originality and denounced as the forerunner of the disastrous decision to despatch two capital ships to Singapore in 1941.[104] Most commentators represent this proposal as a sharp departure from the Admiralty's established 'main fleet' strategy, but this is not entirely true. The 'flying squadron' concept was little more than a plan for dealing with one particular eventuality, and it should be viewed as the logical final chapter in the development of British contingency planning between the wars rather than as a radical departure from the plans that preceded it. By early 1939, the Admiralty had considered virtually every scenario that might arise in the Far East, and circumstances now forced it to face the prospect that the naval force available for the Far East might be not only inferior to Japan's, but significantly inferior. Backhouse and Drax attempted to deal with this problem in a forthright manner, but they still hoped that it would be possible to send a larger fleet to Singapore capable of implementing the plans outlined in the Admiralty's Eastern War Memorandum and the COS's Far Eastern Appreciation. They also believed that a 'flying squadron' was only a temporary expedient, and that it would be necessary to despatch a larger force once Britain's strategic situation had improved.

The flying squadron scheme was still essentially a 'Singapore strategy' in that it involved sending British capital ships to the Far East to defend imperial interests. The only difference from earlier defensive plans is that the emphasis was not on the size of the fleet which could be sent, but on its speed and mobility. The real departure from previous plans was that this one called for a force which, if caught by the Japanese fleet, could not be expected to prevail in battle under any conditions. This was a true fleet-in-being strategy, and it was contentious because of its optimistic assessment of what a very weak naval force could accomplish against a much superior foe.

Although this scheme was received with some apprehension in naval circles, the idea of concentrating naval forces in the Mediterranean for a knockout blow against Italy was generally welcomed outside of the Admiralty, and especially in political circles. This strategy appeared to offer a solution to Britain's three-front dilemma and it accorded well with Britain's growing interests in the eastern Mediterranean at this time. Hence, even though the Cabinet's Strategic Appreciation Committee (SAC) concluded on 17 April 1939 that there were so many variable factors involved in a three-front war that a final decision as to priority between the Mediterranean and the Far East could not be made in advance, it also ruled that: 'Offensive operations in the Mediterranean against Italy offered the best prospects for speedy results and should not, therefore, be lightly broken off.'[105] With this decision, the SAC accepted that a small covering force could defend British interests in the Far East for a prolonged period.

A second school of thought on the problem of a three-enemy war was represented by Lord Chatfield, the former First Sea Lord now serving as Minister for Coordination of Defence. Chatfield was alarmed by the suggestion that Britain should send only a covering force to defend imperial interests in the Far East, fearing that failure to send a strong fleet immediately to the Far East would have serious political repercussions, and might ultimately drive Australia and New Zealand to look to the United States for their protection.[106] He also rejected the contention that there was no possibility of making good on the pledge to despatch a fleet in the event of a three-front war. Pointing to the combined Anglo-French superiority over Germany and Italy in capital ships, Chatfield argued that the British would only need to retain a force of four capital ships in home waters. These ships, together with '5 comparatively modern French capital ships' should be ample to contain the combined German and Italian total of four capital ships and three 'pocket' battleships. It would therefore still be possible to send 7–9 British capital ships to the Far East.[107] Chatfield expected that such a force would be sufficient, given its superior fighting qualities, 'to hold the position and to contain the Japanese fleet, in the same way as a vastly inferior German fleet contained the Grand Fleet for four years.'[108]

Although Chatfield failed to convince the SAC of his views in April 1939, he did manage to get the issue reopened in June. At a meeting of the Cabinet's Foreign Policy Committee,[109] the Minister challenged the COS's conclusion that if war erupted with Japan over the Tientsin crisis they could only send two capital ships to the Far East.[110] At this time, the JPC and COS were working on the assumption that the Mediterranean had priority over the Far East. Chatfield sent them back to the drawing board, and the COS duly produced a new assessment which suggested that it should be possible by August to scrape together a force of seven capital ships if the Mediterranean were abandoned.[111] The COS also laid down the principle that any fleet sent to the Far East must be sufficient to meet the Japanese fleet if it came south in full strength.

The Admiralty was in fact the driving force behind this declaration. The new regime under Admiral Dudley Pound was uncomfortable with its predecessor's plans for a 'flying squadron' and needed little prompting from Chatfield to revert to a more orthodox line. In July, Phillips, the new DCNS, instructed the Director of Plans to omit all references to a 'flying squadron' from the Admiralty's war plans.[112] As a result, revised sections of the Eastern War Memorandum were issued later that month to replace those which had been drafted subsequent to the 17 April meeting of the SAC.[113] The new appreciation acknowledged that in the event of a three-front war it would be necessary to choose between British interests in the eastern Mediterranean and the Far East; but it noted that the decision would have to be based on the circumstances then prevailing. It also laid down the principle that 'if a force is sent to the Far East it must be capable of engaging the main Japanese Fleet under conditions favourable to ourselves. In September 1939, this force must include 7 capital ships.'[114] No mention was made of what was to be done if the politicians decided that British capital ships must be stationed in the Mediterranean and a force this size was unavailable. It appears, however, that Pound believed a small covering force could do no more than secure British communications in the Indian Ocean and deter the Japanese from major operations in the South China Seas or Australasian waters. In the event that the Japanese fleet moved south in strength, he expected that British naval forces would have to retire westwards from Singapore and operate from another base, probably Trincomalee.[115]

After September 1939, the navy continued to view the problem of war with Japan in strictly orthodox terms. It believed that a strong fleet was essential to defend Britain's Far Eastern interests adequately, and that a weak fleet, if that was all that could be sent, would withdraw into the Indian Ocean if threatened by superior Japanese forces. With the fall of France and the entry of Italy into the European conflict in 1940, the Admiralty accepted that it could not send any fleet to the Far East for the foreseeable future.[116] However, during the course of 1941 the United States began to increase its naval assistance to Britain in the Atlantic theater, and by mid-year the British were considering the despatch of naval reinforcements to the Far East. In August the Admiralty concluded that it could put together by March 1942 an eastern fleet consisting of the battleships *Nelson* and *Rodney*, a battle cruiser, four of the old, unmodernized 'R' (*Royal Sovereign*) class battleships, an aircraft carrier, ten cruisers, and 24 destroyers. In the meantime, Pound believed that moving the 'R' class battleships to the Indian Ocean would deter Japan from sending any of its capital ships into the area, while the presence of a battle cruiser and an aircraft carrier would deter the Japanese from using their cruisers to attack British commerce. However, if the government's principal objective was to deter Japan from entering the war at all, he suggested that *Nelson*, *Rodney*, a battle cruiser and an aircraft carrier might be despatched to Singapore before any other movements took place. In the event of war, however, this force would fall back on Trincomalee.[117]

By this stage of the war, the Admiralty knew that the United States might fight at Britain's side against Japan, in which event it was optimistic that Anglo-American naval strength was sufficient to allow the allies to maintain, at the very least, a successful defensive posture in the Far East. Its views on offensive strategy had altered very little since the 1930s, and it hoped that a joint Anglo-American campaign would develop along the lines laid down in its pre-war Eastern War Memoranda. When British and American representatives met in 1940 for the first time to consider strategy for a Far Eastern war, the Admiralty instructed its delegates that the 'Americans should be invited to take [the British] Far East War Memorandum as basis for strategic discussion, [with the] American Fleet taking place of British Fleet in this plan.'[118] In other words, the American Pacific and Asiatic fleets would utilize Singapore as their main operational base, and either Manila or Hong Kong would serve as an advance base for offensive operations. The Americans were unenthusiastic about this idea, however, preferring to remain on the defensive in the Pacific and keep their main naval force at Pearl Harbor. Once the British realized that the United States could not be persuaded to station either of its eastern fleets at Singapore, they turned their thoughts to the best employment of British naval forces from this base.

During the American-Dutch-British (ADB) discussions which took place at Singapore in April 1941, the British contemplated allocating the bulk of their Far Eastern naval forces to the protection of Singapore and British trade routes during the period before relief, leaving the defense of the Malay barrier primarily to the United States.[119] The Americans demurred from this proposal, however, complaining that the British were devoting too few of their own resources to this region.[120] By the time the Americans rejected a revised ADB agreement in October 1941, the Admiralty had concluded that a more aggressive

British strategy had not only become feasible, but would help to secure a greater measure of cooperation with US forces in the Far East.[121] With the possibility of a modest British Far Eastern fleet being formed in the near future, the planners concluded that the distinction between Phases I and II of an eastern war had for the first time become 'largely academic.' Once the proposed redispositions had taken place, the British would only need to despatch cruisers, destroyers, and possibly another aircraft carrier, to bring the fleet up to full strength following the outbreak of war. Planners now began to turn their attention to the use of Manila as a possible advance base for British operations against Japanese communication north of the Malay barrier.[122] At the time of the ADB Conference, both the Americans and the British doubted that Manila was sufficiently secure to fulfil this role, and they had considered withdrawing the American Asiatic Fleet to Singapore in the event of war. By September 1941, however, the Admiralty felt that the recent build-up of Manila's defenses would make it a 'perfectly feasible fleet base from the point of view of air attack, provided reasonable A.A. defence and fighter aircraft were made available.'[123] In November it offered to help the Americans with the construction of underwater defenses for the harbor's protection.[124]

From the Admiralty's perspective, maintaining a British fleet at the Philippines had become both politically and strategically desirable. It provided for increased cooperation between the British and US navies, and hence a greater likelihood of US support in the event of war, and it demonstrated to the Americans a willingness to take a more active role in the defense of Britain's own interests. It was also a logical extension of the navy's pre-war planning. In effect, the Admiralty was reviving the defensive strategy outlined in its most recent War Memorandum. In both cases, a relatively weak fleet operating under land-based air cover in its own waters would protect British interests until more substantial forces could be mustered for offensive operations. The main difference between 1937 and 1941 was that the Admiralty now hoped Manila would serve as its advance base rather than Hong Kong or Borneo, while the presence of a US fleet in the central Pacific reduced the likelihood of the British fleet having to face the full might of the Japanese navy.

The evolution of the Admiralty's plans for a joint Anglo-American war against Japan shows how strongly its 'best case' estimate of 1941 was influenced by its pre-war planning. The same is true of its 'worst case' appreciation. Naval planners were always aware that the United States could not be counted on to enter the war as a belligerent. In the event of a single-handed conflict against Japan, the Admiralty continued to assume that its eastern naval forces would have to fall back on the Indian Ocean for safety.

In the end, only two capital ships, the new battleship *Prince of Wales* and the WWI-era battle cruiser *Repulse*, were sent to Singapore. Historians have often charged that the Admiralty's prewar plans for the despatch of a fleet to the Far East were ultimately responsible for the destruction of these vessels in December 1941.[125] Thus, it is maintained that the navy, unable to abandon its long-cherished goal of sending a battle fleet to Singapore, foolishly despatched two capital ships in place of the larger, balanced fleet it had originally considered necessary. These charges are unfounded. In late 1941 neither the politicians nor the sailors viewed these two ships as a substitute for the fleet envisaged in the navy's prewar plans. They were sent by Britain's political leadership to quiet the latest rumblings emanating from Australia, and to serve as a sign of resolve to deter Japan from war with the British Empire. The Admiralty fought hard to prevent their despatch, and given complete freedom of action it would not have sent these ships to Singapore at all. It certainly did not regard them as a 'flying squadron' capable of defending, even temporarily, Britain's Far Eastern interests. Pound and Phillips gave this idea short shrift in the summer of 1939, and they had no desire to revive this unorthodox scheme in 1941.[126]

When they lost their battle with the politicians, Admiralty officials hoped to reduce the danger to these ships by building up a balanced eastern fleet at the earliest opportunity. Notably, it was at this point that the British began to look seriously at the possibility of using Manila as an advance base for this fleet to operate from. By this time the Japanese decision for war had already been taken, however, and there was insufficient time to reinforce the *Prince of Wales* and *Repulse* before their final sortie on 10 December 1941.

Although charges that the Admiralty acted with particular stupidity in the autumn of 1941 are easily refuted, historians have still fallen over themselves to heap scorn on virtually every aspect of the navy's preparations for war with Japan. The accepted view proclaims that the 'Singapore Strategy' was inherently unsound from the outset. Several reasons for this have been advanced, the most common being that the likely existence of hostile naval powers in Europe made it unrealistic to expect a British fleet *ever* to be spared for the Far East. This criticism contains a germ of truth, but it does not point to any inherent flaw in the strategy itself. This would only be true if there was no possibility of a fleet being despatched to Singapore under any conditions, which is obviously not the case. During the 1920s, Britain possessed a comfortable margin of naval superiority over its rivals, and it might have maintained a large fleet in the Far East and still dominated European waters. This possibility was only undermined by the emergence of a triple threat from Germany, Italy and Japan in the mid-1930s, and it was only precluded by the fall of France in 1940. These events were exceptional and unpredictable. If they had been foreseen, interwar planners would have regarded Britain's position as hopeless. But because this threat seemed remote, they based their plans on the reasonable assumption that British diplomacy could prevent such a threat from emerging. If they had been correct, the rise of a single European naval challenger need not have prevented the transfer of a fleet to the Far East, in which event the navy could still contemplate a defensive strategy in that region.

The despatch of a fleet to Singapore is too often treated as an 'all-or-nothing' proposition. By the mid-1930s the real question for British planners was whether they could send the ships required for an offensive strategy, or only enough for a defensive one. British naval strength was still sufficient to allow a defensive posture in both regions simultaneously. And as long as Britain had a reliable ally, it might even have been possible to assume the offensive in one of these theaters. During the late 1930s Britain had such an ally in France. A two-front naval war need not have posed an insurmountable threat to the British Empire in the 1930s, and if Britain had built up to a full 'two-power standard' in the 1930s, most of the 'inherent' difficulties allegedly facing the Admiralty would have disappeared. A single-handed struggle against three naval powers was another matter, but because British naval strength was insufficient to meet this worst-case scenario, it does not follow that the navy's plan to send a fleet to the Far East could not be implemented under *any* conditions.

The Admiralty's critics have also claimed that developments in air power somehow rendered the whole of British naval strategy irrelevant.[127] The underlying assumption is that any strategy which envisaged the employment of heavily-gunned battleships in any capacity was both antiquated and foolish. Thus, commentators such as Ian Hamill have charged that the 'concept of sea power around which the whole policy revolved was demonstrated to be obsolete. Naval engagements were no longer a simple matter of two battle fleets blasting away at each other.'[128] Statements such as this are riddled with fallacies. The Royal Navy did underestimate the impact of aviation on naval tactics, but this was not done to the extent which is frequently charged,[129] and it does not point to any intrinsic flaw in the Admiralty's strategic thinking. The USN demonstrated during the Second World War that the despatch of a fleet to the Far East was still necessary to secure the defeat of Japan. A better understanding of the effects of modern aircraft on naval warfare would have compelled the Royal Navy to increase both the carrier- and land-based aircraft allocated to its Far Eastern fleet, but its basic strategy would have remained essentially unchanged.

What a superior British fleet could have accomplished at Singapore is a separate issue. Because most commentators dismiss out of hand the possibility of such a force ever being despatched, they usually fail to consider what might have been accomplished if one had. Planners recognized that an offensive strategy by naval forces lacking decisive superiority held out little prospect of rapid success, and during the late-1930s they placed their hopes on winning a prolonged war of economic attrition. In the process, they badly overestimated the navy's ability to inflict decisive pressure on Japan through seapower alone. Ironically, the Admiralty's earlier estimates, as outlined in the 1931 War Memorandum, were more reasonable. At that time, naval planners better understood the need for large-scale combined operations to seize and defend the advance bases necessary for offensive operations against Japan.

American navy planners were far more successful in preparing for war with Japan. The US plan – known as War Plan Orange[130] – dealt with many of the same issues as Britain's Eastern War Memoranda, and was based on many of the same assumptions: that any war would be unlimited in nature, that it would be a predominantly maritime conflict, and that economic pressure would be decisive. American planners expected a Pacific war to unfold in three phases. In the first, Japan would seize American possessions in the Far East and then brace itself for the American riposte. Next, the United States would go onto the offensive. The reduction of Japan's seaborne trade would begin immediately, and a massive battle fleet would make its way westward from Pearl Harbor, securing naval and air bases as it advanced. In the third phase, the American fleet, established by now in the Philippines, would begin a progressive advance northwards. A series of new bases, each one closer to the enemy, would enable American naval and air forces to increase the pressure on Japan. At some point, the Japanese fleet would accept battle with superior US forces and be destroyed. Eventually, a combination of blockade and bombardment would force Japan's surrender.

Although War Plan Orange shares some similarities with the Admiralty's 1931 Eastern War Memorandum, the scale of the proposed US war effort dwarfed anything conceived by the British at this time. American planners realized that large land and air forces would be needed to seize the bases from which naval and air forces could begin to exert decisive pressure on Japan. In 1928, for example, American plans called for the immediate despatch of 36 000 troops to the Far East. By the second year of the war, the strength of the army and marine corps in the principal theater of operations was expected to exceed 400 000. The seizure of an island like Okinawa, in the Ryukyu chain, would employ an estimated 60 000 troops, while an assault on Tsushima Island might require three times that figure. Large American air forces would provide cover for the fleet and amphibious operations from the beginning of the war, and attack 'the military and industrial centers of Japan' as soon as suitable bases could be acquired. It was estimated that at least 360 'bombing planes of the Army Air Corps' would be required for an effective strategic bombing campaign.[131] The maritime blockade alone did not appear to offer much chance of a quick victory. US planners calculated that Japan could obtain virtually all of its essential requirements by the 'short sea routes' to Asia, and that even the destruction of the Japanese fleet would not allow the elimination of this trade until an advance base was acquired at Tsushima Island. Even then, it might take a year or more to force Japan to sue for terms.[132]

War Plan Orange provided a remarkably accurate blueprint for the defeat of Japan, and highlights the most serious shortcomings of the Admiralty's offensive planning. If Britain's resources had been considerably greater during the 1930s, its war plans might have evolved along lines similar to Plan Orange. Offensive planning was effectively derailed during the mid-1930s, however, by the growing reliance on naval forces and economic pressure to defeat Japan. The Admiralty abandoned its most realistic appreciation of the interwar period because it was predisposed to believe that Japan was particularly vulnerable to economic pressure exercised through naval power, and because it appeared to have no alternative. However, this mistake need not have been fatal. It almost certainly made the total subjugation of Japan impossible, but by focusing greater attention on the security of Singapore over Hong Kong, the changes to Britain's war plans in the mid and late 1930s probably resulted in a better prospect of an effective *defensive* strategy being implemented in the initial stages of a war. If Singapore could have been held, Britain might have produced a stalemate which left most of its vital interests intact. With American support and the mobilization of imperial resources, the Royal Navy might eventually have adopted a more aggressive strategy. In any event, the successful execution of the Admiralty's plans for Phase I of a Far Eastern war would have kept the door open for correcting many of the mistakes made by naval planners in their prewar appreciations. The Admiralty's assessment of its ability to exert pressure on Japan was seriously flawed, but it was not in itself responsible for the disasters Britain experienced during the opening stages of the Pacific War.

The navy's critics frequently ask why, given its inherent flaws, the 'Singapore Strategy' was adhered to for as long as it was. The question is often asked rhetorically, as it is usually understood that the explanation lies in the 'sclerotic conservatism'[133] and rampant stupidity which allegedly afflicted naval decision-makers of this period. But even serious attempts to find an answer have been unsatisfactory because the question itself is misleading. Between 1919 and 1941, the British did not adhere to any single naval strategy for a Far Eastern war. In 1929 the Admiralty intended to despatch a superior battle fleet to undertake offensive operations from a base to the north of Hong Kong; in 1939 it expected to send an inferior fleet to operate defensively from Singapore, or possibly Trincomalee. Referring to both of these strategies and the others that were developed as *the* Singapore Strategy only confuses the issue. The one generalization about British naval strategy that holds good for the interwar period is that the Admiralty planned to maintain its principal naval forces in home waters during peacetime, and to despatch the maximum available force to Singapore, at the earliest practical moment, to provide the best possible defense of Britain's Far Eastern interests during wartime. To the extent that a 'Singapore Strategy' can be said to exist, it was nothing more than this. As a component of British grand strategy, the scheme was a tremendous risk. But the Admiralty had no other options. It could neither maintain substantial naval forces in the Far East in peacetime nor abandon British interests in the region to the goodwill of Japan. As long as these choices were denied to naval leaders, a 'Singapore Strategy' of some kind was unavoidable.

British planning for a war with Japan was not based on obsolete conceptions of seapower, outmoded ideas of Jutland-style battle lines, or willful self-delusion regarding the realities of international politics. Naval decision-makers of this period struggled with inadequate resources to prepare the best defense for Britain's world-wide interests. In the end, they failed to preserve all of these interests, but the explanation lies in the magnitude of the threat facing Britain in 1941 rather than in any fundamental errors in the navy's strategic planning.

4

'The Ultimate Potential Enemy': Nazi Germany and British Defense Dilemmas

The German navy was a minor factor in British calculations for over a decade following the scuttling of the High Seas Fleet at Scapa Flow in June 1919. The advent of Hitler in January 1933 was not immediately seen as cause for alarm in naval circles, where the most serious threat still appeared to be in the Far East. Japanese aggression in 1931–2 prompted the COS to ask for the abolition of the 'Ten-Year Rule' in March 1932. The Cabinet accepted this recommendation, but warned that it 'must not be taken to justify an expanding expenditure by the Defence Services without reference to the very serious financial and economic situation which still obtains.'[1] Nevertheless, in November 1933 the government responded to the deteriorating international situation by setting up the Defence Requirements Committee (DRC) to recommend a program for making good the worst deficiencies accumulated by the armed services over the previous decade. This committee, composed of the three service chiefs and the permanent undersecretaries of the Treasury and Foreign Office, identified Germany as the 'ultimate potential enemy against whom all our "long range" defence policy must be directed.'[2] This decision is commonly viewed as a repudiation of Britain's commitment to imperial defense, and thus a crucial turning point in the navy's fortunes.[3] In fact, the DRC never intended to preclude preparations against one potential enemy by assigning precedence to the other. The decisive shift in Britain's priorities away from imperial concerns only began when the DRC's recommendations reached Cabinet level. The Admiralty actually had every reason to be satisfied with the DRC's report, which endorsed the navy's evaluation of the Japanese threat. The committee's response to Far Eastern problems has frequently been misunderstood, however, because historians are usually preoccupied with its views on Germany.

The DRC concluded that Japan posed an immediate threat to British interests, but that the danger from Germany could not become critical for approximately five more years. To avoid facing both threats simultaneously, it recommended concentrating first on neutralizing Japan. As Warren Fisher declared, by 'establishing durable relations with Japan, we can concentrate on the paramount danger at our very threshold.'

> This of course is in the future; but its likelihood will in my opinion become a certainty unless the Germans have every reason to believe that, if and when it might suit them to force a war, they will come up against our maximum strength, undivided and undistracted by Far East complications.[4]

The DRC report recommended 'an ultimate policy of accommodation with Japan, and an immediate and provisional policy of "showing a tooth" for the purpose of recovering the standing we have sacrificed of recent years.'[5] An accommodation with Japan is usually regarded as the goal the committee pinned its hopes on, but only Fisher believed that this could be easily achieved. Convinced that the United States had 'bamboozled' Britain into sacrificing the Anglo-Japanese Alliance for no compensating gains, Fisher advocated a diplomatic accommodation with Japan even at the cost of alienating American opinion.[6] He did not believe that any vital British interests would be threatened if the Americans responded with an increase in their naval armaments, and he assumed that once British 'subservience' to the United States had been renounced, any remaining obstacles to a settlement with Japan could be easily overcome. He therefore advised his colleagues that it was essential

> to get clear of our 'entangling' agreement with the U.S.A. who should be left to circle the globe with ships if they want, to gratify their vanity by singing 'Rule Columbia, Columbia rules the waves,' and to wait and see for how many years the politically all-powerful Middle West will continue to acquiesce in paying a fantastic bill related to no real requirement but primarily to indulge the braggadocio of Yahoodom.[7]

The rest of the Committee rejected Fisher's recommendations, believing that their potential price was too high, and their goal too elusive, to be sensible.[8] The DRC did agree, however, that any improvement in

Anglo-Japanese relations must be accompanied by, and would probably result from, a general refurbishment of Britain's defensive position in the Far East. In practice, this meant expediting work on the Singapore Naval Base and remedying the worst of the navy's deficiencies. It therefore recommended that 'Singapore came first in order of priority for [the] next $3\frac{1}{2}$ years, followed by the situation *vis-à-vis* Germany, together with the possible addition of the Japanese menace.'[9]

The DRC's first report proposed a comprehensive program providing for the needs of all three services and addressing both of the major challenges to the security of the British Empire. There was nothing in its proposals inherently inimical to the navy's well-being. Chatfield himself agreed that 'we have got to prepare ourselves...for a definite European threat of war in, say, 5 years.' In his opinion, Britain's objective should be to 'put ourselves into a secure position during the next 5 years so that we are a Power to be reckoned with, both in Europe and in the East.'

> As soon as that moment has arrived will be the time, in my opinion, to improve our friendly relations with Japan because she will then respect us, which at present she probably does not. Therefore our first policy must be to strengthen the Navy and our bases in the Far East so that we can come to terms with Japan and thus be ready to throw our full weight in Europe if it is required.[10]

The DRC's recommendations were in many respects a significant moral victory for the Admiralty. The committee accepted that the navy's position should be put on a secure basis within a relatively short period, and the Admiralty had no reason to object to the designation of Germany as Britain's 'ultimate potential enemy.' As long as all of the recommendations embodied in the committee's report were carried out, the minimum requirements claimed by the Admiralty would have been met. In different circumstances, this might have led to a substantial rise in the navy's fortunes.

The navy's troubles began when the Cabinet referred the DRC's report to the Ministerial Committee on Disarmament. Neville Chamberlain, the Chancellor of the Exchequer, believed that Britain could not afford to prepare for war against Germany and Japan simultaneously, and advised his colleagues to concentrate on the defense of the British Isles. In his opinion, this meant providing for 'the establishment of an Air Force *based in this country* of a size and efficiency calculated to inspire respect in the mind of a possible enemy.' And to insure against this deterrent failing, he recommended the completion of Britain's anti-aircraft equipment, and 'the conversion of the Army into an effectively equipped force capable of operating with Allies in holding the Low Countries and thus securing the necessary depth for the defence of this country in the air.'[11] To finance these proposals, he believed it would be necessary to cut back spending on the navy, whose programs were principally geared towards a Far Eastern war. He therefore advised that

> while we must (if only out of good faith to the Dominions) proceed to complete Singapore and its essential approaches, we must contemplate its use for the present as a base for submarines and other light craft, and we must postpone the idea of sending out to it a fleet of capital ships capable of containing the Japanese fleet or meeting it in battle. By the adoption of this course we can materially reduce the heavy and increasing shipbuilding programme and can relieve the Navy deficiency programme of the ensuing five years of a substantial sum.[12]

The Admiralty was incensed by these proposals. The DCNS, for example, complained that Chamberlain had rearranged the priorities put forward by the DRC 'not, I think, on account of the real state of world affairs, but in the order in which uninformed public opinion has casually placed them.' Chatfield protested that Chamberlain had

> invented an entirely new Imperial Defence policy, a somewhat bold step, as the new policy is not based on the solid reasoning that has determined our Imperial policy in the past, but upon the question, what is the cheapest way in which we can 'keep face' with the world?

In his view, the Chancellor had 'taken the Daily Mail propaganda very much to heart and is definitely obsessed with the fear of air attack on this country and considers it necessary to put that before everything else.'

> The Dominions are to be abandoned to whatever fate may befall them. The skeleton in the Naval cupboard is to remain locked up, where he hopes it will remain unnoticed by the British public and by the world at large, and we are instead to impress Germany and save England from the certainty of war with Germany in a few years time

of which he seems convinced. We are to keep a few ships in the Far East to keep up appearances but in the event of trouble they are not to be reinforced but are to be sacrificed uselessly …

I am sure this looks as if the Chancellor of the Exchequer's views are supported, we shall have come to the parting of ways as regards Imperial Defence. A bogus Navy inadequate to its responsibilities is not one which any Admiralty could, in my opinion, be responsible for.[13]

The First Lord, Sir Bolton Eyres-Monsell, vigorously resisted Chamberlain's proposals, arguing that they meant 'abandoning our sea power, thereby altering the whole basis of Imperial policy and letting go the principal link which holds the Empire together.'[14] The rest of the Disarmament Committee was unwilling to endorse Chamberlain's proposals, but over the next few years his views gained the tacit acceptance of the majority of his Cabinet colleagues. The fear of aerial bombardment focused politicians' attention firmly on the threat from Nazi Germany and the need to strengthen the RAF,[15] while concerns about Britain's financial strength curbed the pace of naval rearmament. Increasingly, Far Eastern dangers and imperial obligations receded into the background of Britain's defense preparations, and the navy's traditional role as Britain's first line of defense was forsaken with unseemly haste.

Despite the growing attention being paid to Nazi Germany in official circles during the 1930s, the Admiralty continued to focus on the threat from Japan. As a result, some historians have suggested that the navy was unreasonably slow to accept the likelihood of war with Germany.[16] However, this claim rests on the mistaken assumption that the Admiralty measured Hitler's intentions 'solely from the point of view of the size of his navy, and thus Naval intelligence misjudged the possibility of war in Europe.'[17] In fact, naval decision-makers did not regard the size of the German navy as an indication of anything more than Hitler's intentions towards Britain. They correctly assumed during the mid-1930s that Hitler's willingness to limit the size of his navy reflected a genuine desire to buy British friendship, but they also realized that he expected something in return, namely British acquiescence in Germany's expansionist program in eastern Europe.

As long as Hitler's territorial ambitions appeared limited in nature and were directed exclusively eastward, Chatfield and other leading naval decision-makers felt it would be unwise to obstruct Germany at the risk of war. 'If we have to fight her', Chatfield warned, 'it will probably also mean war with Japan and possibly Italy – a world war which may last for years with enormous loss of lives and money and general misery in the world.'

> What are we to get out of such a war, and should we feel in a strong moral position in being a partial cause of this war because we had refused to concede anything to her 20 years after the Great War? And what should we gain at the end of it other than the retention of certain German colonies which we won 20 years ago?[18]

The situation would be different, Chatfield admitted, '*If* we were convinced that by German successes in Czechoslovakia, Poland, Roumania or Danzig, she would eventually dominate Europe and so threaten us at our front door or in the Near East.' If this were the case, he believed that 'it would conceivably be better to fight her to prevent such domination, for the one thing that is quite clear to me is that Germany cannot remain as she is in the world.' He was not convinced, however, that Germany would be strengthened by expansion eastward.

> I can see myself that she [Germany] will run greater risks of disaster unless she is exceedingly limited in what she does in that direction … It is exceedingly doubtful whether any such territorial expansion, or Germanising of the countries on her eastern frontier, would help the people of her country. To dominate Europe Germany needs not only military strength but also economic and financial strength. These she has not got, and without them the further she moves to the east and increases her territory and influence the more a counter force will develop against her that will bring her to rest some time.
>
> Meanwhile, England and France, with their undisturbed financial and military strength would be building up a formidable threat in her rear.

He concluded, therefore, that it would be 'wrong and dangerous' to be drawn into a war over German movements to the east. 'I do not believe that peoples can be conquered and held in subjection nowadays', he wrote in 1937. 'If Germany makes any decided military move to the eastward in her present unbalanced strength she is much more likely to upset her own civilisation, such as it is, and to ride for a downfall internally.'[19]

Chatfield and his advisers correctly judged the basic thrust of German foreign policy during the mid-1930s and, believing that moderate

German expansion would not threaten British interests, urged the government to take advantage of Hitler's goodwill towards Britain. Their most serious mistake was failing to appreciate the extent of Nazi ambitions in eastern Europe, and the degree to which even moderate expansion would strengthen Germany's strategic position. It is wrong, therefore, to characterize the Admiralty's growing concern with the European situation in 1938–9 as a long-overdue realization that Germany presented a real threat to British interests. The Munich crisis did indeed shock the Admiralty into a better appreciation of the scope of German ambitions in Europe, but more importantly it underlined the danger that war might erupt suddenly in this region. The Admiralty responded with a crash program of new construction to provide additional light craft for the protection of British trade against German commerce raiders. That it had neglected to do so earlier is not evidence that the navy underestimated the possibility of war with Germany, just that it was overly optimistic in its appreciation of when it might have to face that danger.

It has also been suggested that the navy's views on the likelihood of war with Germany were distorted by erroneous assumptions about what Hitler planned to use his navy for.[20] This argument wrongly assumes that Hitler always intended to use his navy against Britain, and that the Admiralty believed a German challenge to British maritime supremacy was the sole possible cause of an Anglo-German war. British naval intelligence did indeed conclude during the mid-1930s that the 'keynote of Germany's naval policy is "Supremacy in the Baltic"', but the Admiralty also knew that Britain might find itself at war with Germany even though Hitler did not wish to threaten the British Empire.[21] The navy evaluated the threat from the German fleet on the basis of the damage it could inflict if it were turned against Britain, and it was this assessment which led the Admiralty to play down the German menace.

In the early 1930s, Germany was too weak to pose a serious threat to British security. By mid-decade this was no longer true, but the Admiralty continued to believe that the threat was manageable for a number of reasons. Most importantly, in June 1935 Germany voluntarily concluded the Anglo-German Naval Agreement,[22] which the Admiralty correctly interpreted as a signal that Hitler did not intend to challenge Britain's maritime position with a Tirpitzian building program. The Admiralty willingly accepted the 35 per cent ratio because this figure would permit the navy to face Germany and still meet its commitments in the Far East, as long as Britain maintained the

Washington ratio *vis-à-vis* Japan.[23] The AGNA also committed Germany to respect the qualitative treaty limits then in force, and ensured that Germany would build a 'balanced' fleet of capital ships supported by cruisers and flotilla vessels, rather than a commerce-raiding navy.[24] These developments undoubtedly worked to the navy's advantage. If Germany had concentrated its shipbuilding resources on commerce raiders, the Admiralty would have been compelled to alter the composition of its own forces significantly and at great expense. But as long as Britain maintained its crushing superiority over Germany in heavy ships, a balanced German navy could not challenge Britain directly for command of the seas or inflict crippling losses on British trade. Moreover, the Admiralty's belief that the submarine threat had been mastered, combined with Germany's limited U-boat construction at this time, suggested that the *Kriegsmarine* would be incapable of mounting a successful *guerre de course* with its submarine arm. Planners were also aware that in a European conflict Britain would almost certainly have allies to supplement the Royal Navy's already substantial naval superiority over Germany. These considerations convinced the Admiralty that Hitler's navy, in its current form, was incapable of single-handedly inflicting mortal damage on the British Empire.

The navy's tendency to slight the danger posed by Germany is sometimes depicted as little more than an instinctive attempt to maintain its share of the defense budget at the highest possible level. The underlying assumption is that this is the *raison d'être* of all fighting services,[25] but in this case the motivation ran deeper. The navy defended its programs so vigorously because it believed they were essential for the defense of the British Empire, and because it felt these interests were being neglected. The Admiralty frequently reminded Whitehall that recent developments in the air had in no way reduced the country's need for a powerful navy. Britain still depended on seapower to protect its essential trade and the communications which held together Britain's vast maritime Empire. As the First Lord stated on the eve of the Second World War, it was

perhaps not entirely superfluous to repeat what we all know, that this country is dependent on its seaborne trade, that without imported petrol the RAF cannot fly, that without imported food all our Air Raid Precautions will not prevent us from starving, that without command of the sea we cannot transport our expeditionary forces to the scene of action. If, therefore, our naval preparations are inadequate, the rest is of no avail.[26]

The navy regarded its minimum needs as non-negotiable and feared that a single-minded concentration on the German air threat would only over-insure against one danger – and not necessarily the most serious one – at the cost of leaving Britain vulnerable to others. As Chatfield observed:

> Whatever we may be able to do with our Army or Air Force in preventing our own country from being invaded or attacked, it will never reduce our Naval responsibilities of maintaining our Empire, sea communications and Mercantile Marine, on which our wealth finally depends under our existing system of national economics.[27]

This line of argument struck directly at the politicians' hopes that security might be achieved at an acceptable cost by concentrating Britain's resources against only one of the major threats it faced. The Admiralty believed that Britain's strategic position could only be improved by spending more money on defense or by reducing its global commitments. Until this was done, the problem was how the funds that were available for rearmament could be utilized most effectively. The navy regarded politicians' preference for spending on the RAF to be a fundamentally unsound answer to Britain's problems, and one which was being pursued only in response to the demands of ill-informed public opinion. Leading naval figures did not believe that Britain could maintain both a first-class navy and bomber parity with Germany, and they did not accept that there was any compelling strategic need to do so. As the Plans Division argued, it had 'always been recognised' in the past 'that the price to be paid for naval supremacy must be the acceptance of inferiority on the land, and that the policy of maintaining an army on the continental scale would spell ruin.'

> Financially, that argument now appears to be equally valid with regard to air strength. If it could be shown that a strong air force could relieve us of the necessity of maintaining a strong navy, the two claims would not be incompatible, but there is no evidence to show that this is so. If, on the other hand, it were certain that an air force operating independently could play a decisive part in future warfare, the outlook for Great Britain would be almost hopeless, but there is no reason to suppose in theory and no evidence to prove in fact, that, provided reasonable precautions are taken, aircraft can play a *decisive* part, except in support of an army or navy.[28]

Naval decision-makers also doubted that the public's fears about the effects of bombing were justified. Chatfield, for example, asserted that 'no great people with efficient leaders...would submit to an attack which would be of a terrorising, rather than a dominating, nature.' He did not believe that it would be possible to 'terrorise a whole country in such a way if your defences are acting efficiently, and any London Government that thought of capitulation on the part of the Empire to such an attack would speedily be dethroned by general national opinion. Mothers of murdered children would cry out,' he argued, 'not for mercy, but for revenge and punishment.'[29]

As the decade progressed, the Admiralty was also increasingly inclined to reject the RAF's claims that only a counter-bombing strategy would be effective against Germany. Senior naval personnel disliked the RAF's 'stagnant attitude "You bomb me and I'll bomb you." The very fact that we know we cannot do anything like the damage to Germany that she can do to us does not induce one to put a great deal of faith in the present policy.'[30] In a 1938 critique of the Air Ministry's strategy, the Plans Division asserted that it was 'clearly to our advantage to rely more on fighters and less on bombers for the air defence of Great Britain than is at present proposed.' This would

enable the truly defensive measures to be increased, it will provide a maximum defence during the critical early days of the war, it will destroy enemy air personnel, and his morale, instead of merely his machines, it will provide greater morale support to our own people, and most of all, it will relieve the financial burden on our resources and set free money for expenditure on the main defensive and offensive weapons of our Imperial strategy.[31]

Given the belief that the *Luftwaffe* did not pose a mortal danger to Britain, the Admiralty insisted that the navy's needs must supersede those of the RAF. 'Since...sea power is still our strong suit,' it asserted, 'it is clearly necessary to play it and not against it in the development of our local measures of security.'[32] That this conviction remained strong during the 1930s should not be dismissed as blindness to new technology or a failure to appreciate the danger from a resurgent Germany. Naval conservatism and service egotism undoubtedly influenced the Admiralty's outlook, but naval decision-makers were ultimately more concerned with meeting what they believed were the navy's minimum absolute requirements than with simply preserving their status relative to the other services. The Admiralty accepted that both the army and air force had an essential role to play in home and imperial defense; and they did not object in principle to their needs being met, so long as the navy was maintained at a level commensurate with its global responsibilities. The Admiralty's attacks on the RAF's bomber fleet, and its criticisms of the army's plans for a continental expeditionary·force, stemmed from a desire to prevent too much money being diverted from the one area that was undoubtedly vital into others they believed were of secondary importance.

The inter-service rivalry engendered by financial restrictions should not obscure the fact that the Admiralty always held that the only satisfactory solution to Britain's defense problems was to eliminate the imbalance between its armed forces and its commitments. Senior naval decision-makers were aware that a combination of two or more hostile powers posed potentially insurmountable problems. Chatfield, for example, believed that it was 'exceedingly doubtful, even if we increase our Naval and air strength to the utmost possible limit under voluntary conditions of service, whether we can maintain the Empire if engaged simultaneously east and west. To fight two such wars would be something greater than we have ever done before, and is something which we should not contemplate.'[33] To escape this predicament, the Admiralty concluded that the government must alter its foreign policy so as to reduce the number of potential enemies the Empire faced, or allocate more money for defense. Both courses were urged on the government, in hopes that rapid rearmament would deter potential aggressors and provide the Foreign Office with time to reduce the number of Britain's enemies. Frustrated by the financial impediments to rearmament, Chatfield argued that money must not be allowed to 'stand in the way, as it is not standing in the way of our rivals. Everything that we are doing now to restore our lost military strength should be met by capital expenditure.'[34] To accomplish this, he believed it was necessary to cut expenditure on the social services. In his view, the government was 'looking at these Services from the point of view of a very rich man, yet it is perfectly clear to me that, without increasing taxation, we cannot maintain the Social Services on their present scale and at the same time accumulate enemies.'[35]

In the realm of foreign policy, the Admiralty desired an agreement with either Germany or Japan, and sought to avoid any responsibilities under the League of Nations that might involve Britain in a conflict where its vital interests were not at stake. An understanding with Japan would help to reduce Britain's immediate defense problems, but naval planners also felt that 'so long as the military party in Japan is dominant it can only be a surface arrangement.'[36] Hence, it would still be necessary to maintain a large navy to protect Britain's eastern interests, and little long-term relief could be expected. An agreement with Germany, on the other hand, would mean 'that most of our other defence commitments would largely solve themselves.' Phillips maintained that 'Italy would feel very differently about the situation in Europe and would be very unlikely to make trouble by herself, while even if Japan did not modify her policy, as it is probable she would, we should at least be in a position to deal with her if necessary.'[37] Most importantly, it would allow substantial reductions in the estimates of the army and air force, whose sharp rise was solely attributable to the increased prospect of war with Germany.

From the Admiralty's perspective, financial and strategic imperatives all pointed clearly towards an agreement with Germany. If the British government had been willing to accept Germany's terms, an accommodation might have been reached with little difficulty. An Anglo-German understanding was, after all, a much-cherished aim of Hitler's. The Admiralty was ready to play along at first in the mistaken belief that Nazi Germany did not pose a threat to the European balance of power. It did not recognize until late in the day that Hitler's objectives were essentially unlimited and would have elevated Germany to a position of hegemony in Europe. Of course, the Admiralty was not alone in mistaking Hitler for a reasonable statesman with limited ambitions, but if Germany had been given a free hand in eastern Europe, Britain's security would have been severely compromised.

Despite this failure, the Admiralty was largely successful during this period in evaluating the international environment in which it operated. Naval decision-makers were not unduly slow to recognize or respond to the danger posed by Nazi Germany. Nor did they misunderstand, or misrepresent, the threat from Japan. From the mid-1930s onward, the Admiralty always assumed that war in one hemisphere would ultimately have to be fought in both, and its preparations against Japan were undertaken in conjunction with, rather than as an alternative to, preparations against Germany. Slighting the danger from Germany would only have undermined the navy's case for the adoption of its proposed 'New Standard'. The Admiralty's best chance of securing a greater share of the defense budget was to convince Whitehall that the danger from Germany necessitated simultaneous preparations for war in the Far East.

That the navy failed to meet both of these threats satisfactorily cannot be attributed to a failure to foresee who Britain's enemies would be.

Of all the fighting services, it was the navy which best understood the global nature of Britain's defense dilemmas. The Admiralty attempted to prepare itself for the world war it eventually faced at the end of 1941, rather than the European one it entered in September 1939. It could only have been better prepared for the latter by sacrificing its preparations for the former. Far from acting from an outdated and self-serving desire to preserve the largest share of the defense budget, the Admiralty sought to provide security not only for Great Britain but for the British Empire as a whole. In the 1920s this meant only being able to send a fleet to the Far East while retaining a deterrent force in Europe; in the 1930s it meant being prepared to wage naval war in two hemispheres simultaneously. The navy attempted to meet the latter objective through a long-term program of naval expansion which would restore it to the position of strength it had enjoyed during the 1920s and earlier. Planners hoped that this could be achieved by the mid-1940s, and gambled on war being avoided until then.

The Admiralty firmly believed that a strong navy capable of protecting Britain's interests against both Germany and Japan was one of the British Empire's minimum absolute requirements. If Chatfield's views had prevailed, Britain would have adhered to a policy of limited liability in Europe; the RAF would have been converted to a predominantly defensive force; and the navy would have been allowed to build up to at least a two-power standard relative to Germany and Japan, and possibly to a three-power standard which included Italy as well. Successive governments rejected these schemes for a number of reasons, chief among them being a fear of the financial repercussions and a preoccupation with the air defense of Great Britain. Nevertheless, the conventional view of the navy as the most reactionary and short-sighted of the services during the 1930s is in many respects a complete reversal of the true state of affairs. Of the three fighting services, only the navy possessed a global perspective and tried to formulate coherent policies to meet all of Britain's grand strategic needs.

The Royal Navy's inability to master the U-boat challenge at an early stage of the Battle of the Atlantic has resulted in its prewar planning against Germany being heavily criticized. It is often suggested that the Admiralty should have foreseen Germany's decision to concentrate its naval resources on unrestricted submarine warfare, and that it could have adapted its construction programs and doctrines to meet this challenge sooner than it did. More recently, historians have contested these charges. Andrew Lambert, H.P. Willmott and Joseph Maiolo, for example, have demonstrated that in September 1939 the navy was reasonably well prepared for the challenge that the German navy, *in its then current form*, posed to Britain's maritime communications.[38] The Admiralty's prewar planning against Germany was much better than its critics usually allow. What ultimately upset the navy's calculations was the fall of France in 1940 and Germany's acquisition of naval bases on the French and Norwegian coasts. The navy failed to predict these events, but its record in this respect is hardly worse than that of any other organization. And even if the Admiralty had foreseen Germany's decision to step up U-boat production for an all-out attack on British trade, its ability to prepare for such a threat was severely limited. After 1936, the navy was committed to the construction of new capital ships, and these proved to be essential for the preservation of British seapower in the early stages of the war. A radical shift in naval construction priorities would only have provided Britain with one essential type of vessel at the expense of another. And even if trade defense *had* been given higher priority before the war, the result would have been escorts of limited endurance suited for service in the North Sea and western approaches, not the transoceanic vessels which were later required for Atlantic convoy work.[39]

The navy clearly devoted insufficient attention to the problems of anti-submarine warfare during the interwar period, but the tendency to criticize the Admiralty for failing to prepare for the specific conditions which existed during the Battle of the Atlantic has obscured our understanding of how it attempted to deal with the problems of the 1930s. The Admiralty's strategic thinking during these years was not distorted by the desire to secure a fleet action with its enemies. Planning against Germany focused on the application of economic pressure and the protection of British seaborne trade.

A maritime blockade alone was not expected to bring about Germany's defeat. The Admiralty recognized that Germany was not dependent on overseas sources of supply, and assumed that the coordination of Britain's full range of diplomatic and military resources would be required to undermine the German war economy. In the summer of 1938, for example, the JPC estimated that it would be necessary not just to intercept German seaborne trade, but also to regulate the imports of countries 'with which Germany could communicate by road, rail or river, as was done in 1914–18 by naval, diplomatic and commercial action.' Planners also expected the RAF to contribute to the economic pressure on Germany 'by air attack on manufacturing plant and centres of storage and distribution in Germany itself.'[40] These measures were not expected to have a rapid or decisive effect. Military force would still be required on the continent to ensure Germany's defeat, and the Admiralty expected France to bear the brunt of the fighting on land. The allied blockade was not designed, therefore, to win the war against Germany, but rather to allow the war to be won with other weapons. Germany's ability to fight would be increasingly restricted by economic pressure, while Britain and France mobilized their superior resources for war purposes. The allies would then gradually wear down German strength as they had done in the First World War.

British grand strategy required the navy to enforce a maritime blockade of Germany and protect Britain's seaborne communications. The Admiralty's plans for doing this differed little from the ones it had employed successfully against Germany during the previous war. Britain would concentrate enough capital ships in its northern bases to neutralize the heavy units of the German navy. The navy's numerical advantage in this class of vessel ensured that a fleet action was unlikely to take place. Germany would either keep its fleet intact so as to retain command of the Baltic Sea, or it would disperse these units for attacks on British trade, for 'tip and run' raids along the British coast, or to interfere with the army and air force's communications with France. If any of Germany's capital ships or 'pocket' battleships attempted to break out of the North Sea, superior British forces would always be at hand to hunt them down. In the meantime, light forces would protect British merchant vessels against commerce raiders and cut off Germany's seaborne trade.[41]

The maritime blockade of Germany was expected to be a relatively simple matter. Britain's advantageous geographical position and ample margin of naval superiority meant that it would not be difficult to sever Germany's access to the oceanic trade routes. At the outset of war, the navy would quickly round up German merchant shipping on the high seas and establish naval patrols and contraband control stations to deal with blockade runners. The defense of trade would be more problematical. The main threat to British shipping was expected to come from surface raiders, most likely in the form of disguised merchant cruisers, but possibly from heavy units of the German navy. Germany's relatively small U-boat fleet was at this time composed mostly of vessels of limited endurance. If Hitler resorted to unrestricted submarine warfare, the Admiralty was optimistic that convoy, together with ASDIC, could neutralize the threat. Planners believed that attacks on Britain's trade routes would eventually be mastered, as they had been in 1917–18. As one appreciation stated, this form of attack

> might at first be serious, calling for considerable effort on our part. Germany however has no overseas bases and the attacking forces outside home waters must be made self-supporting. With the passage of time and development of counter-measures the scale of naval attack would certainly diminish and must in the long run be brought to a stand still. Germany with her present limited Naval strength cannot therefore expect to achieve any vital result by naval action against our overseas trade.[42]

The greatest danger would be an unrestricted attack by German submarines and land-based aircraft on British ports and coastal shipping. This course appeared to offer Germany its best chance of fatally disrupting Britain's essential imports, thereby inflicting the 'knockout blow' that British strategists feared.[43]

The Admiralty's plan, therefore, was to remain on the strategic defensive against Germany, as it had during the First World War. As long as Britain retained superior heavy ships at home and possessed sufficient light forces for trade protection and blockade, naval planners believed that the navy could easily fulfil its allotted role in a war with Germany. However, there were those within the service who clamored for a more vigorous and offensive naval strategy against Germany. In 1937, Admiral Drax, the C-in-C Plymouth, sharply criticized the navy's war plans:

> When dealing with a country so inferior to us in Naval strength as Germany or Italy, there is every reason to start with a vigorous offensive. A slow war, ending with economic strangulation as in 1918, would mean economic and financial ruin for us as well. There is therefore the risk that we may lose the next war by stressing too much the need for the passive defence of some 10,000 miles of pencil lines drawn across the seven seas.[44]

Drax wanted the navy's plans completely overhauled, and he recommended the creation of a special planning staff at the Admiralty charged solely with investigating the feasibility of offensive operations.[45] His only practical suggestion was that army and Royal Marine brigades be 'entered and specially trained as an amphibious striking force,' one possible use for which would be subduing U-boat bases on the Spanish coast. Drax was, however, out of touch with the post-1918 trend of naval thought. His ideas appealed to Backhouse, who brought him to the Admiralty in early 1939, and they were attractive to Churchill following his return to the Admiralty.[46] But the weight of naval opinion accepted that seapower was slow acting and did not depend for its success on the destruction of enemy ships. Responsible planners displayed little interest in offensive adventures which risked depleting British naval strength for no tangible benefits. It is hardly surprising, therefore, that Drax's criticisms earned him a sharp rebuke from the First Sea Lord[47] or that the Naval Staff regularly impeded Churchill's quest for more offensive naval action against Germany. As Chatfield noted in 1937, the navy's

> main object has always been and will always be to attack the enemy whenever and wherever he appears and to defeat him. Subsidiary operations may be conceived and would...be welcomed now as always by the Officers of the Fleet, but they are not the primary function of a Navy in a war such as is envisaged in the German War Plan.[48]

The defensive nature of the Admiralty's planning against Germany may have been distasteful to a small circle of aggressive-minded officers, but their objections were more intuitive than reasoned. When the navy's plans are evaluated against its performance during the first eight months of war, they emerge in a relatively favorable light. Until the fall of France completely undermined the assumptions on which naval plans were framed, Britain was indeed able to cut off the enemy's overseas trade with little difficulty, hunt down its surface raiders with superior forces, and keep shipping losses to U-boats to acceptable levels. It is doubtful that a Franco-British blockade would ever have fulfilled Whitehall's high expectations for it, but during the first stage of the war the Royal Navy did succeed in meeting all of the goals it set for itself.

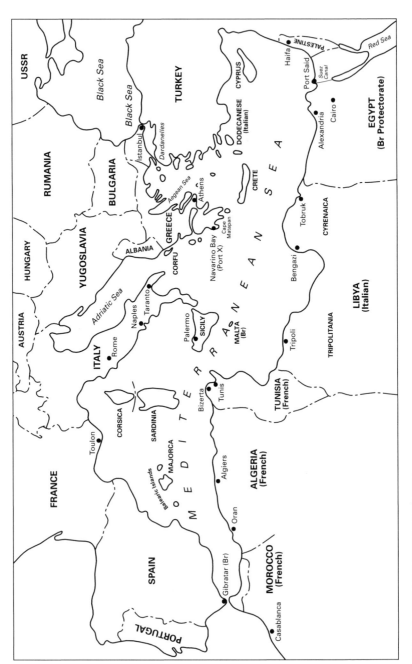

Map 5.1 The Mediterranean Theater

5
The Search for the 'Knockout Blow': War Plans against Italy

The Admiralty only began to think seriously about war with Italy in 1935 as a result of the Abyssinia crisis. Prior to this, Italian friendship had been taken for granted. The decline in Anglo-Italian relations following Mussolini's invasion of the independent east African state of Abyssinia might not have been viewed with particular alarm within naval circles had it not been for the impact of Italian hostility on Britain's strategic position *vis-à-vis* Germany and Japan, and the danger of an estranged Italy moving into alignment with those powers. A three-front war against Germany, Japan, and Italy would stretch British resources to breaking point, and the existence of a hostile Italy athwart Britain's main line of imperial communications would seriously complicate the despatch of a fleet to the Far East. Thus, while Chatfield remarked privately in August 1935 that the 'bumptiousness of Italy is so great that it may be worth fighting her now to re-assert our dominance over an inferior race,' he conceded that since 'a hostile Italy is a real menace to our Imperial communications and defence system' it would be better to avoid war.[1] The Admiralty was confident, however, that Italy's vulnerability to British seapower would make a purely Anglo-Italian conflict a largely one-sided affair – an assessment shared by the Italian navy. In August 1935 the Supreme High Command of the Italian armed forces concluded that 'Italy's total lack of battleship capability and the limited operational value of its air force render the possibility of war against Britain an extremely onerous undertaking.' Admiral Cavagnari, the Chief of Staff of the Italian navy, warned that the prolongation of a war with Britain 'can only act against us, given that Britain, once it has mobilised its awesome war machine, can rely on inexhaustible resources.'[2]

The Admiralty's optimism stemmed in large measure from its assessment of the Italian economy. The Plans Division noted in 1931 that no less than three-quarters

> of the supplies upon which [Italy's] very existence depends come from overseas along lines of communications easily controlled from the naval bases of foreign powers; and six-sevenths of its maritime commerce originates elsewhere than in the Mediterranean.
>
> Thus, so far as supplies are concerned, Italy is, among the greater nations, in a position comparable only with that of Great Britain or Japan. She is, moreover, dependent upon foreign tonnage for the carriage of about half her imports.[3]

'In short,' planners declared, Italy's 'general dependence upon sea-carriage for imports is so extensive that there is scarcely any branch of Italian industrial activity which would not be considerably affected by a successful application of maritime economic pressure.'[4] The RN's crushing numerical superiority over its Italian counterpart seemed to ensure that this pressure could be applied with ease. Britain's control over Gibraltar and Suez would sever Italian imports originating outside the Mediterranean, and this was considered sufficient to ensure Italy's ultimate defeat. Planners never calculated how long it would take maritime pressure to produce decisive results, but the crucial determinant would be the navy's ability to interfere with Italian trade inside the Mediterranean. These operations would be complicated, however, by the lack of a secure naval base in the central Mediterranean. Britain's only first-class base in the region was at Malta, but Italy's ability to concentrate its metropolitan air force in Sicily, a mere 60 miles away, convinced the Admiralty that a British fleet would have to operate from another base in wartime.[5] Alexandria was the obvious alternative, but it was undefended and possessed inadequate docking and repair facilities. Worst of all, it was poorly placed to allow the continuous application of seapower in the central Mediterranean.

This problem shaped the navy's calculations when it suddenly and unexpectedly found itself preparing for war with Italy in late 1935.[6] Alexandria's shortcomings were evident to both the Admiralty and the C-in-C Mediterranean, Admiral Fisher, and plans were immediately developed to improvise an advance fleet base at Navarino Bay, a Greek harbor, in the event of war. This location, codenamed 'Port X,' was still within range of Italian land-based aircraft, but planners hoped that it was far enough from Italy to be relatively safe from air attack.

They realized, however, that when hostilities commenced, the British fleet would have to operate, at least temporarily, from Alexandria. Nevertheless, the navy's plans called for a vigorous offensive posture from the outset.

The need for immediate and relentless action against the enemy is a common theme running through all of the navy's preparations against Italy between 1935 and 1939. This stemmed from the derisive view of Italian fighting abilities prevalent in British naval circles at this time. Richmond, who served as British Liaison Officer with the Italian Fleet during the First World War, formed an especially low opinion of the Italian navy. 'They had better sell their Fleet & take up their organs & monkeys again,' he wrote in 1915, 'for, by Heaven, that seems more their profession than sea fighting.' During the interwar period, the Italian navy was commonly regarded as an unstable and temperamental foe which might crumple quickly if it suffered sharp reverses at an early stage in the war – a character defect which was frequently projected onto the Italian population as a whole. 'If it does come to war,' Backhouse told Chatfield in 1935, 'I'm sure a strong beginning would be important. Italian spirits may now be high, but they are a Latin race & apt to be either high or low & a bad start might lead to early loss of moral[e].'[7] This calculation reappeared frequently in naval appreciations and figured prominently in the debate over British grand strategy in the spring of 1939.

The navy's belief in Italy's weak strategic position and irresolute national character brought out in full measure the offensive spirit that Drax found lacking in the Admiralty's plans against Germany. Sensing a weak and vulnerable enemy, planners in both the Admiralty and the Mediterranean fleet instinctively looked for means to bring direct pressure to bear. The economic blockade was central to the navy's plans, but Italy's colonial presence in Africa offered up other tempting targets. Planners were optimistic that Britain's control of the Suez Canal would isolate Italian forces in east Africa, and that enemy communications with Libya could be severed through naval action. At the same time, warships would be detached to bombard the Italian and Libyan coasts, and aircraft of the Fleet Air Arm (FAA) would attack Italian ports and air bases.

Planners were also confident about Britain's defensive position. Naval forces operating from Gibraltar could easily prevent Italian commerce raiders from getting into the Atlantic, and Britain's Mediterranean trade could be protected by sending merchant ships around the Cape.[8] The only serious threat to British shipping might come in the Red Sea, where Italy would be in a strong position at the outset of the war. Enemy naval and air forces in this region would soon be isolated, however, and British air forces in the Sudan would assist the navy in eliminating this threat.[9] Italy appeared to have no other means of striking at Britain. It was only after the Abyssinia crisis had wound down that the navy became concerned that the enemy might concentrate its land and air forces for an immediate attack on Egypt from bases in Libya. The loss of Egypt and the Suez Canal would transform Britain's strategic position in the Mediterranean, but the navy could only make a marginal contribution to its defense, prompting Chatfield to remark that 'If we have trouble with Italy the Navy can win the war slowly, but the Army and Air Force can lose it in Egypt rapidly, and therefore it is the defence of Egypt that will be our main preoccupation.'[10]

After the threat of war over Abyssinia receded, the navy's attention did not focus on Italy again until the winter of 1938–9. In the intervening years, the Admiralty supported the government's efforts to appease Italy and convert it to a position, if not of friendship, then at least of genuine neutrality. According to Chatfield, Italy 'ought to be our best friend in the future as she has been in the past because her position in the Mediterranean is a dominant one.'[11] The Admiralty's hopes for an Anglo-Italian *rapprochement*, and the reluctance of the COS to base its calculations on the possibility of a three-front war, meant that the navy did not reconsider the problem of war with Italy until after the Munich crisis. In November 1938, Admiral Pound, the C-in-C Mediterranean, submitted an appreciation of the strategical situation in the Mediterranean in the event of war with both Germany and Italy (Table 5.1).[12] Pound was confident that the French navy would tie down a large part of the Italian fleet in the western Mediterranean, thereby easing somewhat the position in the eastern Mediterranean, but he still foresaw considerable difficulties for a British fleet operating from Alexandria. With 'present day communications and long range aircraft the Mediterranean has become a very small place,'[13] Pound observed. The navy should expect to be subjected to steady attrition by Italian air and naval forces, he warned, and British ships would be unable to cross the Mediterranean without a strong escorting force. 'In effect,' Pound noted, 'the movement of a single auxiliary from, say, Malta to Alexandria will become a major operation.'

Economic pressure still provided the most effective means of weakening the enemy, and Pound proposed to use his forces to intercept Italian trade between Italy and the Black Sea. It would only be possible, however, to make 'occasional sweeps from Cape Matapan to the northeast into the southern Aegean.' These operations would be undertaken by a division of destroyers supported by a cruiser, with cover provided

Table 5.1 British and Italian forces in the eastern Mediterranean, October 1938:
Pound's estimates of British requirements and Italian strength

	Britain	Italy	
		Available for use against Britain	*Total strength, Jan. 1939*
Battleships	3	2	4
Aircraft carriers	1	–	–
8" cruisers	4	4	7
6" cruisers	5	6	14
Destroyers	40	30	48
Submarines	21	57	104

Source: Pound, 'Situation in the Mediterranean – 1st October, 1938' and 'The Strategical
Aspect of the Situation in the Mediterranean on 1st October 1938', 14 November 1938,
ADM 116/3900; Roskill, *Naval Policy*, I, appendix B.

by the main fleet. Pound also intended to use the fleet to disrupt Italy's
communications with North Africa, assist the army and RAF in the
defense of Egypt and Malta, and protect supply ships and auxiliaries
between Port Said and Alexandria.

Pound's appreciation also emphasized the need for joint plans with
the other services, and he recommended that consideration be given
to an allied advance into Libya from both east and west by British,
Egyptian, Dominion, and French forces. The conquest of Libya would
improve Britain's position in a number of ways: by discouraging minor
powers in the region from siding with the enemy; reducing the scale of
air attack on the sea lanes between Egypt and Malta; cutting off Italy's
air route to Italian East Africa; and releasing large air and land forces for
other operations. Pound hoped that with Libya in allied hands it would
be possible to build up a strong presence in Tunisia, thus enabling the
allies to obtain air superiority in the central Mediterranean and employ
Malta as a fleet base.

When Pound discussed these proposals with Admiralty officials at
the end of November 1938, he was informed that Britain could not
spare land and air forces for such ambitious operations, and that
British forces in Egypt would remain on the defensive at the outset of
war. In a new appreciation, submitted to the Admiralty in May 1939,
Pound observed that the only 'British force in the Mediterranean
which can take the offensive against Italy is the fleet.'

But in the nature of things the offensive activity of the fleet must of necessity be limited to the exertion of economic pressure by the interruption of Italian sea communications and attacks on his Naval forces found at sea, supplemented by bombardments of Libyan and perhaps Sicilian ports, and possibly by Fleet Air Arm raids on enemy naval forces in harbour.[14]

All of this would be complicated, however, by the Italian air force, which was expected to develop heavy attacks on the British fleet at Alexandria and destroy the dockyards at Malta. The British would be unable to retaliate on anywhere near the same scale, and Pound doubted that France could make good British deficiencies in the air. He recommended, therefore, making immediate arrangements with the French to move British air forces to Algeria and Tunisia, 'whence they can bomb vital points in Italy and Sicily, including the Italian Fleet and dockyards at Taranto and Augusta. Even if the aircraft themselves cannot be sent off till war had broken out, the ground arrangements could be made as soon as possible to collect the stores, reserve equipment and bombs.' Pound also hoped to station British bombers on the Turkish mainland for operations against Italian airfields in the Dodecanese.

These proposals were rejected by both the Air Staff and the COS,[15] which were alarmed by Britain's position in the air relative to Germany and were unwilling to divert aircraft to other theaters. There was, however, considerable interest in Whitehall at this time in a 'Mediterranean-first' grand strategy in the event of a three-front war. Broadly speaking, two different schools of thought developed within the Admiralty on the best solution to this worst-case scenario. The first favored adherence to the principles which had hitherto guided British strategic planning, that Britain should give priority to home defense and the protection of its interests east of Suez. This meant, in practice, that Britain would abandon control of the eastern Mediterranean in order to despatch naval forces to the Far East. The other school of thought proposed that the navy concentrate its resources in the Mediterranean for a knockout blow against Italy, the weakest of Britain's potential enemies, while remaining on the defensive against Germany and Japan.

The latter scheme appealed strongly to offensive-minded officers eager to exploit the Royal Navy's 'Nelson touch' against at least one of its three foes. This offensive school was temporarily in the ascendent at the Admiralty during Backhouse's brief tenure as First Sea Lord. The alternative to a Mediterranean offensive – a predominantly defensive strategy in all three theaters at once – held little appeal to this group. The First

Lord, Lord Stanhope, an early convert, recognized that at the beginning of a three-front war 'we cannot hope to cripple either Germany or Japan by naval action,' but that it might be possible 'to cripple Italy by seizing her colonies, bombarding her oil tanks, stopping her supplies. If so Italy would appear to be the decisive point at the beginning of a war.' Plans for a defensive stance in the Mediterranean afforded 'the Navy no opportunity of helping to win the war & to be purely defensive. We don't want the public to think that the crews of capital ships are about as useful as those who sit in the bottom of a deep air-raid shelter. We shall not get many more capital ships if they do!'[16] In strategic terms it made sense to concentrate Britain's naval forces for a knockout blow against one of its enemies. However, opponents of this scheme raised two fundamental objections. First, they questioned whether Britain's interests in the Mediterranean were sufficient to justify giving this theater priority over the Far East, particularly in view of the difficulties a 'flying squadron' would encounter in defending Britain's interests against Japan. Second, they doubted that a rapid victory against Italy was possible.

These concerns were well-founded. Italy's ability to ward off a knockout blow was never subjected to systematic scrutiny by the proponents of a Mediterranean offensive. Admiral Drax, the leading intellect of the offensive school, thought it was 'obvious that smashing Italy, with the aid of France, should be much easier and quicker than smashing Germany … against Germany our Navy cannot do very much, but against Italy it can do a great deal, mainly in the way of coastal bombardment.'[17] Appraisals such as this, promulgated at the highest levels by the navy's political and professional heads, held considerable allure for politicians looking for a way out of Britain's strategic dilemma; but they were based on little more than blind faith in the offensive value of seapower and a derisive view of Italian national character.

The question of priorities was the subject of extensive debate in the spring of 1939. The political implications of a Mediterranean strategy could not be easily dismissed in view of the repeated assurances given to Australia and New Zealand regarding Britain's commitment to the defense of imperial interests in the Far East. Timing proved to be crucial to the outcome of the debate. In the aftermath of Hitler's move into Prague, politicians and diplomats were eager to back up Britain's new commitments to Greece and Turkey with naval force. Moreover, staff talks were beginning to reveal the full depth of French hostility to British plans for despatching naval forces to the Far East.[18] These concerns eventually tipped the balance of official opinion in favor of a

Mediterranean offensive. However, the wisdom of this decision was questioned by traditional-minded planners inside the Admiralty and the JPC, and when Pound succeeded Backhouse as First Sea Lord, a more conservative approach reasserted itself in planning circles.

Pound, who came to the Admiralty directly from the Mediterranean, was perplexed by the views he found on his return to Whitehall. In a letter to Admiral Andrew Cunningham, the former DCNS and his replacement in the Mediterranean, the new First Sea Lord disparaged the prevailing idea that a knockout blow could force Italy out of a war quickly. 'I do not know who gave the politicians the idea that it could be done,' he complained, 'but it seems that they expect it and they are now undergoing the rather painful process of being undeceived.'

Italy can only be 'knocked out' either by her armies being defeated, or by Italy being laid waste by air. We cannot do either of these things at the beginning of the war and it is left to the Navy to do the 'knocking out.' I can only imagine that they thought the Fleet would steam slowly along the Italian coast and blow it to bits, which, even were it possible would not 'knock Italy out.'

Pound went on to outline his own views on the navy's capabilities in this theater. 'The material damage we can do Italy by bombardment is not great,' he remarked, 'but it will affect their morale to a certain extent.'

My own idea is that the extent to which it will be affected will depend on what damage they do to us in the process. If for the damage (unknown), and which they will tell the world is nil, they can cause us the loss of a battleship (which we shall not be able to hide), then their morale is much more likely to be increased than lowered. Another fallacious idea is that by conquering Libya, which in turn would very likely lead to their losing Italian East Africa, we should 'knock out' Italy.

To my mind cutting off their supplies, interfering with their communications, bombarding their ports, killing their submarines and later on the capture of Libya and some of the Dodecanese Islands are all part of 'throttling' them, not knocking them out. If they are as gutless as we imagine them, in time the throttling may kill them without their being given a knock out blow.[19]

These views typified orthodox naval opinion. Because this school returned to the ascendency after Pound's appointment, the Far East quickly re-emerged as the navy's foremost concern, and plans against Italy assumed more modest objectives. During the last remaining months of peace, naval planners operated on the assumption that it would have to be left to the politicians to decide which theater was to have priority in the event of a three-front war.

This debate over grand strategy did not greatly affect the Admiralty's thinking on naval strategy against Italy. Whether British naval forces were concentrated in the Mediterranean or in the Far East, the navy's basic strategy in the former theater would remain essentially unchanged. Its first objective would be to secure its defensive position in the eastern Mediterranean and take the tactical offensive at the earliest possible moment. As in 1935–6, great importance was attached to striking a hard blow at the Italians immediately hostilities commenced. As one Admiralty official remarked, 'From what is known of Italian psychology there is good reason to believe that an initial and immediate setback would have a profound effect on them and consequently on the result of the war so far as they were concerned.'[20] Such a blow could take several forms, most notably the bombardment of the Italian and Libyan coasts, air attack on Italian warships in harbor, and naval operations against Italy's maritime communications with North Africa.[21]

The degree of success achieved in these operations would depend on the scale of resources allocated to the theater. Inferior naval strength would impose a less ambitious strategy on the Mediterranean fleet, but even a superior British force would be unable to prevent Italy from dominating the central Mediterranean at the beginning of the war. A detailed study by the navy's tactical school in early 1939 concluded that a fleet operating from Alexandria could not sever Italian communications with Libya.[22] It was also clear to senior commanders that local Italian air superiority would impose serious limitations on all naval operations in the Mediterranean. Naval opinion continued to hope that offensive operations against Italy's colonies or coastline could produce spectacular results, but ultimately it was the ability of seapower to strangle the Italian economy and sap the enemy's will to fight that the navy counted on to produce decisive results. Here its assessment was accurate.

6
Neither Corbett nor Mahan: British Naval Strategy and War Planning

British naval war plans during the interwar period were framed on the understanding that Britain's *strategic* objectives in any future great-power conflict would be wholly defensive. The days of empire-building had passed, and the navy's primary mission was to protect Britain's global interests from would-be predators. As Chatfield noted in 1934, 'We are in the remarkable position of not wanting to quarrel with anybody because we have got most of the world already, or the best parts of it, and we only want to keep what we have got and prevent others from taking it away from us.'[1] The best means to protect British interests in wartime was a vigorous *tactical* offensive which would ultimately compel the enemy to accept terms favorable to Britain. How much pressure was required to achieve this was difficult to calculate, but in the aftermath of the First World War planners assumed that it was unwise to prepare for anything less than an unlimited war effort. 'Nothing can be clearer,' the Admiralty asserted, 'than the fact that modern war resolves itself into an attempt to throttle the national life. Waged by the whole power of a nation, its ultimate object is to bring pressure on the mass of the enemy's people, distressing them by every possible means, so as to compel the enemy's Government to submit to terms.'[2]

Whether decisive pressure could be applied by the navy alone depended upon the enemy in question. Naval rhetoric frequently lauded seapower as a decisive weapon, but responsible decision-makers realized that land powers were often immune to naval pressure. In 1920, for example, the prospect of war with Soviet Russia prompted Beatty to question what good ships would be 'against a Power that is without Sea Forces. Blockade, yes, but that amounts to nothing. We can send ships, big ships, into the Baltic to obtain moral effect – but will this accomplish anything? I do not believe the Bolshy cares a cuss for moral effect.'[3]

The Bolsheviks, Beatty asserted, 'understand only the results of heavy blows and as they are far from the sea will not [care or] understand the value of Sea Power!!!'[4] Similarly, when Keyes studied the problem of war with Turkey in 1926, he concluded that 'purely Naval action cannot bring great pressure to bear on Turkey. The role of the navy is consequently to assist the Army which is bringing such pressure to bear.'[5]

If seapower alone was insufficient to overthrow an enemy, a large army would have to be provided by Britain's allies. Naval decision-makers never wavered in their conviction that seapower had always been, and should ever remain, the pre-eminent weapon in Britain's arsenal, and they instinctively accepted the idea of a 'British way in warfare.' This concept, first articulated by Basil Liddell Hart in 1931, maintained that Britain had traditionally refrained from committing large land forces to fight in European wars, relying instead on its naval and economic strength to support allies and weaken enemies.[6] According to this view, Britain had employed its navy since the seventeenth century to strip its enemies of their overseas possessions and seaborne trade, while protecting Britain's own maritime commerce and colonies. Through a combination of economic pressure, seaborne expeditions against enemy territories, and subsidies to continental allies, Britain had defeated continental powers and acquired a great overseas empire. Liddell Hart maintained that this strategy had been effective and profitable in the past, and that it had been a mistake to abandon it for a 'continental commitment' during the First World War.

Naval opinion wholeheartedly embraced this body of ideas, and did so in fact before they were popularized by Liddell Hart in the 1930s. Indeed, the concept of a British way in warfare had already been advanced in the earlier works of Herbert Richmond.[7] However, because this model was derived from Britain's major wars of the eighteenth and nineteenth centuries, it was only relevant to coalition wars against a major European land power. Outside of the European context it held virtually no utility for naval strategists. In the event of war against the United States, for example, allies were unlikely to be found. In a clash with Japan, on the other hand, it was difficult to envisage any role for continental-sized armies. Lacking historical experience to draw upon for planning against non-European powers, and committed in principle to the maintenance of a small British army and air force, the navy looked primarily to seapower for the protection of British imperial interests.

Seapower conferred the ability to pressure an opponent two ways. The first was the transportation of military forces to raid the enemy's territories or seize its overseas possessions. In the years leading up to the

First World War, naval leaders tended to view amphibious operations as the most important means of bringing pressure to bear on a continental opponent.[8] During the interwar period, however, planners attached little importance to combined operations. The Allied failure at Gallipoli in 1915 contributed to the low esteem attached to combined operations during this period,[9] while the impact of technology on coastal defenses and continental communications made it difficult to foresee where combined operations would be feasible in the future. It was only in planning for war with Japan that the Admiralty gave serious thought to joint operations with the British army, and even these plans had to be shelved when the War Office warned that it had no forces to spare for such operations. The days when naval opinion regarded the British army as 'a projectile to be fired by the Navy'[10] had, in fact, quietly passed between 1914 and 1918.

This change in outlook was due in part to the weight attached to the second means of exerting pressure through seapower – the interruption of an enemy's maritime trade. Throughout the interwar period, naval leaders adopted an essentially Mahanian view of the link between overseas trade and national prosperity. As one typical Admiralty memorandum stated, 'The economic existence of all countries depends to a greater or a lesser degree upon oversea trade. Few are wholly self-supporting for food, and nearly all need supplies of some sort from overseas.'[11] The First World War had been crucial in fostering this view. The U-boat campaign highlighted Britain's vulnerability to economic pressure, while the blockade of Germany was often regarded as the decisive factor behind the Allied victory. 'Economic Pressure,' the Admiralty declared 'is nowadays a cardinal doctrine of war...It has been used, in greater or less degree, ever since history began, but its irresistible power when efficiently applied has never been more effectively demonstrated than in the 1914–1918 War.'[12]

As a result of this newfound enthusiasm for blockade, naval planners were increasingly prone to overestimate the economic vulnerability of potential opponents. The ATB concluded in 1927, for example, that the Soviet Union was self-supporting in foodstuffs and most essential raw materials, and would suffer little from British economic pressure.[13] Yet naval planners remained optimistic. One appreciation, prepared in 1932, declared that 'the economic and industrial position in RUSSIA is at present poor and the general conditions are favourable for the exertion of economic pressure in assistance of military operations.' Even if the British blockade 'fell short of isolating RUSSIA from the outside world,' planners believed that it would still 'increase the strain on her industrial resources and means of distribution. The cumulative effect might well be considerable.'[14]

The Admiralty was also optimistic about the role of blockade in the unlikely event of war with France. A memorandum produced by Admiral Wemyss at end of the First World War concluded that the navy's main object in such a conflict 'would probably be to cut off France from the outside world and to immobilise her oversea commerce as in the Napoleonic Wars.'[15] An invasion of France was not considered a serious option, although the possibility of occupying French colonies in Africa, the Far East and elsewhere was not ruled out, especially as this would reduce the overseas bases available for launching attacks on British seaborne trade. In 1930 the Plans Division examined the problem of applying economic pressure on France. It recognized that France could secure most of its essential imports through its land frontiers, but hoped that severing its overseas trade would eventually create crucial shortages of raw materials. To this end planners recommended a naval blockade of the mouth of the river Seine and the port of Marseilles. The economic dislocation resulting from 'the sudden stoppage of the port activities of the three vitally important import centres, Le Havre, Rouen and Marseilles, might well prove to be of eventual decisive value.'[16] Planners also advocated heavy air attacks on French rail centers, inland waterways and industrial centers, especially those in the north and northeast of the country. 'Reconstruction of industries of North France has brought well within the range of Britain's Air Power an area of almost vital importance,' they noted. 'Any measure which could be taken to re-devastate this area by means of air attack at the earliest moment after outbreak of war would be of incalculable value in throwing the internal economy of France into disorder.' Similar attacks on industrial and transportation centers in southern France from aircraft carriers operating in the Mediterranean would also contribute to France's economic difficulties.

The degree to which any state was susceptible to economic pressure would depend on a range of factors. The most vulnerable target was 'a country which is highly industrialised, largely dependent on foreign foodstuffs and raw materials, and whose military strength exceeds its power of economic resistance, by which it is meant that it is easier to wear down its civil population by economic methods than to compel its military forces to submission by strength of arms.'[17] The power most susceptible to this form of pressure was thought to be Japan, an island nation and the center of a maritime empire, like Britain itself. As Britain was vulnerable to economic warfare, it was assumed that Japan, with a less developed industrial base, weaker financial position, and smaller navy, must be even more exposed. European powers, on the other hand, would be less vulnerable to economic pressure. In the case of Italy, naval planners hoped that blockade might prove decisive on its own, but other European states were likely to be more resilient. According to Chatfield, in 'a European war economic pressure would be only a contributing factor to our ultimate victory, albeit a very important one.'

> In a Pacific war, however, it was only by means of economic pressure that victory could be achieved – any idea of an invasion of Japan and her defeat by military action on her own soil was out of the question. The war would be fought at a great distance from a large part of the Empire, only part of which would be affected by it. Except in the Far East, Empire trade would not be interfered with.
>
> Japan, however, could be almost completely isolated by naval action and her national life directly affected. The expansion of Japanese overseas trade meant that she had given a hostage to fortune. Interference with this trade would have fatal consequences for her.[18]

This belief shaped the Admiralty's Far Eastern war plans throughout this period. Given a sufficient degree of naval superiority and secure bases from which to operate, the Admiralty was confident that it could force Japan to accept British terms without the need for allies, and with only modest support from the other services. Similarly, given sufficient naval strength and continental allies to take up the burden of fighting on land, the Admiralty saw no reason to fear war with any single European power.

The navy's experiences in the Great War were also crucial in shaping its views on naval strategy. Prior to 1914, the navy had been preoccupied with the destruction of the enemy's battle fleet, and its planning was indeed 'Mahanian,' in the term's pejorative sense.[19] It is wrong though to attribute the same views to the navy after 1919. The inaction of the German High Seas Fleet during most of the First World War drove home to most officers the truth of Corbett's dictum that a weaker fleet cannot be expected to oblige its opponents by steaming out to its certain destruction.[20] This lesson was not accepted with good grace, however. Many naval officers continued to denounce the idea that the destruction of the enemy's naval forces was not necessary for the effective exercise of seapower. Beatty, for example, informed the 1921 Imperial

Conference that it had 'been said too often that command of the sea means control of communications.'

> This in itself is correct, but control of communications can only be effected by the destruction of the enemy force. Therefore, the real object of the British Navy is the destruction of the enemy force, as a result of which, it will control communications ... There is in some quarters a general idea that until the enemy be properly contained, his destruction is a kind of luxury which may be indulged in only on the condition that the containing force is not unduly risked. This is a fallacy which it is most desirable should be dissipated ... The command of the sea is determined by the result of great battles at sea. To any naval power, the destruction of the Fleet of the enemy must always be the great object aimed at.[21]

Such pronouncements emanated from an almost emotional revulsion within the officer corps to anything which seemed to eschew a vigorous offensive attitude. Notably, however, as C-in-C of the Grand Fleet during the First World War, Beatty adopted a strategy of containment that even the most defensive-minded student of Corbett could not have faulted. Throughout the interwar period, naval planners understood that a great battle between opposing fleets might not happen. War plans were constructed around the assumption that an inferior enemy force would always avoid giving battle on terms favorable to the British, and that any naval war would be a protracted and costly affair. If the opposing fleet could not be destroyed, planners accepted that its containment would meet Britain's essential needs. The destruction of the enemy's main force continued to be desirable, but attempts to bring this about were expected to take place concurrently with operations designed to undermine the enemy's national strength.

While the naval profession attached far less importance to the decisive battle than it had before 1914, the British battle fleet continued to play a central role in naval planning. As one typical appreciation noted, British naval strategy was based 'on the principle that a fleet of adequate strength, suitably disposed geographically and concentrated against the enemy's fleet, provides the "cover" under which security is given to widely dispersed territories and our mercantile marine on the trade routes.'

> This security cannot be given by the same strength of fleet dispersed to afford local protection to particular territories or trade

routes...Whilst, however, the main fleet is the basis upon which our naval strategy rests, naval requirements are not satisfied solely by its provision. The 'cover' it can provide is rarely complete, and instances have occurred in all wars of units detached by the enemy evading the main fleet and carrying out attacks of a sporadic nature on the territories and trade. To deal with these sporadic attacks, cruiser squadrons are required over and above those forming part of the main fleet.[22]

Thus, the primary role of the British fleet was to neutralize the opponent's fleet. It might never succeed in bringing the enemy's main force to battle and yet still exercise a decisive influence on the course of the war, as its very existence would compel an enemy possessing inferior forces to adopt a defensive stance or risk the destruction of its main fleet.

Naval leaders assumed that any British fleet would be dominated by traditional big-gunned battleships, but it is unfair to suggest that the interwar period was characterized by 'tactical sterility' and an obsession with refighting the Battle of Jutland.[23] The impact of aviation on naval warfare was clearly underestimated by the Royal Navy, but it was not ignored. Aircraft carriers were considered an integral part of any British battle fleet, and tactics were developed to take advantage of this new weapon. The navy's experiments with decentralized control, divisional tactics and night fighting during the 1930s also show how far its tactical thinking had developed since the First World War.[24] Nevertheless, battleships were still expected to form the backbone of the fleet – a belief shared at this time by the American and Japanese navies. As a result, British naval rearmament consistently favored capital ships. As long as Britain's enemies possessed these vessels, the Admiralty believed it must do the same. Failure to do so would have jeopardized Britain's maritime security during the early years of the European war, when battleships still had a decisive impact on the outcome of naval battles. The navy's priorities contributed, however, to its growing deficiencies in naval aviation. By 1941, Britain's once-commanding lead in carrier-based aviation had completely disappeared. This was not the result of an irrational obsession with surface fleet engagements, however, but rather stemmed from the RAF's control of the Fleet Air Arm throughout most of the interwar period and a shortage of resources during the 1930s.[25]

Contrary to conventional wisdom, the navy's ideas about maritime strategy owed little to the works of Alfred Thayer Mahan or his successors.

Naval officers were aware of these writers, but few were familiar with or interested in the details of their theories. Mahan's popularity in naval circles stemmed from the authoritative confirmation his works appeared to offer of the importance of seapower – something naval personnel instinctively accepted but usually lacked the ability to articulate. As Richmond complained, the naval officer of this period was

> too often content to say 'Here is the truth; Mahan says it is so. Who am I to question Mahan? I know that this or that saying is true. I am not going to bother my head to read a lot of books to prove it, or to argue with anyone who takes a different view. The authorities are good enough for me.'[26]

Mahan's writings emphasized the interdependence of a nation's prosperity, overseas trade, and seapower. In his view, the ultimate aim of naval strategy was the economic strangulation of the enemy by the destruction of its overseas trade, an objective best achieved through the elimination of the enemy's fleet. Sir Julian Corbett, on other hand, was a more subtle and insightful thinker whose work downplayed the importance of battle in naval strategy. In his opinion, the primary objective of naval forces was to secure a state's maritime communications, and the enemy fleet need only be destroyed if it was in a position to render them unsafe. Corbett also stressed that seapower enabled a state to attack its enemies directly by destroying seaborne trade and launching military expeditions, but he believed that only the latter was capable of producing decisive results. 'Since men live upon the land and not upon the sea,' he noted, 'great issues between nations at war have always been decided – except in the rarest of cases – either by what your army can do against your enemy's territory and national life, or else by the fear of what the fleet makes it possible for your army to do.'[27] Attacks on the enemy's maritime commerce, on the other hand, were principally a means of inducing the enemy to accept battle, and were nota potentially war-winning weapon.

Although historians commonly credit Mahan's malevolent influence with systematically distorting naval policy during this period, the naval profession's ideas about the utility of seapower were only 'Mahanian' in the sense of emphasizing the intimate link between naval power and national economic strength. This conviction could at times be carried to extremes, resulting in a propensity to overestimate the vulnerability of Britain's enemies, and Britain itself, to maritime pressure. This tendency did have a detrimental effect on naval policy between the wars, fostering overoptimistic expectations for a maritime blockade of Japan, hindering the development of more realistic Far Eastern war plans, and inspiring the overly ambitious Mediterranean strategy of 1939. The navy's exaggerated faith in seapower as a weapon against other maritime powers was tempered, however, by a 'Corbettian' appreciation of the limitations of seapower against a predominantly land-based power. The Admiralty's plans for war with Germany in particular demonstrate that decision-makers understood that the navy was only one instrument at the state's disposal, and that decisive results would, in most cases, depend on the mobilization and coordination of the nation's full range of military, diplomatic and financial resources.

Nor was British naval policy distorted at the highest levels by a 'Mahanian' obsession with fleet actions. Corbett's 'heretical' ideas about the role of battle entered the mainstream of naval thinking during the First World War. War plans and strategic appreciations in the years after 1918 directed far less attention to the problem of bringing an enemy fleet to action than to the need for securing bases, defending imperial trade, and enforcing a maritime blockade. The bias which existed within the seagoing navy in favour of the battleship undermined the navy's ability to fulfill these roles effectively when hostilities began, but naval leaders did appreciate that, in the words of Backhouse, 'There are a great many ways of making war without fighting Fleet actions.'[28] The Admiralty's war plans were always framed on the supposition that no enemy would voluntarily fight a battle that it must reasonably expect to lose, and planners eventually admitted that in some circumstances even a British fleet might adopt a fleet-in-being strategy to its advantage.

Throughout the interwar period, the elimination of the enemy's seaborne trade was considered the navy's principal offensive task, an idea more in line with the writings of Mahan than Corbett. To historically minded officers such as Richmond, this was a dangerous development which ignored the lessons of Britain's earlier wars. Other officers feared this trend arose from a deficiency of offensive spirit within the navy's higher ranks. The majority, however, recognized the limitations under which a modern fleet must operate. Remaining on the strategic defensive was preferable to risking valuable vessels in operations which could bring little or no strategic gain. At a time when Britain's naval strength was stretched, it made little sense to contemplate hazardous operations which could only inflict pinpricks on the enemy. Against an opponent perceived to be weak and vulnerable, naval planners showed that they were capable of devising bold offensive schemes.

Some of these projects, such as the bombardment of the Italian coast, were nothing short of reckless. Such operations might have been feasible if the enemy's armed forces proved to be entirely ineffectual, but they were seldom contemplated against adversaries regarded as reasonably competent. Expectations were also influenced by qualitative assessments of foreign navies. Naval leaders firmly believed that British naval personnel and warships were always superior to their foreign counterparts. According to Chatfield, for example, the navy's high standards of discipline and efficiency were 'a national art':

> At the bottom there must be the traditional spirit, handed down through the ages, through British families, from father to son – that inborn sea spirit, the appreciation that nothing but the best is good enough in the Navy and the assumption that it will be achieved; that each individual officer and man intends to and will play his part in accomplishing it. It is that factor, not the mere force of discipline, that is the driving power. It is the torch handed on.
>
> Fortunate we are, as an island race, to have inherited that spirit and to find it pleasing and natural.[29]

This sentiment was shared by both public and elites. In 1921 Lloyd George attributed the navy's successes through the ages 'to the seaman-like qualities of our sailors,' an asset that he advised 'should not be lost sight of.'[30] This exaggerated faith in the navy's capabilities resulted in surprise and indignation whenever it suffered a reverse. As Pound noted in 1940, the British people were 'very funny about the Navy in two ways':

> *Firstly* they think we have unlimited ships and that wherever an enemy ship turns up there should be a superior British force to deal with it ...
> *Secondly*, they imagine one can make war without losing ships. I think it is because they have such supreme faith in the Navy.
> Another curious thing is that the Air Force can allow our cities to be knocked about night after night and no one seems to consider it a reflection on them, whereas if anything comparable happened about the Navy the balloon would go up properly.[31]

Even the best foreign navies were held to be deficient in the intangible qualities that were exemplified by the Royal Navy, most notably the officer corps' affinity for the sea and aggressive fighting spirit. The German navy, for example, was widely regarded as ruthless and efficient, but was also frequently denigrated for its lack of seafaring tradition. Germany was not considered a 'natural' sea power, as its navy had not arisen from a need to protect seaborne trade, as Britain's had, but was the outgrowth of the aggressive aims of German statesmen. France and the United States did possess 'natural' seapower, but not to the same degree as Britain. Thus, while French and American personnel were considered technically proficient and well educated, they were thought to lack the 'sea sense' possessed instinctively by their British counterparts. Italian and Soviet personnel were held to be even more deficient in this respect. The Japanese, on the other hand, *were* regarded as a seafaring race, but their naval officers were thought to lack flexibility and initiative.

These assessments were seldom based on first-hand experience of the navies in question, but rather stemmed from the ethnocentric assumptions of naval officers. To compound this problem, naval attachés serving abroad were encouraged to include a section on the 'national characteristics' of foreign navies in their intelligence reports. 'Each nation has certain special characteristics which will tend to appear in its methods of making War,' the DNI asserted in 1935.

A general idea of a nation's war-like qualities is required. Are they good all-round fighters? Are their discipline, morale and leadership of a high order? Are they quick-witted and excitable, or slow and thorough? For instance, it is characteristic of the average Japanese to work well and efficiently along a carefully thought-out and pre-arranged plan (there are sure to be exceptions, hence the need for reports on individual officers whenever the opportunity offers); but inability to improvise and adjust themselves to unexpected situations tends to handicap them should that plan be upset by their opponent taking the initiative. Nelson's advice to close with a Frenchman and outmanoeuvre a Russian, based as it was on an appreciation of Latin quickness and Slav passivity, is an illustration of the application of this sub-section.[32]

The naval officer's tendency to make sweeping generalizations about his potential enemies did not systematically distort naval planning at the highest levels. The navy always intended to concentrate the greatest possible force against its enemies irrespective of their presumed fighting abilities. War plans were formulated on the basis of straightforward material calculations and 'bean-counting' estimates, with British and enemy vessels of comparable size rated roughly equal in fighting power. Assumptions about the Royal Navy's inherent qualitative superiority suggested that some enemies might prove less formidable than they appeared on paper, but planners seldom considered this a reliable basis for its war plans. As Beatty noted in 1921, 'Superiority of personnel was an asset to be kept up the sleeve, but not one to gamble with.'[33] Only in the case of Japan did racial stereotypes cause the British seriously to underrate an enemy's fighting ability and technical accomplishments, but this did not appreciably distort the navy's Far Eastern war plans. Conversely, the navy's low opinion of the Italian navy did have a significant influence on naval planning for war in the Mediterranean, but in this instance its appreciation did not prove to be far wrong.

While the navy's assumptions about its potential enemies tended to be crude, its ideas about the utility and application of seapower in wartime were far more sophisticated than has been acknowledged. The British naval officer corps may not have been teeming with intellectuals, but neither was it composed exclusively of idiots. Britain's naval elite understood that there were clear limits to the offensive tasks that navies could perform: at most they might destroy an enemy's warships, annihilate its seaborne trade, or transport forces belonging to the other fighting services. The means the navy possessed and its plans for employing them varied little from one enemy to the next. However, the navy's objectives changed considerably depending on the opponent it faced. Against some enemies seapower might inflict decisive pressure; against others it would be all but useless. In most cases, however, it would be simply one of several weapons required to produce a British victory.

7

'Showing the Flag': Deterrence, and the Naval Armaments Industry

Like most naval strategists, Mahan and Corbett were preoccupied with the application of seapower in wartime; their writings pay little attention to the navy's utility during periods of peace. For British decision-makers, however, the latter issue was often of real and immediate concern. The navy was the most visible symbol of British power and prestige abroad during the interwar period, and the Admiralty never questioned the link between naval strength and national influence. 'The navy is the chief sanction of our Foreign Policy,' Madden wrote in 1929; 'it is hardly an exaggeration to say that every Foreign Office telegram is backed by it.'[1] How to use the navy as a diplomatic tool in peacetime could be a complicated matter, particularly when the disposition of major fleet units was involved. The Admiralty regarded its main fleet as the most effective deterrent to hostile powers, and it was loath to disperse its forces for diplomatic effect. As long as foreigners knew that the navy could respond promptly to an attack on British interests, it assumed that the threat was unlikely to materialize. Politicians and diplomats generally shared these views, but were more likely to consider the movement of major warships as a means of sending signals both to friends and potential enemies. This is particularly true in the case of Japan.

The idea of modifying Japan's behavior by substantially strengthening Britain's naval forces in the Far East was raised on several occasions prior to the outbreak of the Pacific war. In 1937, a Cabinet committee recommended the despatch of two battleships to the Far East to induce Japan to cease its interference with British shipping in the region. Chatfield strongly opposed the idea, however, on the grounds that such a weak force would invite attack by offering the Japanese 'a possibility of defeating the divided British forces in detail.' If capital ships

138

were to be despatched, he insisted that they must be 'in sufficient strength to defeat the full strength of the Japanese Navy.'[2] The movement of capital ships was suggested again in November 1938 by Sir Josiah Crosby, the British minister at Bangkok, who felt that such a move would help to 'recover a measure of that prestige which we have been losing to Siam by comparison with our more blatant and brutally forceful opponents.' Crosby later asserted that what was wanted 'in this part of the world is a real sight of the British Navy in real force here and now, and less of indefinite assurances that we shall see it when the time comes.'[3] Sir Robert Craigie, the ambassador to Japan, also felt that the despatch of capital ships 'at this juncture would afford a powerful deterrent against Japanese co-operation with the axis Powers.' In his view, the Admiralty's policy of concentrating its forces in European waters 'has created here a false impression of British naval *impotence* in Far Eastern waters but there is still time to destroy this impression even on the assumption that no more than three capital ships could be spared for the purpose at present.'[4] If the government could be persuaded to give British diplomats in the Far East 'a little straw with which to make our bricks,' Craigie suggested that the 'psychological effect on Japan would be greater if the ships were … sent out one by one at intervals of about a month.' Such an unorthodox suggestion would give the Japanese 'less to get excited about than would be the case if the whole squadron were to proceed together but it would at once raise the question in their minds "How many are they going to send?" The uncertainty would be salutary.'[5]

The Foreign Office agreed that capital ships at Singapore would provide a powerful deterrent to Japan, but doubted that this could be achieved without weakening Britain's position in Europe. As one official remarked, 'the question of peace time dispositions depends on whether we consider that the deterrent effect on Germany (and Italy) of maintaining greatly superior forces in home waters is greater than the deterrent effect upon Japan of depleting our strength at home and in the Mediterranean in order to send forces to the F.E.'[6] The Foreign Office decided to approach the Admiralty on this question after a lengthy memorandum by one of its legal advisors, G. G. Fitzmaurice, argued that a small fleet at Singapore could 'produce a very great, and probably a decisive, deterrent effect', and that such a force could be provided if the five *Royal Sovereign* ('R') class battleships were not scrapped as planned in 1942–4. These ships were too old to be of much use in European waters, Fitzmaurice conceded, but they might still have a role to play in the Far East:

> To put it at its lowest, it would seem that these five ships would be better than nothing at Singapore. If the alternative is to scrap them altogether, would it not be better to keep them and put them in the Far East for what effect they can produce? At least we should be no worse off than we are at present when we have no capital ships there, and we may be considerably better off, for ... these ships [would] produce at least some appreciable deterrent effect ...[7]

The Admiralty's reaction was mixed. Backhouse, unlike Chatfield, accepted that a small force of capital ships 'should be quite capable not only of looking after itself but also of safeguarding our trade and our communications', but he had 'no use' for the 'suggestion to send out the 5 Royal Sovereigns, which are too slow and unsuited for that part of the world.'[8] He also did not think the time was right to send *any* reinforcements to the Far East given the current shortage of operational battleships and the declining political situation in Europe. Backhouse admitted that he had

> often thought that we should 'show' our Fleet more than we have done in recent years, but one 'crisis' after another and our large Capital Ship reconstruction programme has left us nothing to spare in the way of capital ships ... The moral to be drawn from the situation we now find ourselves in is that our foreign policy should be largely governed by the strength of the Navy.[9]

In replying to the Foreign Office, the Admiralty seized the 'opportunity of emphasising the close relation that exists between naval strength and foreign policy.'

> Unless the Navy is maintained at a strength sufficient to secure our position in those parts of the world which are vital to the existence of the Empire, it is impracticable to carry out our chosen policy as and when we wish. But while, in theory, naval strength must be based upon foreign policy, in practice, there is a limit, governed by money, men and material, and determined by the Government of the day, beyond which our armaments cannot be advanced; and when this is reached the tables are turned, and foreign policy must depend upon naval strength, unless the risk of war, and even of unsuccessful war, is to be incurred.

The Admiralty's opposition was decisive on this occasion, but the idea of maintaining a small fleet in the Far East continued to appeal to civilian decision-makers even after the onset of the European war. In November 1940, for example, R. A. Butler, Parliamentary Under-Secretary at the Foreign Office, suggested that a battle cruiser and an aircraft carrier at Ceylon would be 'useful in connexion with current difficulties in India' and 'strategically well placed to reinforce the Far East if the occasion arose.'

Meanwhile they would have a stimulating effect upon the morale not only of countries such as Indo-China, Thailand and the Netherlands East Indies which are most susceptible to Japanese pressure, but also upon the people of China and upon our own peoples in Malaya and Burma. The despatch of the ships would also hearten Australia and New Zealand and help to reassure them as to the safety of their lines of communication with Africa, the Middle East and Europe.[10]

The Australian government also routinely lobbied for the despatch of capital ships to Singapore. In December 1940, Sir Robert Menzies, the Australian Prime Minister, pressed Churchill for the transfer of three or four vessels to Singapore from the Mediterranean fleet. When Menzies visited London in March 1941, he again urged the Admiralty to reinforce its naval forces in the Far East. This appeal was renewed in May, following a reduction in American naval strength in the Pacific, and again in August, when Menzies telegraphed to Churchill that 'an early despatch of capital ships east of Suez would itself be [a] most powerful deterrent.'[11]

As British leaders became more confident of American support, they began to give the idea serious consideration. On 25 August 1941, Churchill told the Admiralty that it 'should be possible in the near future to place a deterrent squadron in the Indian Ocean.' In his opinion, such a force should 'consist of the smallest number of the best ships. We have only to remember all the preoccupations which are caused us by the *Tirpitz*... to see what an effect would be produced upon the Japanese Admiralty by the presence of a small but very powerful and fast force in Eastern waters.' Churchill therefore favoured the despatch of one of Britain's new *King George V* class battleships to serve as the nucleus of a 'formidable, fast, high-class squadron', which he hoped to have operating in 'the triangle Aden-Singapore-Simonstown' as early as October 1941.[12]

The navy was unenthusiastic about this proposal and insisted on retaining all three of its *King George V* class battleships in home waters in case of a breakout by the powerful German battleship *Tirpitz*. On 28 August, Pound informed Churchill of the Admiralty's plans to build up a Far Eastern fleet. Between mid-September 1941 and early January 1942, four of the unmodernized 'R' class battleships would be sent to the Indian Ocean, where they would initially serve as troop convoy escorts, and between November 1941 and mid-January 1942, the battleships *Nelson* and *Rodney* and the battle cruiser *Renown* would be moved to either Trincomalee or Singapore. The addition of an aircraft carrier, cruisers and destroyers would create a balanced fleet by March or April 1942. In the meantime, Pound hoped that the presence of heavy ships in the Indian Ocean would 'go some way to meet the wishes of Australia and New Zealand for the Far East to be reinforced,' and deter Japan from sending any battleships or large cruisers into the Indian Ocean in the event of war.[13]

Although there was much to be said for these plans, Churchill was swift to reject them. 'It is surely a faulty disposition', he complained on 29 August, 'to create in the Indian Ocean a fleet...consisting entirely of slow, obsolescent, or unmodernised ships which can neither fight a fleet action with the main Japanese force nor act as a deterrent upon his modern fast, heavy ships, if used singly or in pairs as raiders.' More importantly, he suggested that Japan would be unwilling to contemplate war with the 'combination now forming against her of the United States, Great Britain, and Russia, while already occupied in China.' It was very likely, he claimed, that Japan 'will negotiate with the United States for at least three months without making any further aggressive move or joining the Axis actively. Nothing would increase her hesitation more than the appearance of the force I mentioned, and above all of a K.G.V. This might indeed be a decisive deterrent.'[14]

The Admiralty was not persuaded by this argument, and the matter was allowed to drift until the Foreign Secretary, Anthony Eden, revived it in September 1941. Like Churchill, Eden was optimistic that Japan could be deterred from war. On 12 September he informed the prime minister that the Japanese were 'hesitating', but that their 'better mood has only been brought about by the contemplation of the forces that may confront them.'

Russia, the United States, China and the British Empire, to say nothing of the Dutch, is more than this probably over-valued military power is prepared to challenge. Our right policy is, therefore, clearly to keep up the pressure. ... We want the Japanese to feel that we are in a position to play our hand from strength.[15]

Eden concluded that the time had come to consider the movement of naval reinforcements to Singapore. Britain and the United States were both in the process of strengthening their defensive position in the Far East at this time. The transfer of American B-17 bombers to the Philippines and the gradual increase of British air strength in Malaya were regarded by London as significant deterrents in their own right. Eden hoped to impress the Japanese with a further show of strength, a course also being recommended by leading civilian and military figures in the Far East, including the Commander-in-Chief Far East, Sir Robert Brooke-Popham, and the Commander-in-Chief China Station, Vice-Admiral Sir Geoffrey Layton, who emphasized the 'propaganda value of even one or two battleships at Singapore.'[16] It was the fall of the Konoye government in Japan, however, that made a decision on naval movements critical. On 16 October, Eden warned Churchill that the new Japanese government would likely be under the influence of 'extreme elements', but that it should still be possible to deter them from war. 'There is nothing yet to show in which direction they will move, if any', he observed. 'But it is no doubt true that the stronger the joint front the A.B.C.D. [American, British, Chinese, Dutch] powers can show, the greater the deterrent to Japanese action.' He therefore advised that the 'possibility of capital ship reinforcements to the Far East ... has now become more urgent, and I should be glad if it could be discussed at the Defence Committee tomorrow afternoon.'[17]

This matter was taken up by the Committee the following day. Over the course of two meetings, on 17 and 20 October, Pound and Phillips fought to prevent the despatch of a small capital ship squadron to Singapore, arguing that all of the *King George V*s were needed in home waters in case of a breakout by German capital ships.[18] They also questioned whether the *Prince of Wales* and *Repulse*, the two ships preferred by Churchill, would in fact deter Japan, which could 'easily afford to put four modern ships with any big convoy destined for an attack in Southern Waters.'[19] In their view, the only real deterrent was a fleet of at least six battleships. Such a force would compel the Japanese to detach a large proportion of their fleet for any southward advance, leaving Japan itself exposed to the American navy at Pearl Harbor. They knew that two capital ships at Singapore could do no serious harm to Japan, and feared that their presence in eastern waters would demonstrate weakness and vulnerability rather than resolve and strength.

Churchill insisted that the despatch of a fast striking force would be an effective deterrent, and was 'scathing in his comments on the Admiralty attitude to this matter.'[20] Eden also urged the Defence Committee to despatch a modern ship to the Far East. Unlike the prime minister, however, he did not dwell on what this vessel might hope to accomplish in the event of war, but rather focused on the problem of deterring Japan from war altogether. The despatch of a 'modern ship, such as the *Prince of Wales*, to the Far East would have a far greater effect politically', he argued, 'than the presence in those waters of a number of the last war's battleships. If the *Prince of Wales* were to call at Cape Town on her way to the Far East, news of her movements would quickly reach Japan and the deterrent effect would begin from that date.' In the end, the civilian members of the Defence Committee agreed that the political advantages of this course were great enough to justify the risk.

Like most civilian decision-makers of this period, Churchill and Eden believed that the movement of capital ships was sufficient in itself to demonstrate resolve, bolster British prestige, reassure friends, and threaten potential enemies. In their eyes, the *Prince of Wales* symbolized Britain's still considerable national strength, rather than its present naval capabilities, and it was hoped that this latent threat would help to deter Japan from war with the British Empire. Notably, these two ships were not the only deterrent Britain employed at this juncture. During the last months of peace in the Far East, London also tightened economic sanctions against Japan and asked the Canadian government to despatch reinforcements for the hopelessly exposed garrison at Hong Kong.[21] This was all part of an attempt to create an impression of growing British strength and resolve in the Far East. But even this was not expected to deter Japan. Ultimately, it was the *combined* strength of Britain and the United States which Churchill and Eden counted on to restrain Japan's leaders. British efforts to impress Tokyo were therefore aimed at Washington as well. By the summer of 1941, British decision-makers believed that they must follow the United States' lead in matters relating to Japan,[22] and the despatch of capital ships to Singapore was meant to reassure the Americans of Britain's support and resolve. Keeping in step with American actions seemed to offer the best means to encourage Anglo-American collaboration and present the sort of joint front that would overawe Japan's new leaders.

The loss of the *Prince of Wales* and *Repulse* at the beginning of the war has focused attention on Churchill's disagreements with the Admiralty over what these vessels might hope to accomplish if they failed in their deterrent role. That debate says much about Churchill's qualities as a naval strategist, but it had little bearing on the decision to send capital ships to Singapore in the first place. Their mission was to prevent a war, not fight one. Churchill clearly overestimated the impact of a modern battleship on Japanese naval strategy, but that mistake was not the primary reason that the *Prince of Wales* was despatched. The origins of Force Z lie in the assumptions of British decision-makers about the symbolic value of capital ships and the willingness of Japan's leaders to resort to war. There is no doubt that Churchill and Eden erred on both counts, but to appreciate why the despatch of capital ships to Singapore was on the agenda in October 1941 it must be recognized that the use of battleships as a diplomatic tool held a strong appeal for civilian decision-makers in Britain and Australia. The idea was raised over and over again during the years 1937–41, and had taken on a life of its own long before Churchill suggested it to the Admiralty.

Britain's civilian decision-makers had a long history of employing warships for political purposes in peacetime, and when the stakes were great enough, they were prepared to overrule their professional naval advisers. Opinions also frequently differed over the political utility of minor warships in peacetime. The routine movements and dispositions of detached naval squadrons did not normally have a bearing on issues of peace and war, but it was widely thought that by 'showing the flag' in distant waters, these vessels would bolster Britain's national and naval prestige, stimulate trade, and ensure the security of British interests and nationals abroad.

The importance naval leaders attached to 'showing the flag' between the wars is best demonstrated by the Admiralty's interest in South America. In 1921, the Finance Committee of the Cabinet proposed to withdraw all British naval vessels normally stationed in South American waters. The Admiralty objected to this measure on the grounds that these vessels – a squadron of light cruisers – were 'required to carry out a variety of duties in peace.'

Apart from the general stimulus which their presence gives to British prestige and British trade in foreign countries, their services are frequently requested by the Foreign Office or Colonial Office for the direct protection of British interests or maintenance of order. From the naval point of view these squadrons are well placed to take up their war stations and afford invaluable opportunities to Officers and men of becoming acquainted with the water which, at some future date, may be the principal theatre of naval operations.[23]

To strengthen its case, the Admiralty approached the Foreign Office for support. Lord Curzon, the Foreign Secretary, replied that the withdrawal of the squadron would in fact be 'most regrettable. The visits of H. M. Ships to South American ports are invariably productive of satisfactory results, and international courtesies of this nature are highly valued by the Latin American countries.'[24] The Cabinet's Finance Committee was intent on securing extensive economies, however, and the Admiralty had no choice but to accept the abolition of the South American cruiser squadron.

With many of the navy's most important programs under attack at this time, the Admiralty was not prepared to put up more than a token fight over what it regarded as a secondary issue. Indeed, the Admiralty was so little concerned about the navy's prestige in this region that it did not object to the withdrawal of its two naval attachés from South America. These positions had been created during the First World War, but after the abolition of the South American cruiser squadron, the DNI concluded that these officers were no longer required.[25] By late 1922, however, the Admiralty was beginning to regret its lack of representation in this part of the world. The DNI noted that 'time had shown that 'the economies effected have been too drastic and that complete withdrawal [from South America] has resulted in a most damaging effect on naval influence with its consequent reaction on British prestige and interests.'

The field has been left open to the U.S.A. who are taking full advantage of the opportunity given them of belittling the value of British Naval training and British Naval material. A great deal of headway is being made by them, especially in Brazil.
    Strong representation on this subject has been put forward by ambassador in Brazil, Rear Admiral Sir W. Cowan, our Naval and Military Attaches, and the firms of Armstrongs, Vickers, and Thornycroft. They point out that although the U.S.A. with the aid of their Naval Mission are now predominant, we can still retrieve our position by taking advantage of their mistakes.[26]

He therefore proposed that British warships visit this region more frequently and a naval attaché be assigned to South America. These measures would, he hoped, restore the navy's 'position and prestige.' It was 'most undesirable,' he maintained, 'that the U.S. should be allowed to "Americanize" the South American Navies.'[27] The Director of the Operations Division [DOD] proposed to go further and seek Cabinet approval for the re-establishment of the South America squadron. In his view, there were great 'advantages entailed by the display of the White Ensign in South American Waters, the presence of Officers and Men of H. M. Ships at the annual celebrations of the various Republics, and the increase of prestige which is thereby occasioned to the British Flag, with its corollary of improved trade.'[28]

Keyes, the DCNS, concluded that it 'would be quite out of the question' to consider the revival of the South America Squadron 'during the coming financial year when pressure is being applied to make reductions in every direction.'[29] However, he approved the appointment of a resident naval attaché in South America. According to Keyes, the number of naval attachés and assistant naval attachés employed by the leading naval powers at this time were:

USA – 18; France – 10; Japan – 8; Great Britain – 7; Italy – 6.[30]

In view of these figures, he believed that an increase in the number of naval attaché positions was justified. The Treasury disagreed, however, and only assented to the South American appointment when the Admiralty agreed to abolish the post of naval attaché to the Hague in return.

It was only in late 1924 that the Board of Admiralty decided to take up the question of re-establishing the South America squadron. Its first move was to solicit the support of the Foreign Office and the Board of Trade (BOT).[31] Officials at the latter were enthusiastic about the proposal, which they believed would give a general impetus to British trade in the region. But they also admitted that it was 'extremely difficult to estimate with any accuracy the effect on British trade of such periodical visits by British warships.'

While, however, there is no concrete evidence in the Department that visits by British ships in the past have led to the placing of orders in this country, there is a general consensus of opinion, both in official and in business circles, that the indirect advantage derived by British trade from such visits is very considerable. It is reasonable to suppose that the visit of a British warship to a South American port being regarded as a compliment to the nation visited, turns the thoughts of the population to things British and fosters an interest in the produce and manufactures of the Empire.

In a similar vein, they concluded that 'it is not possible to say with any certainty that the withdrawal of the British squadron has had any pronounced effect in diminishing orders for British yards.'

There is evidence, that the withdrawal of our naval attaches in South America and the appointment of American "Naval Commissions" has had the effect of increasing the interest taken in the shipyards of the United States as against those of this country. On this analogy the assumption is justified that the periodical visit to a South American port of a smart British unit, followed by the establishment of friendly relations between the officers of the ship and the naval authorities of the port, will necessarily arouse a keener interest in British shipbuilding industry as a means of replenishing the naval requirements of the country.[32]

The Secretary of the Board of Trade, Sir P. Cunliffe-Lister, did not share this enthusiasm. He informed the Admiralty that if it was simply a case 'of considering the re-establishment of a ship as an isolated proposition,' he might concur with his officials, 'though I hold rather strongly the view that a big ship is the only thing that strikes the South American imagination.' But while he was 'prepared to accept generally the view of the Department as to a [light] ship having some value, I feel that I must personally attempt to assess that value in relation to cost. If, therefore, I were asked whether I would rather have the ship or ships, or the equivalent economy to assist in the reduction of taxation, I should certainly plump for the economy.'[33]

The reply from the Foreign Office was similarly mixed. Austen Chamberlain, the Foreign Secretary, was principally concerned about the navy's ability to protect British interests in the region during periods of unrest. 'There can be no doubt in my mind as to the desirability of the navy being permanently represented in South American waters,' he wrote.

I am informed that, taking this year alone, considerable difficulty was experienced in finding ships belonging to the North American and West Indies Station to go to Mexico and Brazil in connection with revolutionary disturbances there, and that in the case of Brazil the inevitable delay might well have had serious consequences. We were also unable to find a suitable ship to send to Lima in connection with the recent celebration of Peruvian independence. All that was available was a small sloop, which was considered to be unworthy of the occasion.

But in the end, financial considerations shaped his response also. He informed the Admiralty that he was 'entirely favourable to the re-establishment of two ships on the South American station,' but that he did not 'consider that we should go outside the estimates for these ships, which I feel can well be provided from your existing resources.'[34] In view of this 'lukewarm support' from both the Foreign Office and Board of Trade, the Admiralty decided in January 1925 that it would not be prudent to press the issue.[35]

In October 1926 the question was raised again by William Fisher, the DNI, who voiced the Admiralty's growing concern over the health of Britain's naval armaments firms. Prior to the Washington Conference this had not been a serious issue. Indeed, during the summer of 1921 the future of this industry looked secure, with orders going out for four new capital ships and the possibility of naval competition with the US looming on the horizon. By the mid-1920s, however, the effects of the Washington shipbuilding holiday and the reluctance of successive governments to spend lavishly on naval construction was beginning to undermine the well-being of the naval armament industry, whose health was one of the pillars on which British seapower rested. Naval decision-makers were acutely aware of this and sought to maintain the state's capacity for producing naval armaments at the highest possible level.

The most effective means to accomplish this was for the Admiralty to keep up a large and steady flow of orders for warships, as it had done since the late nineteenth century. Failing that, it might provide subsidies directly to armament producers. The former solution was preferable, from the Admiralty's perspective, as it would ensure that essential armament firms remained in peak condition, while the navy was supplied with a steady stream of the most modern warships. But the latter course would at least guarantee that Britain maintained its ability to produce warships quickly and in large numbers. In the years following the First World War, the Admiralty pursued both of these courses, but with only limited success.[36] Studies of the relationship between the navy and the armaments industry during the interwar period have emphasized the Admiralty's efforts to deal with this problem by prising money out of a reluctant Treasury for new construction or subsidies. But from the mid-1920s onward, the Admiralty began to think that it might solve, or at least alleviate, the problem of industrial decline by helping British firms attract shipbuilding orders from abroad.

Fisher noted with alarm that Britain had 'almost lost what practically amounted to a monopoly as regards foreign war ship building, with the result that the political and naval advantages associated with the development of Minor Navies is passing into the hands of our rivals and British Armament plants, an important reserve in times of emergency, are being converted to other uses.'[37] The relatively high prices charged by British shipyards deterred many potential customers, but Fisher believed that this disadvantage could be offset by establishing British naval missions in prospective client states, offering instructional facilities to foreign officers, and increasing the visits by British warships 'to those countries which normally see little of the excellence of British design and workmanship'. To this end he suggested that the Admiralty either maintain a cruiser continually in South American waters or else extend the boundaries of 'the North American Station to Cape Horn,' to allow vessels from this station to make regular visits to South America. 'For the encouragement of trade,' he concluded, 'it appears more important to show the flag in S. America than in the maritime provinces of Canada, the U.S.A. and West Indies.'[38]

This latter suggestion found general acceptance and in mid-1927 the North America and West Indies Squadron was refurbished as the America and West Indies Squadron. When Andrew Cunningham, then Flag Captain to the C-in-C, complained that the two cruisers detached for service in South America 'would become rather inefficient at gunnery and so on,' he was informed that this 'must be accepted as being of less importance than flag showing.'[39] Shortly after this decision was taken, the question of the navy's prestige in South America was reopened by the British ambassador to Argentina, Malcolm Robertson. In letters to the Foreign Office and Beatty, Robertson urged that a British cruiser be permanently stationed in South American waters and that the Admiralty appoint a second naval attaché to the continent. 'At this moment', he stated, 'we are making an effort to recapture lost ground in South American markets.'

Being a naval people it does not redound to our prestige not to be able to show the white ensign permanently on the coast, for that ensign is the symbol of all our greatness. We now have one naval attaché for the whole of South America, whereas the United States have a naval mission at Rio, besides naval attachés at Buenos Aires, Santiago and elsewhere. This will never do. We cannot take a back seat in naval matters. Cost what it may we must have a British cruiser here. I am convinced in my own mind that had we had one last year or, at least, a naval attaché permanently on the spot instead of having to wander around from post to post, the Argentine order for cruisers would have come to us and not gone to Italy. Even as regards Brazil, their British built battleships were overhauled (most unsatisfactorily) in the United States Naval Yards. It is humiliating.[40]

Robertson's appeal prompted the Director of Plans to propose that a South American squadron be formed by reducing the strength of the Mediterranean fleet and the America and West Indies station by one cruiser each.[41] The only disadvantage of this scheme, which would leave the total number of cruisers in commission unchanged, was that it meant the 'loss of one Cruiser to the Main Fleet to the East' in event of war with Japan. The new DNI, Barry Domvile, and the DCNS, Frederick Field, both endorsed this proposal. In the latter's opinion, 'the Government by their decision in 1921, committed themselves to a "penny wise pound foolish" policy and, if the Squadron had been maintained, the expense would probably have been counter-balanced by the greater volume of trade, especially warship construction, which would have resulted.' Domvile also recommended that the Treasury be asked to sanction an assistant naval attaché to South America, although he warned that 'any growth of our interests in South America is looked on with disfavour by U.S.A. and will be an increasing source of friction. This is unfortunate but ought to have no deterring effect.'[42] In November the Board of Admiralty accepted both recommendations.[43]

A South America squadron was established as a result of this decision.[44] In 1931 the Board decided that the 'extent of the America & West Indies Station has made it impossible for any single Flag officer to keep in personal touch with the whole of his command, and favourable opportunities for advancing the interests of British trade had been lost.' It therefore recommended that the squadron be established as a separate unit, as this would 'be likely to do much to further British prestige and British trade.'

The Board's recommendation for the appointment of a second naval attaché did not fare as well. In January 1928, the Admiralty's first request for the additional funds met with a flat refusal from the Treasury. A second approach in August attempted to strengthen the Admiralty's case by pointing out that since a British naval mission 'has been resident in Chile orders for 6 Destroyers and 3 submarines have been placed with British firms, undoubtedly due to the beneficial influence of the Mission.' It also cited Robertson's opinion that while the Treasury 'may have saved a relatively trifling amount in salaries, British shipyards have lost millions of pounds' worth of contracts and considerable amounts are being paid in unemployment relief to workmen who might otherwise have been well employed.'[45] The Admiralty secured the

Foreign Secretary's endorsement, but the Treasury remained unmoved. 'My Lordships [of the Treasury] are not satisfied,' the Admiralty was informed 'that the proposed appointment would have such influence as is suggested...on international competition for the shipbuilding contracts of the countries of South America. They understand that the French and Italian Governments have each only one Naval Attaché in South America, who is also accredited to rival countries.'[46]

Domvile complained that the 'Treasury are apparently determined not to part with another penny to further our interests in South America,' However, he felt that the reasons they gave were 'very poor'.

> [T]he French and Italian Attaches are mentioned because it suits the Treasury argument, but they make no mention of the 4 United States Naval Attaches; and it is with the United States interests that we are principally called upon to contend. Moreover, the lower prices the Italians are able to quote give them an advantage equivalent to several extra attaches.[47]

He felt that one final attempt should be made and proposed that the position of vice consul at Callao be abolished in return for the establishment of the assistant naval attaché. The Foreign Office agreed to this proposal, but the Treasury strongly opposed it, claiming that 'each service Department has a single attaché in South America at present and we should be very loth to see this standard set aside by the appointment of a second Naval Attaché for reasons which are very much more Commercial than Naval.'[48] The Admiralty went without its second attaché.

Despite this setback, the Admiralty's efforts to increase the navy's presence in South America from 1922 onward were largely successful. That its motives were increasingly linked to the well-being of the British armaments industry is highlighted by the Admiralty's marked lack of interest in providing for the protection of British interests and nationals during outbreaks of political unrest. This form of activity was of considerable interest to the Foreign Office, a fact the Admiralty exploited whenever possible, but naval opinion was inclined to think that there was, 'as a rule, not much a British warship can do unless in exceptional circumstances to evacuate the British population.'[49] There were undeniably advantages to having warships on hand if their presence was actually required, but the Admiralty believed that in many cases 'the ship never reaches the country in which the disturbances occur and when she does, usually no action is required.'

On the other hand, the fact that one of H.M. Ships is en route has a reassuring effect on the British community and her presence has a steadying influence generally and strengthens any representations that our diplomatic representative may have to make. The fact that we demonstrate that we are able to send a warship is also no doubt of considerable value from the point of view of general prestige.[50]

The principal problem, from the Admiralty's perspective, was that the unscheduled movement of ships disrupted the navy's training activities and meant increased expenditure for the Admiralty. It therefore tried to persuade the Foreign Office to limit its requests for naval assistance, for as Admiral Drax commented, if 'we encourage British [diplomatic] representatives to think that a warship will come along every time they whistle for one, the demands will be unceasing.'[51]

Naval missions offered a more direct and potentially more effective means of fostering Britain's naval prestige and promoting orders for its shipyards. However, in the years immediately following the First World War, the Admiralty's interest in this activity was minimal. In 1919, for example, Admiralty officials were unhappy about the possibility of a British naval mission being sent to Poland, and only agreed to it under pressure from the Foreign Office. 'It is a bad policy to encourage these small navies,' wrote the First Sea Lord, Admiral Sir Rosslyn Wemyss. 'I have before stated that I am against a naval mission. ...I suppose that [it] is to be used solely for the purpose of preventing other nations establishing such, in which it is possible to conceive that it may be of some use as a counter against intrigues.'[52]

News that Romania might request a British naval mission also met with a lukewarm response from the Admiralty. The commercial advantages of such a mission were emphasized, however, by the British naval attaché to Italy and the Balkans, who reported that France was pressing the Romanian government to accept a French naval mission 'with the further end in view of the reorganisation of Roumanian Commercial ports and water ways etc, which would given them great power and influence over Roumanian trade in general.'[53] This view was supported by Admiral Charles Ottley, who informed the DNI that as 'small as is the Roumanian Navy, I regard it as most important that the Navy should be trained and moulded *not* by France, or by Italy or by the U.S.A. but by England.'

The future wealth & prosperity of Roumania is assured, she is the one Balkan State that gives signs of future stability, and her geographical position and long frontage upon the Danube are assets of real value. Galatz and Braila must tend more and more to be the great entrepots of the fluvial transportation system, – if France or another power gets indirect control of them (through the Roumanian Naval Influence) then good-bye to British commercial success in this area.[54]

In the end, the DNI agreed to the proposal, in large measure to forestall the French. 'If France succeeds in her efforts to establish a Naval Mission to Roumania,' he wrote, 'the position created for this country on the Danube by Admiral Troubridge will be very much prejudiced. Apart from her natural resources and the commercial importance of the Danube, Roumania is the back door into Russia, whose recovery may not be so long delayed as is commonly thought.'[55] Still, when negotiations with the Romanians dragged out for well over a year, the exasperated DNI claimed that the 'Admiralty attach no naval importance to the establishment of this Mission, and have only consented to finding officers for it in deference to Foreign Office wishes.'[56]

The only naval mission the Admiralty could muster real enthusiasm for at this time was the one it had maintained in Greece, off and on, since 1911. Its interest here was mainly strategic. Greece occupied an important position in the Mediterranean and naval decision-makers believed that close relations with the Greek navy would be of considerable value in wartime. In 1919 Wemyss informed the new head of the mission that he was 'looking forward to the Greek Navy under your guidance becoming almost an integral part of the British Fleet in the Mediterranean.'[57]

By the mid-1920s, the Admiralty was increasingly eager to send naval missions to any state which could be persuaded to accept one. This change in attitude is attributable to a growing awareness that the United States, France and Italy were striving to increase their influence over minor powers through naval missions, a feeling that British naval prestige was adversely affected whenever its competitors secured one, and hopes that British missions would induce foreign governments to purchase British warships. The latter consideration is illustrated by the Admiralty's actions during 1925, when the Greek government linked the renewal of the British naval mission to its ability to secure a loan in Britain for the purchase of warships. When the poor state of Greece's finances made it appear unlikely that it would succeed in raising a loan, the DNI suggested that

In view of the deplorable state of the shipbuilding industry in this country – and particularly owing to the fact that so few warships are being built, this is tending more and more to reduce the skilled labour available for this class of work – it is for consideration whether some effort should not be made to induce the Foreign Office and Treasury to finance in some way or other a Greek order for armaments.[58]

The Treasury insisted, however, that there was no possibility of the British government making a loan to Greece.[59] The DNI was undeterred, and reminded his colleagues that 'many skilled men from the Clyde and Tyne shipbuilding yards are emigrating to the U.S.A. and that more are on the waiting list for the 1925–26 quota.' It was his opinion 'that the Admiralty can only view with concern the turn over of this skilled labour to a country with a Navy as large as ours, and that Admiralty influence might have some effect in modifying the Treasury attitude.'[60]

This warning was strengthened by the Director of Naval Construction, who noted that it was

repeatedly being stated by Shipbuilding and Armament Firms that they have already lost a number of their best men by emigration and judging from the delays that are occurring in providing armament for our own New Construction this is probably only too true. The effect on any future British programme of Naval Construction may become very serious unless something happens to improve the prospects of these Firms.[61]

The Admiralty secured the support of the Foreign Office, but the Treasury insisted that there was 'nobody in England foolish enough to lend money for this purpose.' Moreover, it questioned whether an order for warships, 'if placed, would be any help to the British industry. …Of course, if somebody gave John Brown £$2\frac{1}{2}$ millions, John Brown would be very happy to have £$2\frac{1}{2}$ millions, but if it came out of British pockets and was in fact not repaid by Greece, as is not unlikely, the benefit to British industry as a whole would be absolutely nil.'[62]

The Greeks, unable to secure a loan in Britain, ordered new warships from France. The Admiralty was not pleased by this outcome, but given the undeniably poor state of Greek finances it was not prepared to press its case. However, when the Treasury refused the Admiralty's requests for a similar loan to Portugal the following year, Admiralty officials were incensed. Murray noted that the Treasury's policy 'does not seem to prevent our debtors from placing orders with our other debtors, but merely precludes our distressed shipbuilding firms from getting any share in the orders.' Chatfield, the Controller, complained that it was 'intolerable that all these chances of trade should be denied this country & given to debtor countries instead.' In his opinion, it was 'not apparent that this Treasury standpoint is helpful to this country.'[63] But while Chatfield and Field, the DCNS, wished to take the matter to the Cabinet, the First Lord did not think it would be wise to challenge the Treasury's decision. He was willing, however, to consider raising 'the general question of assisting British firms to get orders for foreign warships in this time of depression.'[64]

This suggestion does not appear to have been pursued, but in 1927 the Admiralty did succeed, with the support of the Foreign Office and the other service departments, in persuading the Treasury to pay half the cost of British missions abroad. Prior to this, the entire expense of these missions had been borne by the host country. The Admiralty pressed for a change because it believed that 'the high cost of a British Mission made Foreign Governments hesitate to employ one, and, our whole argument was based upon the desirability from the general point of view of increasing the number of missions in foreign countries.'[65] Despite this victory, by the early 1930s Admiralty officials were beginning to face up to the fact that the 'principal object of the missions, as represented to the Treasury – namely, obtaining foreign orders for war material – has failed to materialize in the case of most of the countries to which missions have been sent.'[66] Even the mission to China, the contract for which stipulated that the Chinese government must order warships in Britain, failed to produce any work for British firms. The stumbling block in this case, as in most others, was price. When the Chinese government decided to purchase a light cruiser it offered the work to British firms, but when none could match the lower prices offered by Japanese builders, the order was placed in Japan.[67]

The lack of tangible results did not diminish the Admiralty's enthusiasm for establishing naval missions abroad. In 1933, for example, the ACNS noted that a 'study of the list of warships built for small navies since the war shews that up till 1930 Great Britain did fairly well but that since that date the majority of the orders have gone to Italy.' He believed, however, that as 'the Italian shipbuilding firms are heavily subsidised British firms are at a great disadvantage and are only likely to secure orders if the ground is well prepared by full facilities being afforded to foster appreciation of British methods and material.'

The advantages resulting from Missions to Foreign navies are political and industrial. The only naval advantage comes indirectly from the industrial. How seriously the Navy will be handicapped in the next war, as compared with the last, by the grave decline of the Armament and Shipbuilding industries in this country (caused principally by a lack of foreign orders) is shewn in the Report of the Principal Supply Officers Committee. ...

For this reason I feel that the Admiralty should make every endeavour to increase the influence of the British Navy with the smaller, and particularly the South American navies: the fruits of such a policy might not be seen for several years and until the world economic state has improved, but the small sums involved might in the long run prove a valuable investment.[68]

The Admiralty also sought to attract orders for British firms by allowing foreign naval officers to receive instruction in RN training establishments and on British warships. Foreigners were regularly given such opportunities during the nineteenth and early twentieth centuries, but in 1912 the Admiralty decided for reasons of security to stop training on seagoing ships.[69] After the First World War, naval leaders were initially reluctant to depart from this principle, which was reaffirmed by the Board of Admiralty as late as July 1925.[70] This policy was reconsidered, however, in 1926 when the Admiralty became aware that Italy was vigorously pursuing shipbuilding orders in South America. According to the Foreign Office, 'Mussolini had been approaching various South American countries with a view to obtaining orders for Italian firms at prices which left no margin for profit'. The Admiralty feared that the 'effect of this, might be to divert to Italy orders which would almost certainly come to firms in this country if there were a chance that certain Officers of the countries concerned could be given a course of training afloat in the British Navy'.[71]

The Board of Admiralty felt 'that it was very desirable to do everything possible to assist firms in this country to receive orders from abroad'. As one official remarked, there 'is no doubt that if the South American countries took to placing orders in Great Britain, it would have an appreciable effect on unemployment in general and particularly on certain specialised trades, which we are anxious to keep alive.'[72] The Board decided therefore that restrictions on training foreign officers afloat could be loosened for countries which had accepted British naval missions.[73] It was stipulated, however, that these officers should not be present in the main fleets when exercises were being carried out in which aircraft carriers were employed. In 1927 the Board removed this condition, on the grounds that it was 'very desirable to do everything possible both to encourage Foreign Powers to invite the services of British Naval Missions and to assist firms in this country to receive orders from abroad.'[74]

Over the next five years, officers from six countries received training in seagoing squadrons, but in 1932 the wisdom of this policy was called into question by the ACNS, who believed that the navy must 'not risk compromising our superiority in fighting methods now that the size of the Fleet is limited and we no longer possess the same numerical superiority over other Navies.' Besides the danger of information being passed on to potential enemies, he pointed out that minor powers simply did not need experience in handling large fleets. He therefore suggested that the Admiralty only continue to give 'facilities for the training of foreigners in schools and establishments and their tenders.' As long as this was done, he believed that the 'withdrawal of facilities for training afloat would not affect to any appreciable extent the placing of orders in England.'[75] These recommendations were endorsed by the Board in October 1932,[76] but the Admiralty's enthusiasm for training foreign officers remained strong throughout the remainder of the decade. In 1937, for example, the DNI observed that there was

> something to be said for a long view in the question of assisting British firms to obtain orders; no doubt the time will soon be upon us when the country will be thankful to get these orders, and, as so much war material is being obtained by foreign Governments, orders for war material may become a larger proportion of our national exports than heretofore. Hence, it seems desirable to use instruction of Foreign Officers as a lever to obtain orders.[77]

The Admiralty also attempted to assist British firms by allowing them to use RN designs when building warships for foreign navies. Naval decision-makers were wary, though, about providing other powers with vessels built to the same specifications as British ships. As Chatfield noted, these designs 'are our only stock in trade, everything is against us except our special knowledge. If we give away that for nothing,' he asked, 'how do we keep any advantage?'[78] But naval leaders also believed that the more closely British firms could copy British warships, the better their chances of securing foreign orders. By the mid-1920s, the need to keep British armament firms busy was seen to outweigh the benefits of secrecy.

The issue was raised in late 1925, for the first time since the end of the War, when two different firms enquired about the Admiralty's policy. Chatfield felt that it was 'most desirable to encourage foreign construction in this country, from the purely naval point of view, as every ship built helps to lessen the cost of similar types of vessels being built for the Admiralty.' He therefore had no objection to these firms using Admiralty designs provided modifications were made to omit 'certain secret fittings related to fire control, communications, asdics, etc.'[79] He was supported by the DNI, who complained of the 'tendency to exaggerate the importance of secrecy in naval matters. This may handicap us commercially in obtaining orders and politically with regard to naval missions.'[80] In January 1926, at a conference held in the Admiralty, it was observed that British shipbuilding and armament firms, which had been fully employed before the War, were now 'in a very depressed condition.'

There had been no men-of-war built in Great Britain for foreign countries for some years and several firms had lately represented to [the] Controller that they might be handicapped from obtaining orders, owing to an impression which existed in certain Foreign countries that the Admiralty imposed greater secrecy now over their designs than they did before the war. It was very desirable that the Admiralty should take all possible steps to assist them in obtaining foreign orders, which would not only relieve unemployment but would materially assist in keeping valuable productive plant in being, which was a matter of great national importance.[81]

The Admiralty thereafter allowed British firms to make use of 'Admiralty hull and machinery designs' in preparing their own drawings for foreign warships, 'subject to any particular restrictions which might have to be imposed' and only after the Admiralty was satisfied 'that the firm will actually receive the order.'[82]

Nor did the Admiralty's desire to secure foreign orders end after rearmament had begun and British firms were working at nearly full capacity. Naval decision-makers were conscious during the late 1930s that if the Treasury had its way, new construction programs would be severely cut back sometime between 1939 and 1941. Foreign orders offered a potential means of keeping the armaments industry employed if and when demand from the Admiralty tapered off. Thus, when Chile attempted to order two cruisers from British firms in 1937, the Controller recommended that the Admiralty give its approval: 'I think it is so very important that, when our re-armament programme is easing up, our armament and shipbuilding firms should have regained as far as possible the markets of the world – for it is by foreign orders that they will be helped to keep going.'[83] However, whenever these orders threatened to slow down the pace of British rearmament, the Admiralty insisted that they be declined, as happened in 1937 when it appeared that the production of gun mountings for Turkey would jeopardize Britain's capital ship program.[84] However, when the Controller concluded in 1939 that building cruisers for Chile would have 'a very material delaying effect on one or more of our own cruisers,' he still recommended that British shipbuilders be allowed to tender for the order in view of 'the importance to our shipbuilding industry of obtaining foreign orders where possible, and of the fact that a ship under construction for a foreign power is potentially available to this country in case of war.'[85] The First Sea Lord disagreed, but still hoped that the Chilean cruisers could be built in Britain if their construction was spread over a longer period.[86]

In the decade following the First World War, the navy's attitude towards peacetime activities intended to bolster British prestige were transformed. At the beginning of this period, naval leaders looked on these endeavours with indifference. They accepted that 'showing the flag' was a worthwhile undertaking, but one which was of more interest to diplomats and statesmen than to the navy itself. Anything which took sailors and ships away from the more important task of preparing for war was viewed as a distraction, and in most instances the Admiralty only consented to these activities in deference to the wishes of the Foreign Office. But by the mid-1920s this attitude was changing. As the health of the British shipbuilding and naval armaments industry deteriorated, naval decision-makers came to believe that by actively promoting the navy abroad they were helping British armament firms to secure foreign orders. As a result, the Admiralty began to take a strong interest in 'showing the flag', on the assumption that the more foreigners saw of its naval personnel and warships, the more likely they would be to place orders for naval material in Britain. However, the assistance the Admiralty could offer was limited and largely indirect, and its efforts were often impeded by Treasury officials and others who doubted that the tangible benefits of 'showing the flag' were as great as the navy and its supporters maintained.

The connection between naval prestige abroad and industrial strength at home has gone largely unnoticed because the Admiralty's efforts to foster it were generally unsuccessful. By the 1930s, however, naval decision-makers took for granted that a link existed between the navy's prestige and the number of orders for foreign warships placed in Britain, and this conviction did not materially diminish before the outbreak of the Second World War. But while British firms fared poorly in the competition for foreign orders during the interwar period, the Admiralty's efforts to assist them were not necessarily misguided or wasted. These firms may not have attracted work from abroad on a large scale, but they did not fail entirely in this respect, and there were instances where the Admiralty's assistance contributed to their success. Given the relatively low cost of the programs adopted by the navy to enhance its prestige abroad and stimulate foreign orders, it is arguable that they were at least cost-effective, even if the Admiralty's more ambitious goals were not met.

8
'Something Very Sordid': Naval Propaganda and the British Public

In the years following the First World War, naval leaders were increasingly worried that the navy could not count on the same high level of popular support that it had enjoyed prior to 1914. By the mid-1930s, they were openly alarmed by the public's growing fascination with aerial matters, which appeared to be undermining official support for the navy. Chatfield, for example, complained that when he went to the Admiralty as First Sea Lord in 1933, he had 'found a pernicious propaganda against the Navy started in the Houses of Parliament and all over London.' According to its opponents, the navy 'was an obsolete service! There was no more use for it! The future lay in the Air. The Navy would never be able to command the seas. It was as dead as the bow and arrow. The sailor stood up for the Navy as he was interested in it – and so on –.'[1] Naval decision-makers believed that irresponsible statements in the popular press were at the root of the government's preference for increased spending on the RAF during the 1930s, and some high-ranking officials outside of the Admiralty shared this view. Sir Edward Hardinge, the Permanent Undersecretary at the Dominions Office, complained in June 1934 about Neville Chamberlain's readiness to focus on the threat from Germany to the exclusion of all else. Public opinion was, in his view, 'not infrequently extremely ill-informed about the world situation and about our defence situation in particular'

> & because a certain section of the population have been stirred up by the penny papers to think we were being menaced by Germany, is that any reason why we should pander to what we know to be a fallacy at the present time and probably for some years to come, and entirely ignore the whole weight of expert opinion which realises full well that the Achilles Heel of the British Empire is in the Far East.[2]

The navy lamented its declining popularity, but pride in its reputation as the 'silent service' hindered its ability to put its case directly to the British public. Senior naval officers were not always above feeding information to the press from time to time to further specific ends, but most looked upon anything resembling straightforward publicity as vulgar and undignified. Historians have been strangely silent on the question of naval propaganda during this period. Recent works on popular images of the military and empire in nineteenth- and twentieth-century Britain have almost completely overlooked the Royal Navy.[3] Moreover, studies which have considered aspects of the navy's propaganda activities concentrate on the two world wars, leaving the mistaken impression that the service maintained a rigid silence in peacetime. In fact, the navy employed a variety of means to keep itself in the public eye and present a positive image to the British people during the interwar period. Most importantly, it attempted to reach a mass audience through the use of films and 'navy weeks.'

This chapter examines why Britain's naval elites became involved in these activities, how they attempted to manipulate public opinion, and the ideas they sought to disseminate. The naval profession's opposition to self-promotion gradually decreased between the wars, but the ideal of a 'strong, silent navy' continued to exercise a powerful hold on naval decision-makers. As a result, opportunities to advance the navy's case were undoubtedly lost. Propaganda offered the service a means to shape popular perceptions about seapower and enhance its popularity with the general public. The navy's declining fortunes could not have been reversed by this means alone, but its position might have been improved if this tool had been more willingly and effectively exploited.

The navy first became directly involved in the production of propaganda during the First World War. A handful of naval officers, led by the Chief Naval Censor, Rear-Admiral Douglas Brownrigg, accepted this development with good grace, but most officers, and especially those afloat, adopted an obstructive attitude and only cooperated under pressure from above.[4] When the state's official propaganda machinery was dismantled after the Armistice, the Admiralty hoped to distance itself from this distasteful activity as quickly as possible.

One of the first opportunities to do so occurred in early 1919, when it insisted on the recall of a naval officer, Captain Alfred Carpenter, who was in the midst of an official lecture tour on the Zeebrugge raid in the United States and Canada. According to Keyes, who had led the raid, 'That a Naval Officer should behave as Carpenter is doing has disgusted our Service, and his proceedings and the daily advertisement of the Dover Patrol which I have been unable to stop in the Northcliffe Press is almost more than we of the Dover Patrol can bear.'[5] At around this same time the Admiralty also had to consider the publication of *The British Naval Effort, 4th August 1914 to 11th November 1918*, a document the War Cabinet had ordered the naval staff to prepare at the end of the war.[6] As a chronicle of the navy's wartime achievements this monograph was notable only for the modesty of its claims; its main objective was to show that the navy had in fact made a contribution to the Allied victory. In the early postwar years, naval decision-makers were troubled by charges that the navy had not pulled its weight during the war, but they opposed the publication of this or any other official document which might present the navy's achievements in a favorable light. According to Rear-Admiral Rudolph Bentinck, the Naval Secretary, this sort of publicity 'would do more to influence the best public opinion adversely to the Service, than anything else.'

> Moreover, I believe that those Officers, to whom the Service looks with the highest respect, and in whom the highest ideals of the Service are embodied, would experience an intense feeling of repulsion at this blazoning forth of the deeds and acts of what they have always been proud to think was a 'Silent Service.'[7]

Significantly, however, at least one officer spoke out in favor of publication. The Organising Manager of Convoy suggested that 'Parliament and the People are entitled to some account of the *work done* by the Navy – as they have to find the money.' 'It should be possible now,' he concluded, 'to give a clear statement of facts and to draw conclusions without any undue advertisement. "Silence" certainly won't prove "golden" when Naval estimates are presented.'[8] In the end, a compromise was reached: the offending document was scaled down and published as part of the First Lord's annual statement on the Navy Estimates for 1919/20.

The idea that publicity was desirable as a means of increasing public and political support for the navy carried little weight in naval circles in 1919, despite fears that the army's wartime accomplishments had undermined the navy's popularity. Shortly after becoming First Sea Lord, Beatty concluded that 'History is repeating itself as far as the Navy is concerned and the one idea on the part of our rulers is to minimize the part played by the Navy and use the resulting arguments to cut the Navy down altogether.' Notably, he attributed this problem to the inability of politicians to understand the navy's proper role in British defense policy. 'There is not one among them that has a proper conception of Sea Power', he complained.

They are all military mad and fed by the War Office have come to consider the Navy as an appendage to military forces and only exists for the purpose of carrying the Army and keeping the Road open for them and we are in their eyes no longer the Spear Head of Great Britain which we have been for four hundred years. Well they will have to be educated thats all & I must see that the education is thorough. That in itself will provide food for thought for our Political rulers as to the value of Sea Power and may provide a valuable object lesson.[9]

The possibility that this education might be realized by a propaganda campaign directed at the British public was not considered. By the mid-1920s, however, naval officers were slower to dismiss the possibility out of hand, and many junior officers hoped that a modest measure of publicity would halt the steady decline in the size of naval estimates. In 1927 one of these officers, Lt T. Davys Manning, contributed an article to the *Naval Review* lamenting the lack of naval propaganda emanating from the Admiralty. Davys claimed that it was 'the unsound policy of a "Silent Navy" that has caused the people of Britain to grow up in abysmal ignorance of their first line of defence. For, though the term was stressed during the war, the spirit of independence and indifference to public opinion is deep rooted and of long standing.'

Before the war the Germans carried out a great deal of propaganda for their Navy with the result that a non-maritime race took a keen interest in the building up of a great fleet. In the United States to-day there is an intense campaign of publicity for the U.S. Navy going on, chiefly to aid recruiting, and it is the writer's opinion that a quiet campaign of naval propaganda in this country is urgently required to-day...Such a campaign must not be aggressive like the German system or tub-thumping like the American way of introducing the Navy into the homes of the people, but must be a gradual course of 'peaceful penetration' which will educate the people and make them regard a strong Navy as being absolutely essential.[10]

The view that the navy needed to take steps to promote itself was confirmed by its supporters outside of the service. In 1926, for example,

Lord Burnham, the proprietor of the *Daily Telegraph*, suggested to Archibald Hurd, a prominent writer on naval affairs, that the navy's

> policy of silence had been carried too far and I honestly believe that there is appreciably less enthusiasm for the Navy now than there was not only immediately after the war but also in the latter years before the war. It is obvious that if you shut down the discussion of naval problems and the recital of naval achievements you must damp down the ardour and appreciation of the nation, which has to be stoked up and kept if not at fever heat at least at a reasonably high temperature.[11]

The Admiralty remained reluctant to provide substantial assistance to those who wished to publicize the navy. In 1926 Hurd judged that the Board of Admiralty was 'still very opposed to anything in the nature of propaganda.' He noted, however, that the situation had improved slightly, as the Admiralty no longer intended 'to pursue a policy of secrecy, which really served no useful purpose and indeed did, I am sure, a great deal of harm to the service, as all the younger officers have felt for a long time.'[12] Hector Bywater, another prominent naval writer, also complained that the 'silent service' tradition was being overdone. In *A Searchlight on the Navy*, Bywater questioned whether 'the shabby treatment of the Navy, as compared with the sister services, in respect of pay, allowances, and other cognate matters [may not] be due in part to the halting and deprecatory manner in which its case has been presented?' There was, he complained,

> an ultra-conservative element in the Service which abhors publicity of any kind. It resents the mildest curiosity on the part of laymen, and would, if it could, place an impenetrable screen round the fleet and its doings. When this mentality is analysed it is found to be largely composed of mawkish sentimentality, which finds expression in worship of the more emotional aspects of naval tradition and a morbid distaste for innovation of any kind.[13]

One reason that the navy's leaders were slow to make concessions in this area is that a reasonably efficient propaganda machine already existed in the Navy League. This organization had been created in 1895 to 'impress on the people of the country the necessity of maintaining an adequate navy,'[14] and it continued to operate throughout the interwar period. The League's willingness to criticize official policies before 1914 had frequently strained its relations with the navy, but as it became clear after the war that the League was willing to support the Admiralty uncritically, relations between the two bodies steadily improved. With steady pressure being exerted on the navy to reduce expenditure, and public support for the service apparently declining, the value of a well organized lobby group was increasingly evident to naval leaders. Beatty, for example, concluded that it was 'wholly desirable that there should be some such organization as the navy League supported by those who have influence with the Country,' especially at a time 'when every form of pressure is likely to be brought to bear to reduce the standard of naval strength to a dangerous minimum.'[15] Chatfield declared that 'If we had not a navy League now we should have to create one.'[16]

Naval decision-makers valued the Navy League because it could and did appeal directly to the public, something the navy felt itself unable to do. Much of the organization's work was aimed at educating the British people on the importance of seapower. In the words of the naval historian Geoffrey Callender, the League's primary task was 'to act as the Fleet's interpreter; to remind each generation of the lessons of the past; to awaken the intelligence of Britons at home and abroad by an educative process to a living sense of their Imperial needs.'[17] This it did by providing textbooks to schools, giving public lectures, distributing films and pamphlets, hosting public meetings, sponsoring the sea cadet corps, sending letters to the press, and a variety of other methods. At the same time, when the League felt that the Admiralty's advice on major issues was being ignored it did not hesitate to attack the government publicly. It did so most vocally in 1924, when the Labour government cancelled the Singapore Naval Base, and again in 1930 when the London Naval Treaty imposed a limit of 50 cruisers on the navy. On both occasions, the League bombarded the press with letters critical of the government and organized public meetings featuring prominent opposition politicians as the principal speakers.[18]

Because the Navy League engaged in these overtly political activities, the Admiralty was careful to keep it at a discreet distance. Thus, while retired naval officers formed a significant portion of the League's membership, their colleagues on the active list were seldom seen on a Navy League platform. The only notable exception was the League's annual Nelson Day dinner, an event regularly attended by the navy's political and professional heads. In this way, the Admiralty provided the Navy League with a clear vote of confidence and a measure of moral support, but it seldom provided direct assistance for the League's propaganda activities. The Admiralty did allow the use of some naval facilities in the production of a League propaganda film, and for a time it provided financial assistance to the sea cadet corps, but for the most part the Navy League was no better off than any other organization when it came to securing the navy's active cooperation.

The British film industry also enjoyed an ambivalent relationship with the Admiralty between the wars. The navy first became involved in the production of films in 1915 when Balfour, the First Lord, persuaded Admiral Sir John Jellicoe to allow film-makers to take footage of the Grand Fleet for *Britain Prepared*, the first official British propaganda film of the First World War.[19] The navy's involvement in film-making then lapsed almost completely for over a year, only to revive suddenly in mid-1917 as the result of mounting pressure from the Department of Information and the Foreign Office. During the final year of the war no fewer than ten full-length propaganda films on naval topics were produced. The navy was unenthused about this sudden surge of publicity, however, and officers afloat were, at best, reluctant collaborators in this process. According to Brownrigg, every 'artifice and stratagem down to downright lying and misuse of high officials' names' had to be put in use to succeed in planting…professional photographers and cinematographers on the fleet.'[20] To overcome this resistance, Eric Geddes, the First Lord, found it necessary to write directly to Admiral Beatty, reassuring him that he knew 'very well the natural aversion of the service to being "filmed" or "written up"' – but also asserting that 'from time to time it really is essential that they should submit to treatment of this kind.'[21] Appeals such as this helped to secure the cooperation that film-makers required, but the majority of naval officers were undoubtedly relieved when the navy got out of the film business almost immediately the war ended.

The Admiralty produced very few films for public consumption during the interwar period, but it sometimes allowed the use of naval facilities in the making of commercial pictures. The navy's cooperation with the British film industry did not arise out of a desire to publicize the navy, however. In 1920, the Admiralty's Sports Control Board decided to generate funds by selling the rights to film naval events,[22] and tenders were invited for the Prince of Wales' forthcoming trip to Australia on the *Renown*. The resulting film, *50,000 Miles with the Prince of Wales*, proved to be a financial success both for its producers, the Topical Film Co., and the Sports Control Board. Over the next few years, the Board continued to sell the film rights for naval events, but by 1923 the film industry's interest in naval topics was waning and no tenders were submitted for the empire cruise of the Special Service Squadron.

This event was only filmed when a last-minute appeal resulted in British Instructional Films Ltd accepting the contract.[23] The resulting film, *Britain's Birthright*, proved to be a commercial failure, but by producing it, the film company won the Board's gratitude. The rights for the Prince of Wales' next tour were awarded to British Instructional Films without first being put out to tender, and the Sports Control Board arranged for naval cooperation in several of this company's historical productions, most notably *Zeebrugge* (1924), *Nelson* (1925), and *The Battles of the Coronel and Falkland Islands* (1927).

The commercial success of the *Zeebrugge* film renewed the film industry's interest in naval subjects and prompted complaints from other film-makers about the privileged position enjoyed by British Instructional Films. In 1925 the Admiralty twice refused assistance to Astra National Production Ltd for *The Flag Lieutenant*, a naval story based on the play by Drury and Trevor, on the grounds that it would be unfair to British Instructional Films to grant facilities to its competitors. Only through persistent lobbying and the support of Viscount Curzon, the chairman of the Navy Committee of the House of Commons, did this company succeed the following year in overcoming the Admiralty's objections. Other producers soon began to request the use of naval facilities for their productions, and in late 1927 the Board of Admiralty decided that the time had come to give the matter its consideration.

In a memorandum for the Board, Sir Oswyn Murray suggested that commercial films might be classified into three categories. The first was the 'Pictorial Record' of actual events, such as the cruise of the Special Cruiser Squadron. Murray believed that this type of film had 'a real historical value,' but he also recognized that 'such films have insufficient appeal to the general public (though in a hundred years' time they might awaken enormous interest), and in a number of cases a heavy financial loss resulted to the producing Companies.' The second category was the 'Historical Film,' such as *Zeebrugge* and *Nelson*, which provided 'an imaginary pictorial record, as accurate as possible, of important Naval events of the past.' This type of film, which was popular at this time, usually involved a greater demand on naval facilities, but Murray suggested that this was offset by the fact that 'their propaganda value is probably great, particularly in foreign countries and the Dominions.' Finally, there was the 'Romantic Film,' which was 'merely an ordinary story, with a Naval Background, or with Naval incidents included.'[24]

Opinion within the service was divided over which types of film, if any, the navy should cooperate in. The attitude of many senior officers was summed up by the C-in-C the Nore, who complained that 'this sort of publicity is likely to do harm to discipline and efficiency in the Service, as it is apt to encourage eye service and disinclination to disagreeable work when out of the limelight.' In his view, the navy's popularity was due in large measure to its 'unobtrusiveness and efficiency when called on,' and he feared that this popularity would be adversely affected 'if the present day fashion of advertisement and propaganda is followed.'

> Publicity of genuine work, such as parades, reviews, etc., etc. is justifiable as these are public functions, but I am unable to believe anything but harm can come of detailing H.M. Ships and personnel for romantic and semi-comic scenarios which, it is submitted, are not in keeping with the traditions and dignity of the Service.

A more progressive view was articulated at this time by a naval committee on recruiting, which regarded films as 'a medium of great influence among the younger generation.' It complained that 'Boys see on the screen far too much of the American Navy, and too little of our own.'

> We do not think that the best means of securing publicity is by the provision of a special Naval film. The cost and trouble is very great; the launching of the film is speculative, and its popularity is uncertain. We think that greater opportunities might be given to Film Companies to use the Navy as a background for their ordinary productions.[25]

In the end, the Board outlined a compromise. Naval facilities would continue to be granted for 'pictorial and historical films of a suitable nature,' but the Admiralty would not cooperate in 'romantic films, on the ground that they are becoming a serious tax on the time of officers and men.'[26]

The following year, the Admiralty considered becoming directly involved in the production of 'pictorial' films after it received a report from the naval attaché in Rome stressing the Italian government's extensive use of naval photographs for propaganda purposes. Fisher, the DCNS, suggested that the navy might in future employ its own cameramen to film naval events for theatrical release. He was quick to add, however, that there was

> no need to advertise the Navy in the ordinary vulgar sense of the word nor is there any lack of pictures showing ships in motion during Gunnery and other exercises, but the Navy does so many other

things which I think might be of great interest to the public. Instances that occur to me are – Admiral Tyrwhitt's recent visit to Japan; the cruise of the 'Wistaria' up the Amazon, 'Cornwall's' visit to South America and Honolulu; the Prince's voyage in the 'ENTER-PRISE'; the work done by 'DESPATCH' in the Solomon Island, etc.

'Good cinema records of such events would,' he believed, 'be a popular feature in any topical programme,' and he suggested that a small committee be set up to 'examine the question which would comprise the instruction in cinema work at Tipnor [site of the RN's photographic school], the drafting of certain selected ships of naval ratings trained in cinema work, the provision of cameras, the disposal of the films to the Trade, the circulation of copies to other units of the Fleet, etc.' Such an enterprise would, he hoped, 'provide a useful and interesting record besides being entertaining and instructive to the public.'[27]

A Naval Cinematograph Films Committee was formed in early 1929, but it advised against expanding the navy's existing film service on the grounds that 'pictorial' films would have little or no commercial value. 'Generally speaking, and excepting a few special war pictures, films to be successful from the public standpoint must contain a romantic and love interest, a type which could scarcely be produced by the Navy alone, even if it were thought politic to do so.' The only pictorial films to make a profit had been those featuring the Prince of Wales, and their popularity was attributed to the Prince rather than the navy. The Committee suggested, however, that the service's existing film-making organization might be put to better use and employed to record 'scenes which might be of commercial value,' and especially tours made in 'HM ships by members of the royal family or other notable personages.'[28]

This interest in sustaining the pictorial film genre suggests that naval decision-makers had no strong objection to the navy being placed before the public on the movie screen as long as it was done in a sufficiently dignified manner. Moreover, it demonstrates that the Admiralty was conscious of film's ability to reach a mass audience and that it wished to exploit this to the navy's benefit. The problem that it increasingly encountered was that the type of film it considered acceptable held a limited (and diminishing) appeal to the theater-going public. 'Romantic' films remained anathema to many senior officers. As C-in-C Mediterranean, Fisher later complained that his

experience of Naval Films is there is something so *second rate* about the parts of them, that the service is not benefited – the invariable scene of film actors aping Naval Officers cutting for drinks in the Ward Room & discussing their love affairs makes me sick. It's not good for the Lower deck to see night after night either. If the real Navy is to be on the screen only first rate actors should collaborate and the 'book' should be written by someone of birth and good taste.[29]

Opinions such as these ensured that the Admiralty's injunction against romantic films was strictly enforced after 1927, with the exception of British International Pictures' *The Middle Watch*, for which limited facilities were given to film incidents in a ship's normal routine. In 1931 the Admiralty also received a request from London Screen Plays Ltd to use naval footage from Astra-National's *The Flag Lieutenant* in a new sound version of the film. This request was granted even though this new production clearly fell into the 'romantic' category, and despite a serious dispute between the Admiralty and Astra-National over the payment of royalties from the original film. This matter had been resolved in the law courts, but the decision had gone against the navy and, to make matters worse, the judge had condemned the service's involvement in commercial films, stating that it was

quite lamentable that our ships and our seamen should be used to produce films, not for one Company but for many companies: Britannia Films, Gaumont Films, and National Productions Ltd. They were brought into being, as I believe and hope, for a totally different reason, and to my mind there is something very sordid in the fact that our great ships and our sailors should be used for purposes of this sort.[30]

Discussion about the new production of *The Flag Lieutenant* prompted the First Lord to refer the question of films to the Board of Admiralty for reconsideration. The matter was taken up again in June 1932 and the Board reaffirmed its previous decision not to provide facilities for the production of romantic films. But at the same time it decreed 'that all possible steps should be taken to interest the Film Companies in current Naval incidents, so that they could be introduced as often as possible in the Topical News items which are shown in cinema theatres throughout the country.' This activity was to be handled by the Press Section of the Naval Intelligence Division, but it appears to have accomplished little if anything in this direction.[31]

In any event, the Board's film policy was not rigidly enforced. Over the next year and a half, naval facilities were granted for three separate 'romantic' films. By the autumn of 1933, it was becoming clear to all concerned that this type of film offered the only viable means of keeping the navy before the film-going public. The DNI suggested that the Board remove its restrictions on the production of such films 'in the interest of naval propaganda, and as a counterblast to the United States' Film Companies, who make free use of the United States' Navy.'[32] The DNI's request coincided with a similar appeal from Lord Lee of Fareham, the vice-president of Gaumont-British Pictures and a former First Lord. In a memorandum for the Admiralty, Lee spelled out the issues at stake for the navy:

> It is a fine tradition that the Navy should be 'silent' but, in these days, silence in the face of perpetual agitation may be misconstrued as 'consent,' and the case for an adequate Navy needs to be kept prominently before the present and rising generation, whose sympathies have to be aroused before their support can be counted upon. There are few ways in which this can be done more effectively than by the wide circulation of Naval Films which are sufficiently entertaining or exciting and which yet present a reasonably true and creditable background of life aboard His Majesty's Ships, whether in peace or war.[33]

When the matter was taken up again in November 1933, the Board decided that future applications from film makers would 'be considered on their merits, regard being had to the suitability of the story and nature and extent of the facilities asked for – especially the demands to be made on Naval personnel.'[34] In December, a small standing committee was set up under the DNI to review applications from film companies. The Board made clear, however, that in taking this step it did not

> accept the view that the RN stands in need of advertisement by means of Naval story films, and the rôle of the Committee is not to try to encourage the films companies to produce more Naval story films, but to exercise supervision over the making of such films by conditioning the grant of facilities upon the adoption of suitable stories and the elimination of all undesirable features.[35]

With this decision, the Admiralty tacitly admitted that the navy did in fact need publicity. This had been apparent to many officers for some time, but naval leaders only dropped their objections to romantic films when it became clear that no other means existed to entice the

British film industry to take on naval subjects. The Admiralty's only positive aim in all of this was to ensure that the Royal Navy appeared regularly on British theater screens. It assumed that this would in itself promote popular interest in the navy. The Admiralty was not in a position to do much more than this, as the film companies were responsible for the subject matter of their films. The Admiralty's only means to influence their content was to place restrictions on the types of film that it helped to make and to exercise its rights of censorship over films that it cooperated in. The alternative, producing its own films, was never seriously attempted, although the Admiralty did collaborate with the Empire Marketing Board to produce two documentary films in 1932 chronicling the *Challenge* expedition to Labrador.[36]

The navy found greater scope for presenting a positive message to the public through the annual 'navy weeks' held at the navy's home ports between 1927 and 1938. Initially, however, the goal of these events was to raise money for naval charities. Prior to 1927, the navy had collected funds for this purpose by holding 'flag days' and naval pageants at each of its home ports. In October 1926, Admiral Brock, the C-in-C Portsmouth, appointed a committee to consider the feasibility of raising money by 'holding an annual Naval Pageant in Portsmouth that would attract the public in the same way as the Aldershot Tattoo and the RAF Display at Hendon.'[37] The committee concluded that the proceeds from such a pageant would probably not surpass the costs and recommended instead holding an annual naval charities 'week' at the dockyard. For a small admission fee, members of the public would be permitted into the dockyard and given access to a dockyard museum, HMS *Victory*, and a number of modern warships. Brock forwarded this proposal to the Admiralty, where it met with a mixed reception. Some were concerned that such an event would interfere unduly with the regular work of the dockyards, and one official feared that 'it might be difficult to confine the week to Portsmouth Yard, if it proved a success.'[38] The Board of Admiralty decided nonetheless that Brock could proceed with the week in 1927 as an 'experiment.'[39]

To minimize the disruption to the dockyards, the event was held at the beginning of August when workers were on leave. Brock reported afterwards that the results 'far exceeded expectation.' 'The love of the British public for the Navy is well known,' he remarked, 'but I was astonished at the interest shewn in the ships and the frequent remarks that they had never had an opportunity of going on board a man-of-war in their lives and of seeing the various vessels which make a modern fleet.'

Brock also drew the Admiralty's attention to the propaganda value of the event. 'It is eminently desirable in these days that the Navy should be better known to the public,' he wrote, 'both from the recruiting point of view, and the more general one of educating those who have to pay for it in the work and life of the Service.'[40]

The timing of this report was propitious, as there was a growing distaste within naval circles for the usual means of raising money for naval charities. In the words of one C-in-C, 'the majority of Officers and a large proportion of the Lower Deck' were of the opinion 'that the spectacle of the Navy annually appealing to the Public for money by pageants, flag days, etc., is highly undignified and unworthy of the service.'[41] This opinion was shared by most of the officers directly involved in fund-raising activities. In March 1928 the Board took up the question of naval charities. It concluded that 'navy weeks' offered the least objectionable means of raising money, and decided that they should be held that year at all three of the home ports.[42] These events also proved to be a success, drawing over 198 000 visitors and raising a total of £11 355.[43] The Admiralty therefore gave its approval for these events to be held annually. Their popularity with the public over the next decade is attested to by contemporary press reports and the size of the crowds they attracted. By 1931, attendance at the three ports surpassed 300 000, and in 1938, the last year Navy Week was held, the figure reached 415 000[44] (Table 8.1). The navy helped to ensure their success with a vigorous advertising campaign, which included supplying articles to local and London papers, distributing posters and leaflets, and enlisting the assistance of the BBC.

The propaganda value of Navy Weeks was evident at an early stage, and junior officers were often eager to exploit this to the navy's benefit. The chairman of the Plymouth Navy Week Committee believed, for

Table 8.1 Navy Weeks: admission figures, 1927–38

Year	Admissions	Year	Admissions
1927	48 764	1933	245 667
1928	198 348	1934	301 655
1929	235 273	1935	333 007
1930	288 688	1936	434 764
1931	316 506	1937	387 655
1932	281 883	1938	415 560

Sources: ADM 116/2478; *The Times*.

example, that the 'value of Navy Week should be measured not only by the sum of money made available for naval Charities,'

> but also by the public interest aroused in the Navy through articles and pictures in the press and by the opportunity given to the public to see men-of-war of all types and in all stages of construction, and the weapons used in sea warfare.

If Navy Weeks at the three Home Ports can be made annual events, equal in public interest to the Aldershot Tattoo or the R.A.F. display at Hendon, they may go far to educate public opinion on the value of the Navy to the Empire and thus assist to reduce parliamentary and newspaper pressure for the reduction of Naval strength below that which the Admiralty considers essential.[45]

In 1934, the officers charged with organizing Navy Weeks recommended expanding the scale of these events in order to increase their publicity value. Senior officers tended to be less enthusiastic about the propagandistic side of Navy Weeks, however, and the Board decided that these proposals 'should be discouraged.'[46] Its objective was not to avoid giving publicity to the navy, for as the Second Sea Lord remarked, 'the Navy requires all the right sort of publicity it can get,'[47] but to ensure that publicity did not interfere with the navy's regular work and training, as was held to be the case with the Aldershot Tattoo and the Hendon Air Pageant.

Naval leaders and retired admirals were perfectly willing, though, to use Navy Weeks as a platform from which to remind the British people of the need for a strong navy and to deplore reductions in the navy's strength. Audiences were frequently told by distinguished speakers and official souvenir literature that the navy's most important role was ensuring the safety of British trade in wartime, and in particular Britain's food imports. According to the souvenir program:

> A strong Navy is essential to preserve an Island Kingdom and a world-wide Empire. The greater part of our food and raw materials come to us from overseas. Stoppage of supply for a few weeks only means disaster. Co-operation between the Mother Country and the Dominions in defence of the Empire is possible only when the ocean routes are open. The Navy guards them.
>
> Navy Week is being held to give the public an opportunity to see the most modern types, from battleships to submarine, of the vessels which protect their homes and their trade.[48]

This message was reinforced by speakers such as Jellicoe, who informed listeners in 1933 that two-thirds of Britain's food came from overseas, but that Britain's cruiser strength had been reduced by 50 per cent since the end of the war. Similarly, Admiral Tyrwhitt told crowds in 1936 that: 'When war broke out in 1914 we were able to protect our trade routes; now, to put it bluntly, we could not. Our trade routes were the pulse of the Empire. If the pulse stopped beating that would be the end of the Empire and we should starve.'[49] The navy also used these opportunities to emphasize the work it carried out in peacetime, presenting itself as a great international police force which protected the interests of Britain and all nations on the high seas and ashore. In 1938, for example, the First Lord told a Navy Week audience in Portsmouth that Britain's 'great modern warships were not only mighty weapons of war, but they also kept the peace. Wherever there was trouble in the world the presence of a British man o' war reassured people that law would be maintained.' 'During the past 12 months,' he asserted, 'the British navy had been carrying out services in the cause of world peace and humanity.'[50]

These themes were reinforced by the special displays put on at these events.[51] The protection of British trade against submarine attack was a popular subject, and mock engagements between British Q-ships and 'enemy' submarines, which invariably ended in the latter's destruction, were a regular feature throughout this period. In 1938 the familiar Q-ship was replaced by a defensively armed merchant cruiser, assisted by the timely arrival of naval aircraft. Notably, it was only after the navy regained control of the FAA that aircraft began to play a prominent part in Navy Week displays. These usually took the form of mock air attacks on British ships, and always ended with the ships still afloat and several of the attacking aircraft 'destroyed.' Displays showcasing the navy's peacetime work were also common. One example is the 'Santa Maria' display at Chatham in 1933, which centered on an imaginary seaport 'somewhere between the Balkans and the Far East' where an insurrection was taking place against 'King Hildebrand of Santa Maria.' A British cruiser on foreign service in the region promptly arrives to protect British interests, a goal it accomplishes by sending ashore an armed party which 'quickly succeeds in restoring order.'[52]

Navy Weeks were thus the most overtly propagandistic of the navy's activities between the wars. Indeed, by the mid-1930s it had become commonplace within the service that the principal objective of Navy Weeks was, in the words of Admiral John Kelly, 'to educate the Public of this Country in the meaning of and necessity for the Navy, and to make them Naval-minded.'[53] In public, the navy continued to stress the charitable aspects of these events, but this was increasingly a convenient façade to give them an air of dignity and allay the misgivings of officers who still found this type of activity objectionable.

The naval profession's aversion to self-promotion significantly diminished during the course of the interwar period. At the end of the First World War, the navy looked back on its wartime propaganda activities as an unfortunate but necessary response to the demands of total war. It immediately sought to distance itself from this type of work after the armistice, but soon found that it was being drawn back in despite the resistance of many senior officers. To a large extent, this was simply an instinctive reaction to diminishing naval estimates. But it is also attributable to a growing fear that the navy's popularity was waning.

The impact of the Admiralty's propaganda efforts is impossible to calculate, but the decline of the navy's popularity after the First World War was not entirely a figment of the Admiralty's imagination. Even a non-partisan observer such as Sir John Simon could claim in 1934 that he was 'doubtful whether the Navy has not lost its hold on public imagination.'[54] However, there is ample evidence that the navy remained genuinely popular with the British public during these years, and that politicians were conscious of this fact. Hence, the government's readiness to increase spending on the RAF during the 1930s was at least partially balanced by the reluctance of ministers to countenance Neville Chamberlain's schemes for a drastic curtailment of naval construction and the virtual abandonment of Britain's eastern empire. In 1934, for example, Baldwin informed his colleagues that

> it was necessary to do something to satisfy the semi-panic conditions which existed now about the Air and for obvious reasons. It was true that, from the political point of view, there had so far been no trouble in respect of the Navy but, even at the present stage, the Committee ought to have in their minds possible activities on the part of the Navy League and other similar organisations.

The Admiralty's political power remained stronger during the 1930s than naval officials cared to admit. According to Lord Trenchard, the former Chief of Air Staff and a seasoned bureaucratic infighter, the navy not only had 'much greater political influence and power in Whitehall' than the RAF, but also 'many more people to put their case forward' in Parliament and the press.[55] Chatfield noted that Parliamentary proponents of air expansion believed that the Admiralty, 'because of its well dug-in position and experience,' was able to obtain a dispropor- tionate share of British defense spending.[56] Chatfield denied this charge, but there is no doubt that the government spent lavishly on the navy once rearmament was under way. Until 1935, expenditure on the navy nearly equaled that of the air force and army combined, and it was not until 1938 that Britain began to spend more on the RAF than its navy.[57] Moreover, politicians allowed the Admiralty to build to the limits of Britain's industrial capacity from 1936 to 1939, despite the strong opposition put up by the Treasury. Thus, in the short term, a more extensive propaganda effort could not have allowed the navy to extract significantly more money from the government than it actually did. The navy's forays into the publicity field may even have con- tributed to the Admiralty's successes against the Treasury during these years. However, the Admiralty's reluctance to put up a more deter- mined fight for the 'hearts and minds' of the British public did nothing to reverse the service's declining popularity, and if the Second World War had not broken out when it did, the navy would have been in a difficult position to withstand Treasury attacks when the debate over naval expansion was resumed.[58]

Conclusion

In the decades following the First World War, the sea and the navy continued to play a central role in British national mythology. The British people were disposed to view themselves as a seafaring race, with a special affinity for the sea and an unmatched aptitude for maritime pursuits. In the words of Lloyd George, 'we are naturally sailors and an amphibious race.'[1] Since the reign of Alfred the Great, and possibly even before, British ships and sailors were believed to have been superior to all others simply by virtue of being British.

The Royal Navy was considered crucial to the acquisition of the British Empire. Britons proudly recalled how their fleet had prevailed against its enemies time after time, and how Britain had stripped its rivals of their overseas possessions. But even though the navy had achieved its greatest glories in wartime, it was not regarded as a tool of aggression. Indeed, it was accepted that Britain's seapower had always been a defensive weapon. Its primary task was to protect Britain, its empire, trade, and vital food supplies. Moreover, it was widely believed that Britain had traditionally exercised its seapower for the good of all states. The Royal Navy had been Britain's principal weapon against continental states seeking to dominate Europe. It was instrumental in securing the defeat of Napoleon and Kaiser Wilhelm II, and it had repeatedly curbed the ambitions of France's Bourbon monarchs. Britons also took pride in the navy's role in suppressing the slave trade and piracy during the nineteenth century, and were inclined to view it as a sort of high seas police force offering protection to the maritime traffic of all nations.[2] In 1930, for example, Lord Lloyd asked when 'the British Navy, even when it dominated the world, [had] ever committed aggression like the armies of Napoleon or those of the Kaiser?'

The whole history of the British Navy has been one of defence, sometimes of our own coasts, more generally defence of world freedom from one new tyrant or another. Its strength, as Admiral Mahan has recorded, has always been employed in defence of liberal civilisation, the freedom of nations and individuals. It is to-day, and has for centuries been, the only effective and honest police force of the seas...

For centuries past the British Navy... has been the chief agent for the suppression of gun-running, the chief liberator of slaves. In the Persian Gulf, the Red Sea, and in China Seas our smaller vessels, gunboats and sloops are continually engaged in this necessary work... *I say, without hesitation, that it will take centuries of effort by the League of Nations to achieve as much at Geneva for peace, freedom and honour as has been achieved by the British Navy on the high seas of the world.*[3]

The British navy was thus regarded as fundamentally different from the armies of continental states, which had traditionally been employed for aggressive purposes: its mission was to ensure international peace and stability, punish aggressors, and protect Britain from aggression.

The role that seapower had to play in the modern world was a more contentious issue. There were doubts in some quarters about the continued importance of the sea to Britain, but public and elites were still predisposed to believe that seapower remained crucial to Britain's prestige, prosperity, influence, and security. Trenchard, for example, dismissed the 'extreme' view which was 'sometimes put forward in the Press and elsewhere by wild men about the air force making the Army and Navy unnecessary. As regards the Navy in particular I have always expressed the view... that the strength and prestige of the Navy is an essential bulwark against utter disaster to the Empire.' This consensus seldom led to agreement on broad issues of policy, however, because there was no agreement on the requirements of seapower.

Throughout most of this period, Britain's maritime needs were loosely defined in terms of naval standards, which laid down the ideal strength of the navy in relation to other powers. In practice, however, these standards regulated only one class of vessel – capital ships – and did not commit Britain to any absolute level of strength. Hence, standards cannot be taken as a measure of Britain's actual seapower. A one-power standard was not a sign of imperial decline, as some historians have suggested, nor was it insufficient to provide full security for British interests during the 1920s. Naval standards were only meant to provide a rough guide for policy-makers' calculations. They were open to a wide range of inter-pretations, and could be modified or replaced whenever they ceased to reflect Britain's genuine strategic needs. However, standards were super-seded throughout most of this period by treaty restrictions, which placed absolute limits on the size of the navy. Moreover, they were disregarded whenever politicians concluded that diplomatic or economic needs must take precedence. Between 1929 and 1935, the navy was crippled by a combination of treaty limitations, liberal internationalism, and the effects of the Great Depression, not by the one-power standard.

What type of naval standard Britain required was decided by the gov-ernment, which estimated which power or powers threatened British interests, what size navy was needed to meet this threat, and how much Britain could afford to spend. Opinions on these issues could and did vary greatly during this period. The naval profession naturally took the widest view of Britain's needs and always interpreted naval standards generously. It appreciated that seapower depended not only on a powerful battle fleet, but also on a network of naval bases, a large merchant marine, and a healthy shipbuilding industry, and it sought to ensure that Britain retained all of these essential elements in peace-time. Seapower was something that could not be improvised in an emergency, nor quickly revived if allowed to decline. As Chatfield noted in his memoirs, 'the Admiralty knew well that great navies can-not be built in a night.'

> Sea power is like an oak, of slow growth. Once the tree is grown and sea superiority is attained, a nation's position is assured, secure from challenge. But if it is allowed to fail, its roots to wither, it cannot rapidly recover, and years of anxiety and expense must ensue before safety is again reached.[4]

The navy believed that the greatest danger to the 'roots' of Britain's seapower was the decline of the naval armaments industry. Throughout the interwar period, naval decision-makers struggled to ensure that Britain did not lose its ability to construct warships quickly and in large numbers. During the Washington Conference, Britain's naval leaders opposed the idea of a building holiday because they knew it would deprive British firms of the steady flow of orders that their well-being required. In 1930 their successors protested against an extension of the Washington building holiday, which they knew would further damage the already-struggling armaments industry. During the 1920s and early 1930s, the Admiralty fought for the construction of cruisers and other vessels which were not limited by treaty so as to provide orders for British shipbuilding firms. It also dispensed subsidies to key armament suppliers, and attempted to stimulate foreign orders for British-built warships by 'showing the flag' and increasing the number of naval attachés and naval missions abroad.

The most pressing concern for naval leaders was securing the warships and other instruments of seapower that were essential to Britain's security. The Admiralty maintained that the navy must be capable at all times of meeting any threat to Britain's vital interests. Thus, at the end of the First World War it insisted on a large program of capital ship construction to maintain Britain's naval superiority over the United States. Failure to do so, it argued, would undermine British prestige and influence, and leave Britain vulnerable to American pressure. After the Washington Conference, Japan increasingly occupied naval minds, and the Admiralty fought for the construction of a naval base at Singapore and the accumulation of large fuel reserves. With the rise of Nazi Germany in the 1930s, the navy demanded a full two-power standard of naval strength relative to Germany and Japan, without which it could not protect British interests in both hemispheres simultaneously. And by the late 1930s, it held that Italy must also be taken into the navy's calculations. The Admiralty asserted that the empire's vital maritime communications would be imperilled if these demands were not met. It recognized that financial considerations must act as a brake on naval expenditure, but because Britain's wealth and prosperity were ultimately dependent upon overseas trade, it believed that starving the navy for the sake of the economy would be counterproductive. Without a strong navy, it maintained, British trade would be destroyed and the economy would collapse.

Admiralty officials also insisted that the navy's needs must take precedence over those of the other fighting services. They believed that Britain could not afford to spend lavishly on more than one service, and that only the navy could meet the most serious threats Britain faced – the loss of its eastern empire and the destruction of its overseas trade. It was understood that British security would be endangered if any single power gained hegemony over Europe, but the Admiralty believed this threat could be met as it had been in the past, by providing naval and financial support to continental allies. The danger to Britain from the German air force, on the other hand, was regarded as greatly overrated, as indeed it was. Naval leaders concluded that the air threat was best countered by a predominantly defensive air force, rather than one designed for a counter-bombing strategy. Hence, it appeared that Britain could safely forgo a continental-size army and a strategic air force as long it possessed powerful allies in Europe. The navy's needs could not be neglected, however, without endangering Britain's essential maritime communications, on which the security of the empire ultimately depended.

The navy's self-confidence stemmed from a conviction that seapower remained a potent weapon of warfare, and one which could produce decisive results against a non-European power such as Japan. It was not, however, obsessed with fighting a Far Eastern Jutland. After the First World War, the navy increasingly viewed seapower as a means to exert economic pressure on an enemy and protect Britain's seaborne trade. As a result, fleet encounters never dominated naval war planning or grand strategy. The navy expected any Far Eastern war to be a long and costly struggle of attrition in which seapower would play the dominant role.

During the 1920s, when Britain possessed a comfortable margin of naval superiority over Japan, the Admiralty confidently prepared to project British power into the Far East. Planners intended to despatch a powerful fleet to an advanced eastern base, whence it could neutralize the Japanese battle fleet and provide cover for combined operations and detached cruiser squadrons. By the mid-1930s, however, the decreasing ability of a British fleet to operate from Hong Kong or seize an advanced base to the north of it compelled the Admiralty to rely on plans to cripple Japan with an economic blockade. As the strength of the fleet available for the Far East diminished, planners were also forced to consider defensive strategies. The navy consistently overestimated what it could accomplish against Japan; but, contrary to conventional wisdom, it was fully aware of the effects European complications would have on its calculations, and it always had an accurate idea of what forces would be available for despatch to the Far East. Most of the criticisms leveled at the navy's Far Eastern war planning are based on the erroneous assumption that the navy possessed a single 'Singapore strategy' which it adhered to throughout the interwar period despite mounting evidence of its infeasibility. In fact, the navy developed a number of schemes which can be described as 'Singapore strategies,' and none of these was responsible for the destruction of the *Prince of Wales* and *Repulse* in December 1941. Given complete freedom of action, the Admiralty would not have despatched these two vessels to the Far East at this time. The decision was taken by civilian decision-makers who possessed an exaggerated faith in the deterrent value of capital ships.

Britain's Far Eastern war plans were increasingly complicated by the need to retain in home waters sufficient naval forces to deal with the threat from Germany and Italy. Planners were confident that they could manage the naval threat posed by either of these powers individually; but they rightly feared that war on two or three fronts simultaneously would stretch Britain's naval resources to breaking point. Historians have frequently attributed the navy's failures in the Battle of the Atlantic to causes stemming from the interwar period, including a mistaken belief that war with Germany was not a serious possibility, a fixation with decisive battles and fleet actions, and a preoccupation with Japan, which has itself been attributed to the navy's selfish desire to retain the largest share of Britain's defense budget. None of these explanations is satisfactory. In the first place, leading naval decision-makers always recognized that war with Germany might erupt for any number of reasons, and it is for this reason that Chatfield and his advisers supported Chamberlain's policy of appeasement. The navy also expected that war with Germany would automatically mean war with Japan as well, and it always held that it must be prepared to face both threats simultaneously. Hence, it was not considered strategically sound to neglect capital ship construction. It was only because the navy attempted to meet the worst-case scenario of a two- or three-front war that it failed to prepare more fully during the 1930s for an unrestricted submarine campaign. However, its record in this respect is better than Roskill and others have allowed.

The navy was unable to secure everything it wanted during this period because the government usually held different views on Britain's strategic needs. The leaders of the Labour Party disagreed with nearly all of the navy's fundamental assumptions, and their willingness to disregard naval advice resulted in the temporary cancellation of the Singapore Naval Base in 1924, its suspension in 1929, and the conclusion of the London Naval Treaty in 1930. Other politicians shared a greater measure of common ground with the Admiralty, but they could still disagree over how much insurance the empire required. Throughout this period, civilian decision-makers feared that over-spending on defense would diminish Britain's economic strength and undermine its strategic position, and successive governments limited peacetime defense expenditure to the lowest level they considered commensurate with British security. As long as the likelihood of war appeared remote, governments were usually willing to cut down or reject programs that the Admiralty insisted were vital. Thus, during the 1920s, the navy struggled to secure money for new warships and the Singapore Naval Base because politicians did not believe that Japan or any other naval power posed an imminent threat to British interests.

Similarly, Britain accepted capital ship parity with the United States because the government was not convinced that prestige was sufficient justification for an expensive naval arms race. Politicians were always reluctant to build warships that might never fire shots in anger, and they usually sought to postpone new construction until the expense was justified by a clear threat to British interests. It was hoped that this would strengthen the economy by reducing unproductive expenditure, thereby improving Britain's ability to pay for naval expansion at a later date if it became necessary. It would also ensure that when a threat did emerge, the navy would not be encumbered with obsolescent warships. However, the case for delaying expenditure rested on two faulty assumptions: that Britain would have ample time to rearm once a threat was identified; and that Britain's naval armaments industry would always be capable of matching foreign construction.

The need for the state to take an active role in sustaining the naval armaments industry in peacetime was not appreciated by politicians and Treasury officials of this period. This industry possessed a large degree of over-capacity during the 1920s, and civilian decision-makers failed to appreciate the need to preserve the largest possible part of it for the day when naval expansion might become necessary. Few realized that this industry could not be rapidly revived by an infusion of funds at a date in the distant future, while others blithely assumed that Britain would always possess unsurpassed shipbuilding resources because it had always done so. When Winston Churchill sought to cut the Admiralty's cruiser program in 1927, for example, he confidently asserted that Britain was 'in the very good position, the unique position, ... of being able to build much faster and on a larger scale than other Powers, so that we can, in fact, at any time set on foot a programme which is necessary to meet a forthcoming period of danger three years later, if danger does intervene.'[5]

The government's failure to maintain excess industrial capacity in peacetime resulted in the precipitous decline of the British naval armaments industry after 1929. This was not the worst of the navy's problems, however. The government's reluctance to meet the Admiralty's demands during the 1920s and early 1930s meant that the instruments of seapower were also allowed to deteriorate below the point of safety. By the time rearmament began in the mid-1930s the fleet had been significantly reduced in strength and efficiency, and Britain remained incapable of effectively projecting its power into the Far East.

The emergence of major threats to British security during the 1930s ensured that the government was willing to increase spending on defense, but the funds available for naval rearmament failed to keep pace with the Admiralty's growing demands. Financial considerations imposed important constraints on British rearmament, but the navy's bargaining position was also undermined by the government's strategic priorities. Because Nazi Germany threatened the very heart of the empire and was the most serious single danger Britain faced, politicians preferred to concentrate their limited resources on home defense, and priority was given to the RAF. In 1939 the government also accepted a continental commitment in order to provide support for France, Britain's only major ally. As long as politicians believed that Britain was unable to defend itself against Germany, the needs of imperial defense were allowed to take second place. And because Germany alone did not appear to pose a serious threat to British seapower, the Admiralty was unable to secure all of its demands. It did, however, secure most of them. Between 1936 and 1939 British shipyards were building as many warships as its diminished capacity would allow, and the Admiralty succeeded in compressing its five-year building program into three years. But even though the navy won most of its major ` battles with the Treasury during this period, it was losing ground relative to the other services, and unless this trend changed, Britain's ability to defend its imperial interests would have significantly declined in the long term.

The navy was not easily deflected from policies it believed were in Britain's best interest. Naval leaders were unwilling to endorse the government's policy of tacitly writing off Britain's eastern empire, and they refused to decouple the threats posed by Germany and Japan. In their view, Britain's armed services had to be prepared for simultaneous wars in two hemispheres, and their rearmament program was designed to create a margin of superiority over the combined naval strength of Germany and Japan. Politicians allowed the navy to pursue these objectives as best it could because they were not prepared formally to abandon the defense of Britain's eastern empire. But from 1934 onward, the government believed that it was both politically and strategically expedient to concentrate its resources on home defense. This was not the radical departure from Britain's traditional grand strategy that naval leaders perceived it to be. Statesmen had always been willing to divert expenditure from the navy whenever seaborne threats were overshadowed by other dangers, and the circumstances of the 1930s induced them to do so again.

The navy's difficulties might have been alleviated if a greater effort had been made to win the support of the British public, but naval propaganda was hindered from the outset by the service's aversion to publicity. When the navy did finally attempt to place itself in the public eye, its only objective was to reinforce the idea that seapower still mattered to Britain. It did not attempt to educate the public about how seapower operated or, more importantly, what was required to maintain it. Naval leaders simply hoped that bolstering the navy's popularity would improve the Admiralty's bargaining position in Whitehall. It failed to achieve this goal, however, and it is unlikely that even a prolonged and intensive propaganda campaign could have given the navy the leverage it desired. The navy remained genuinely popular during this period, but the British public's revulsion against war, its high hopes for the League of Nations and disarmament, and the growing demand for social services ensured that it could not count on unconditional popular support in the absence of a clear threat to vital British interests. When such a threat emerged, it was the German air force that captured the public imagination, not the German or Japanese navies. As a result, Britain's civilian decision-makers could often overrule their naval advisers with little fear for the political consequences. Indeed, the political disadvantages of heavy naval expenditure appeared at times to outweigh the advantages, particularly during the years 1929–35.

The Admiralty's inability to dominate Britain's strategic policies proved to be a mixed blessing. Some of the navy's demands, such as naval competition with the United States, were indeed extravagant, and the government was wise to reject them. The Admiralty's views on grand strategy during the late 1930s were also flawed, and not all of its prescriptions would have improved Britain's strategic position. However, more money could have been spared for the navy during this period, and savings could have been effected at the expense of the strategic bombing force. The government's failure to consider these options placed unnecessary restrictions on the pace and scale of naval rearmament, and weakened Britain's ability to defend its global interests. More seriously, by disregarding the Admiralty's advice on questions relating to the maintenance of seapower, successive governments took many poor strategic decisions, such as the disastrous London Naval Treaty of 1930 and the failure to maintain Britain's industrial infrastructure.

One of the essential foundations of seapower is a government willing to nourish the state's maritime resources in peacetime, and this proved to be lacking for Britain between the wars. As one editorial writer quipped, 'He would be a bold man … who would say that there was any large proportion of men among our politicians with any real knowledge of the inner meaning of sea power in Imperial Defence.

They pay lip-service to it; they have not the time to understand it.'[6] Richmond was probably correct in thinking that this obstacle could only have been overcome by explaining 'to these inconceivably stupid people [i.e. Britain's politicians] what the meaning of the words "Sea Power" is.'

Most of them seem to suppose that it means strength in fighting ships and no more in spite of all that Mahan (whom they now consider out of date) said about it sixty years ago. Ships are one of the elements of which sea power consists. Sea power is the power of using the sea for one's own purposes and depriving the enemy of its use – a totally different thing. Its elements are all those types of vessels and craft capable of taking an effective part in the direct operations at sea of which the aim is the control of the sea, the bases without which those craft cannot operate, and a merchant navy and shipbuilding industry sufficient to carry our trade and troops across all the seas and to repair and replace losses. The blindness and ignorance of our politicians, and the apathy or cowardice of the successive Boards of Admiralty, during the last 25 years have allowed all these three elements to be emasculated.[7]

The navy's leadership was less culpable in this process than Richmond suggests. Successive Boards of Admiralty explained the workings of seapower to civilian decision-makers at every opportunity, and they attempted to exploit what popular support they had to prise concessions from the government. There were limits to what they could accomplish, however, and Richmond clearly overestimated the navy's political strength at this time. The Admiralty was in fact largely powerless to prevent the government undermining the foundations of British seapower after the First World War. Between 1921 and 1934, civilian decision-makers could have averted this decline if they had listened more carefully to their naval advisers, and in so doing, they would have greatly strengthened Britain's strategic and diplomatic position during the 1930s and early 1940s. The navy did make many mistakes of its own, both before and during the Second World War, but few of its failures were the result of a fundamental misunderstanding of the nature and application of seapower.

Notes

Introduction

1 First Plenary Session of the London Naval Conference, 21 January 1930, 'Documents of the London Naval Conference 1930,' ADM 116/2748.

2 Letter to a public meeting of the Navy League, *The Navy*, May 1924, p. 132.

3 CID 134th Mtg, 14 December 1920, CAB 2/3.

4 Quoted in John Ferris, 'The Symbol and Substance of Seapower: Britain, the United States and the One-Power Standard, 1919–1921,' *Anglo-American Relations in the 1920s*, ed. B. J. C. McKercher (Edmonton, 1990), pp. 56–7.

5 For example, Paul Kennedy, *The Rise and Fall of British Naval Mastery* (London, 1976); Correlli Barnett, *The Collapse of British Power* (London, 1970).

6 2 vols, London, 1968 and 1976.

7 See in particular the articles by Gordon Martel, Keith Neilson, John Ferris, and Brian McKercher in a special issue of *The International History Review*, XIII (November 1991).

8 Joseph Maiolo, *The Royal Navy and Nazi Germany, 1933–39* (London, 1998); John Ferris, 'The Last Decade of British Maritime Supremacy, 1919–1930,' and Orest Babij, 'The Royal Navy and the Defense of the British Empire, 1928–1934,' both in *Far Flung Lines*, eds Keith Neilson and Greg Kennedy (London, 1996); Jon Sumida, '"The Best Laid Plans": The Development of British Battle-Fleet Tactics, 1919–42', *International History Review*, XIV (November 1992); Geoffrey Till, *Air Power and the Royal Navy* (London, 1979); Clare Scammell, 'The Royal Navy and the Strategic Origins of the Anglo-German Naval Agreement of 1935,' *Journal of Strategic Studies*, 20 (June 1997), 92–118.

9 Mahan himself never precisely defined seapower in his many works on the subject. Philip A. Crowl, 'Alfred Thayer Mahan: The Naval Historian,' *Makers of Modern Strategy from Machiavelli to the Nuclear Age*, ed. Peter Paret (Oxford, 1990), p. 451.

10 Admiral Sir Herbert Richmond, *Statesmen and Sea Power* (Oxford, 1947), p. ix.

11 On the 'rational actor' decision-making model see Graham Allison, *Essence of Decision* (Boston, 1971).

12 For example, Keith Neilson, *Strategy and Supply* (London, 1984); B. J. C. McKercher, *The Second Baldwin Government and the United States, 1924–1929* (Cambridge, 1984); D. C. Watt, *Succeeding John Bull: America in Britain's Place, 1900–75* (London, 1984).

13 Mahan's most important works are *The Influence of Sea Power Upon History, 1660–1783* (Williamstown, KY, 1978) and *The Influence of Sea Power Upon The French Revolution and Empire 1793–1812*, 4th edn (Boston, 1894). Corbett's ideas are clearly outlined in *Some Principles of Maritime Strategy* (London, 1988), which includes a valuable introduction by Eric Grove and an appendix containing Corbett's 'Green Pamphlet.'

14 The exception is the navy's plans against Nazi Germany, which have been thoroughly treated in Maiolo, *Royal Navy*.

1 The Politics of Seapower: the 'One-Power Standard' and British Maritime Security

1 Minute of 21 July 1937, ADM 116/4434.
2 On the Washington and London Conferences see in particular Ferris, 'Symbol and Substance' and 'Last Decade'; Babij, 'Royal Navy'.
3 *Hansard*, 3rd Series, CCCXXXIV, col. 1328: 1 April 1889.
4 On the history of the two-power standard see E. L. Woodward, *Great Britain and the German Navy* (Oxford, 1935), Appendix II.
5 *Hansard*, 4th Series, CXXX, cols 1528–9: 9 August 1904.
6 Draft Parliamentary paper by Lord Cawdor, 15 November 1905, ADM 116/1658.
7 Churchill memorandum, 'Naval Estimates, 1914–15,' 10 January 1914, ADM 116/1677.
8 *Hansard*, 4th Series, LXII, col. 860: 22 July 1898.
9 Ibid., CXXX, cols 1409–10: 1 March 1904.
10 Ibid., CXLIII, col. 617: 21 March 1905.
11 Ibid., CLXXXVI, col. 524: 18 March 1908.
12 Ibid., CXCVI, col. 560: 12 November 1908.
13 Ibid., CLXII, cols 1395–6: 2 August 1906.
14 Minute of 21 November 1918, ADM 116/1605.
15 Minute of 22 November 1918, ADM 116/1605.
16 Ibid.
17 See, for example, Walter Long's letter of 8 April 1919 to Lloyd George, quoted in Ferris, 'Symbol and Substance,' p. 66.
18 Cabinet paper GT 7646, 'Navy Votes: Memorandum by the Chancellor of the Exchequer,' 8 July 1919, CAB 24/83.
19 Board of Admiralty memorandum, 'Suggested Memorandum for War Cabinet: Naval Policy,' undated, ADM 167/59.
20 'Naval Policy and Expenditure', ADM 167/56; also circulated to the Finance Committee as FC 18, 24 October 1919, CAB 27/72.
21 Cabinet Paper GT-7975, 'Post War Naval Policy,' Walter Long, 12 August 1919, CAB 24/86; see also *The Beatty Papers*, ed. B. McL. Ranft (Aldershot, 1993), II, p. 52.
22 Cabinet Conclusions, 15 August 1919, CAB 23/15.
23 Ferris, 'Symbol and Substance,' p. 69.
24 FC 18, 'Naval Policy and Expenditure,' 24 October 1919, CAB 27/72.
25 Ibid.
26 Walter Long, 'Naval Estimates and Naval Policy,' 13 February 1920, ADM 167/61.
27 *Hansard*, vol. 126, cols 2300–1: 17 March 1920.
28 Chatfield, 'Naval Policy – Relative Naval Positions of Great Britain and U.S.A.,' 6 May 1920, ADM 167/61.
29 Beatty, 'Naval Policy and Construction,' 8 July 1920, ADM 167/60.

30   Walter Long memorandum, 'New Construction Programme,' 7 October 1920, ADM 167/62.
31   Long to Lloyd George, 13 December 1920, *The Beatty Papers*, II, p. 110.
32   CID 134th Mtg, 14 December 1920, CAB 2/3.
33   Ibid.
34   Lloyd George to Long, 14 December 1920, Walter Long Papers, British Museum, Add. 62425. This passage is omitted from the copy published in *The Beatty Papers*, II, pp. 113–15.
35   Long to Lloyd George, 17 December 1920, Walter Long Papers, Wiltshire Record Office, 947/716/2.
36   CID 135th Mtg, 23 December 1920, CAB 2/3. Roskill notes that the Cabinet's decision to examine naval policy resulted in the formation of the Bonar Law Committee, but he does not appreciate that this represented a retreat from Lloyd George's original intention of convening an inquiry into the future of the one-power standard. Roskill, *Naval Policy*, I, p. 221.
37   COS 207th Mtg, 18 June 1937, CAB 53/7.
38   Warren Fisher to Stanley Baldwin, 7 January 1925, T 161/243/S25613/ANNEX/5. On another occasion Fisher wrote that: 'A navy is an element in national insurance and the extent of such insurance should depend on (a) the measure of risk and (b) the purse of the insured. What should we think of a man who insisted on insuring his life against drowning to an amount that crippled the resources necessary for his existence? (Anyone dependent on him would be tempted to encourage him to realise the risk and drown himself.)' Fisher to the Chancellor of the Exchequer, 16 November 1922, T 161/119/S9627/01.
39   CID 134th Mtg, 14 December 1920, CAB 2/3.
40   Undated Treasury memorandum, 'Committee on National Expenditure: Special Report by the Treasury on Navy Expenditure,' T 163/11/4. See also the comments by Barstow in his memorandum, 'Naval Policy and Expenditure,' 15 June 1921, T 161/800/S18917/1.
41   Quoted in CID 244-C, 'Naval Policy: The Development of Imperial Defence Policy in the Far East', 24 March 1925, CAB 5/5.
42   'Admiralty Memorandum in reply to Paragraph 101 of Questionnaire [from the Geddes Committee],' undated, ADM 1/8615/200.
43   Ibid.
44   Barstow, 'Reports of the Geddes Committee and Churchill Committee,' 20 February 1922, T 172/1228.
45   Ibid.
46   CP-3692, 'Report of Committee Appointed to Examine Part I (Defence Departments) of the Report of the Geddes Committee on National Expenditure,' 4 February 1922, CAB 24/133.
47   Barstow, 'Naval Policy & Estimates,' 1 February 1924, T 161/227/S23175.
48   See, for example, Barstow, 'Reports of the Geddes Committee and Churchill Committee,' 20 February 1922, T 172/1228.
49   Keyes to Churchill, 21 March 1925, *The Keyes Papers*, ed. Paul G. Halpern (London, 1980), II, p. 110.
50   CID 193rd Mtg, 5 January 1925, CAB 2/4.
51   CID 165th Mtg, 30 November 1922, CAB 2/4.

52 CID 193rd Meeting, 5 January 1925, CAB 2/4. Bridgeman made similar comments in his memorandum of 5 February 1925, circulated as CP 67(25), CAB 24/171.

53 Pound to Richmond, 13 August 1924, Richmond Papers, RIC/7/4.

54 Barstow, 'Naval Policy and Expenditure,' 15 June 1921, T 161/800/S18917/1; see also his memoranda of 26 February and 1 March 1924, T 161/800/S18917/2.

55 Barstow, 'Singapore,' 1 March 1924, T 161/800/S18917/2.

56 Ibid.

57 On the course and outcome of this struggle over the Navy Estimates see in particular John Ferris, *Men, Money and Diplomacy* (Ithaca, NY, 1989), chapter 10; also B. J. C. McKercher, 'A Sane and Sensible Diplomacy: Austen Chamberlain, Japan and the Naval Balance of Power in the Pacific Ocean, 1924–1929', *Canadian Journal of History*, XXI (1986), 193–200; Roskill, *Naval Policy*, I, pp. 445–53; and Martin Gilbert, *Winston S. Churchill* (London, 1976), V, chapters 4–5. Historians frequently but erroneously treat Churchill's attacks on the navy while Chancellor as a skeleton in his closet. See in particular Ian Hamill, 'Winston Churchill and the Singapore Naval Base, 1924–1929,' *Journal of Southeast Asian Studies* (September 1980) and David MacGregor, 'Former Naval Cheapskate: Chancellor of the Exchequer Winston Churchill and the Royal Navy, 1924–29,' *Armed Forces and Society* (Spring 1993). Jon Sumida, 'Churchill and British Sea Power, 1908–29,' *Winston Churchill: Studies in Statesmanship*, ed. R. A. C. Parker (London, 1995), presents a more balanced view.

58 NP (25) 8th Meeting, 30 June 1925, CAB 27/273.

59 This principle was endorsed by the Cabinet the following year when it accepted a statement by the COS that the one-power standard required the 'maintenance of all other types of ship [than battleships and aircraft carriers] at such strength as will assure adequate security of sea passage to and from all parts of the British Empire, which is the basis and foundation of our system of Imperial defence, and without which all other measures of defence can be of little avail.' COS 41, 'Review of Imperial Defence, 1926,' 22 June 1926, CAB 53/12.

60 NP (25) 1st Mtg, 2 March 1925, CAB 27/273.

61 CID 199th Mtg, 2 April 1925, CAB 2/4.

62 Cabinet 24 (25), Conclusion 3, CAB 23/50.

63 CID 199th Mtg, 2 April 1925, CAB 2/4.

64 NP (25) 2nd Meeting, 5 March 1925, CAB 27/273.

65 Ferris, 'Last Decade.'

66 Ferris, *Men, Money and Diplomacy*.

67 Undated Admiralty memorandum, 'Answers to Questions Asked by Colwyn Committee,' ADM 116/2282.

68 On the background to this decision see Babij, 'Royal Navy.'

69 Minute by Oswyn Murray, 18 November 1928, ADM 116/3629.

70 Minute by W.W. Fisher, 7 November 1928, ADM 116/3629.

71 On perceptions of Japan in Whitehall after the Manchuria incident see Antony Best, 'Constructing an Image: British Intelligence and Whitehall's Perception of Japan, 1931–1939,' *Intelligence and National Security*, 11 (July 1996), 403–23.

72 DRC 11th Mtg, 19 February 1934, CAB 16/109.
73 'Memorandum by the Chief of the Naval Staff in Preparation for the 1935 Naval Conference,' Appendix to N.C.M. (35)1, CAB 29/148.
74 Ibid.
75 Ibid. (italics in original).
76 The final report of the DRC not only implies that this definition had official acceptance, but also antedates it to 1932. These details were repeated in the report of the DPR (DR) Committee and reappeared in virtually all subsequent Cabinet documents on the subject. That a new definition of the one-power standard had been laid down in 1932 was accepted by Treasury officials and, more recently, by historians of British rearmament, most notably Peden, Gibbs, and Gordon. The latter wrongly concludes that Field put this definition forward in his 'S/L Memorandum' of 14 November 1932. G. A. H. Gordon, *British Seapower and Procurement Between the Wars* (Annapolis, MD, 1988), pp. 107–8; DRC 37, 'Third Report of Defence Requirements Sub-Committee,' 21 November 1935, CAB 16/112; DPR (DR) 9, Report, 12 February 1936, CAB 16/123; minute by Bridges, 'New Construction Programme 1937,' 6 January 1937, T 161/755/S36130/37; N.H. Gibbs, *Grand Strategy*, (London, 1976), I p. 334; G. C. Peden, *British Rearmament and the Treasury: 1932–1939* (Edinburgh, 1979), p. 113.
77 DRC 33, 'Naval Defence Requirements', memorandum by the First Sea Lord, 9 October 1935; DRC 18th Mtg, 14 October 1935, CAB 16/112.
78 DRC 37, 'Third Report of Defence Requirements Sub-Committee,' 21 November 1935, CAB 16/112.
79 DPR (DR) [Sub-Committee on Defence Policy and Requirements: Defence Requirements Enquiry] 5th Mtg, 20 January 1936, CAB 16/123.
80 Ibid.
81 DPR (DR) 9, 12 February 1936, CAB 16/123.
82 Hoare later admitted this to the Defence Plans (Policy) Sub-Committee of the CID, DP (P) 2nd Mtg, 11 May 1937, CAB 16/181. In contrast, the Navy Estimates for 1935/36 stood at just over £60 million.
83 Board of Admiralty minute 3380, 24 June 1936, ADM 167/94.
84 Cabinet 10(36), 25 February 1936, CAB 23/133.
85 Board of Admiralty minute 3380, 24 June 1936, ADM 167/94; DPR 88 (Revise), memorandum by the First Lord, 'Practicability of Accelerating the Naval Programme and the Effect on the Programmes of the Other Services,' 25 June 1936, CAB 16/140.
86 The Admiralty program was contained in a draft memorandum by Hoare, DPR 88, 22 June 1936; for the reaction by Treasury officials see in particular the minutes by Bridges and Hopkins, 22 June 1936, T 161/713/36130/36/01.
87 Minute by Bridges, 22 June 1936, T 161/713/36130/36/01.
88 Minute by Hopkins, 'Accelerated Naval Building Programme,' 25 June 1936, T 161/713/36130/36/01. The Admiralty's revised proposals are contained in DPR 88 (Revise), 25 June 1936, CAB 16/140.
89 DPR 24th Meeting, 2 July 1936, CAB 16/136.
90 Coxwell, 27 November 1936, ADM 116/3596; Board of Admiralty minute 3421, 16 November 1936, ADM 167/94.
91 Board of Admiralty minute 3421, 16 November 1936, ADM 167/94.
92 Ibid.

93 Minute by Bridges, 'New Construction Programme 1937,' 6 January 1937; Barlow and Hopkins concurred in this assessment, but Warren Fisher minuted on 11 January that he felt 'sure that there can be no conscious intention to conceal on the Admiralty part.' T 161/755/S36130/37.

94 Bridges, 'Naval Construction Programme,' 8 February 1937, T 161/755/S36130/37.

95 Chamberlain, 28 January 1937, T 161/755/S36130/37.

96 DPP 2nd Mtg, 11 May 1937, CAB 16/181.

97 Ibid.

98 Ibid.

99 DP (P) 3, 'A New Standard of Naval Strength,' memorandum by the Board of Admiralty, 26 April 1937, CAB 16/181.

100 Ibid.

101 DPP 2nd Mtg, 11 May 1937, CAB 16/181.

102 Minute by Bridges, 27 April 1937, T 161/780/S42000.

103 Ibid.

104 Hopkins, 'Control of Defence Expenditure,' May 1937, T 161/783/S48431/02/1.

105 Peden, *Rearmament*, pp. 39–42.

106 CP 165 (37), 'Control of Defence Expenditure,' CAB 24/270.

107 CP 256 (37), 'Defence Expenditure in Future Years', 18 August 1937; CP 257 (37), 'Defence Expenditure in Future Years: Summary of Forecasts Submitted by the Defence Departments and the Home Office', Memorandum by the Chancellor of the Exchequer, 22 October 1937, CAB 24/272. A record of the meetings held by Inskip can be found in T 161/855/S48431/04.

108 CP 316/37, 'Defence Expenditure in Future Years: Interim Report by the Minister for Co-ordination of Defence,' 15 December 1937, CAB 24/273.

109 The Admiralty's proposed program consisted of 3 capital ships, 2 aircraft carriers, 7 cruisers (4 'Fiji' class, 3 'Dido' class), 8 destroyers, 7 submarines, 4 small minelayers, 2 escort vessels, 4 minesweepers, 2 patrol vessels, 2 river gunboats and miscellaneous small vessels. The total cost of these vessels was estimated at £70 028 850 spread over five years. CP 29 (38), CAB 24/274.

110 T. S. V. Phillips, 'Notes on CP 316/37,' 21 December 1937, ADM 116/3631.

111 CP 316/37, 'Defense Expenditure in Future Years: Interim Report by the Minister for Co-ordination of Defence,' 15 December 1937, CAB 24/273. The modernization of Britain's older battleships had been approved subsequent to the DRC report and the Admiralty was understandably reluctant to scrap these vessels almost immediately the renovations were complete. The preferred solution was to retain these vessels and increase the total number of this class to be kept in service. This was the course advocated by the Secretary of the Admiralty, who recommended that in putting this proposal forward 'it would be undesirable that the Treasury should learn that we are departing from the original D.R.C. standard without telling them.' See the minute of 1 December 1937 from R. H. A. Carter to the First Sea Lord and the First Lord of the Admiralty, both of whom concurred in this suggestion. ADM 116/3631.

112 CP 29 (38), 'New Construction Programme, 1938', memorandum by the First Lord, 11 February 1938, CAB 24/274.

113 Minute by Hopkins, 19 January 1938. The only dissenting voice belonged to Warren Fisher, who, possibly inspired by his high regard for Chatfield, minuted that he did 'not think the Admiralty w^d consciously aim at short-circuiting a decision. It surely must be misunderstanding. I think the attention of the Admiralty sh^d be drawn to the proper meaning of the interim decision.' Minute of 20 January 1938, T 161/824/S36130/38/1.

114 T. L. Rowan, 'Naval New Construction Programme 1938', 3 January 1938, T 161/824/S36130/38/1.

115 The revised 1938 program consisted of 2 battleships (later cancelled), 1 aircraft carrier, 4 'Fiji' class cruisers, 3 'Dido' class cruisers, 3 'Triton' class submarines, and a number of small craft. Board of Admiralty minute, 3530, 25 February 1938, ADM 167/100.

116 CP 24 (38), 'Defence Expenditure in Future Years: Further Report by the Minister for Co-ordination of Defence,' 8 February 1938, CAB 24/274.

117 Inskip to Duff Cooper, 11 March 1938, ADM 116/3631.

118 Duff Cooper to Inskip, 29 March 1938, ADM 116/3631.

119 Minute by Duff Cooper, 4 April 1938, ADM 205/80.

120 Minute by the D of P, 4 April 1938, ADM 205/80.

121 Ibid. Proposals to improve the navy's defenses against air attack were put to the Cabinet the following week. See CP 92 (38), 'Measures of Acceleration Proposed in Consequence of the International Situation,' CAB 24/276. Treasury officials were not fooled. Bridges suggested, for example, that 'the real urge behind this paper is that the Admiralty fear that the Air Ministry may get away with an increase in expenditure and that they want to get something for themselves while the going is good.' Minute of 12 April 1938, T 161/936/S43880/1.

122 Record of a meeting held in the First Lord's room on 5 April 1938, ADM 205/80.

123 Draft memorandum by the First Lord for the Cabinet, 'Defence Expenditure in Future Years: Naval Policy,' 28 April 1938, PREM 1/346. This document was numbered 'CP 104 (38)' but does not appear ever to have been circulated to the Cabinet.

124 Inskip to Simon, 19 May 1938, T 161/936/S43880/1.

125 Duff Cooper to Chatfield, 9 May 1938, ADM 205/80.

126 Minute by Barlow to Hopkins, 17 June 1938, T 161/936/S43880/1.

127 Simon to Chamberlain, 24 June 1938, PREM 1/346.

128 CP 170 (38), 'Naval Expenditure,' memorandum by the Minister for Co-ordination of Defence, 12 July 1938.

129 Duff Cooper to Inskip, 21 July 1938, T 161/936/S43880/2.

130 Duff Cooper to Hankey, 21 July 1938, PREM 1/346.

131 Cleverly to Hankey, 22 July 1938, PREM 1/346.

132 Inskip to Duff Cooper, 21 July 1938, T 161/936/S43880/2.

133 Minute by Rowan, 21 July 1938, T 161/936/S43880/2.

134 Notes of a meeting between the Chancellor, the First Lord and Inskip, 25 July 1938, T 161/936/S43880/2.

135 Minute by Rowan to Gilbert, 28 February 1939, T 161/905/S35171/39.

136 See, for example, the First Lord's letters to the Chancellor of the Exchequer of 24 February 1939 (ADM 167/106) and 21 June 1939 (ADM 167/104);

and Admiralty letter to the CID, 3 April 1939, enclosing an undated memorandum, 'Long Term Projects Recommended by the Admiralty for Supplementing and Accelerating the Naval Defence Programme,' ADM 1/10012.

137 Chancellor of the Exchequer to the First Lord, 9 May 1939, ADM 1/10012.

138 DP (P) 63, 'Capital Ship Position,' memorandum by the First Lord, 27 June 1939, CAB 16/183A; CID 364th Mtg, 6 July 1939, CAB 2/9.

139 Claims that the navy secured approval for its 'new standard' during the final months of peace are wrong. The source of this error is M. M. Postan, *British War Production* (London, 1952), p. 58, which mistakenly claims that in July 1939 the CID approved the Admiralty's plans for the development of additional shipbuilding capacity.

140 Gordon, *Seapower*, chapter 21.

141 Ibid., p. 259. The document Gordon cites here is the Board memorandum of 26 April 1937, ADM 1/9081.

142 For example, Roskill, *Naval Policy*, I, p. 215, *passim*.

2 'Main Fleet to Bermuda': Naval Strategy for an Anglo-American War

1 Cabinet memorandum, 'Cruisers and Parity', 20 July 1927, *Winston S. Churchill*, ed. Martin Gilbert (London, 1979), vol. V, part 1, pp. 1030–5.

2 See, for example, the Admiralty memorandum, 'Imperial Naval Defence,' October 1919, ADM 167/56; Wemyss' memorandum, 'Future Naval Programme', 24 March 1919, ADM 167/58; and PD memorandum, 'British Imperial Naval Bases in the Pacific,' 26 April 1919, ADM 1/8570/287.

3 Minute of 13 June 1919, signed by K. Dewar for D of P, ADM 1/8570/287. This minute also suggested the assignment of a single officer to study war with Japan.

4 The Plans Division also produced a brief memorandum entitled 'Headings: War with USA and Japan' for the benefit of the Capital Ship Committee: *Beatty Papers*, II, pp. 138–40. This document was not formally circulated to the committee, however, and was probably only seen by Beatty and Brock.

5 Other notable witnesses include Richmond, Keyes, and the Chief of the Air Staff, Sir Hugh Trenchard. All witnesses were examined individually and many also submitted memoranda. Oral testimony is located in CAB 16/37/1, and memoranda in CAB 16/37/2. The latter generally duplicate the former, but tend to be less candid. The committee was made up of Arthur Bonar Law (Lord Privy Seal), Robert Horne (President of the Board of Trade), Eric Geddes (Minister without Portfolio), Churchill (Secretary for War and Air, and later Colonial Secretary), Long (First Lord) and Beatty (First Sea Lord). Its final report, dated 2 March 1921, was circulated as paper N-11, CAB 16/37/2.

6 Beatty, 'Naval Policy,' 7 January 1920, ADM 167/61. One who did disagree with Beatty was Brock, who felt that the 'Americans are absolutely different from us. We are two distinct races. My experiences of Americans is that we do not think on the same lines, and in addition to a certain amount of racial

antipathy, which I am quite certain exists, we have the Press on both sides which is a most dangerous factor.' NSC [Sub-Committee on the Question of the Capital Ship in the Navy] 5th Mtg, 11 January 1921, CAB 16/37/1.

7 Beatty, 'Naval Policy,' 7 January 1920, ADM 167/61.

8 Admiral Sir Barry Domvile, *By and Large* (London, 1936), p. 134.

9 NSC 5th Mtg, 11 January 1921, CAB 16/37/1. Such views were common at this time. See, for example, the Admiralty memorandum 'Naval Policy and Expenditure,' 24 October 1919: 'The United States are building up a Mercantile Marine with the idea of competing with Great Britain in the world-carrying trade. They propose to protect that trade with a strong Navy, and the fact cannot be denied that conflict of interests may arise with the United States in the same way as with other powers in our history.' FC 18, CAB 27/72.

10 Leveson to Admiralty, 24 April 1924, ADM 116/3124.

11 Keyes to Churchill, 20 January 1928, *Keyes Papers*, II, p. 239.

12 NSC 5th Mtg, 11 January 1921, CAB 16/37/1.

13 On 7 February 1921, Lady Lee, wife of the First Lord, recorded in her diary that 'Geddes says the Sea Lords have very inflated ideas, and even talk of wanting new docks built at Bermuda in case we should have to fight America!' This proposal never appeared in the minutes of the Capital Ship Committee, and if accurate was based on informal comments. *'A Good Innings': The Private Papers of Viscount Lee of Fareham*, ed. Alan Clarke (London, 1974), p. 205.

14 NSC 6th Mtg, 13 January 1921, CAB 16/37/1.

15 NSC 3rd Mtg, 5 January 1921, CAB 16/37/1.

16 Michael Vlahos, *The Blue Sword: The Naval War College and the American Mission, 1919–41* (Newport, RI, 1980), pp. 105–8.

17 Meeting of 7 November 1922, *Hearings Before the General Board of the Navy 1917–1950* (Wilmington, DE), reel 5.

18 Joint Army and Navy Basic War Plan-Red, 8 May 1930, *American War Plans: 1919–41*, ed. Stephen Ross, 2, p. 308. See also *Strategic Planning in the U.S. Navy: Its Evolution and Execution, 1891–1945* (Wilmington, DE, n.d.), roll 4.

19 Admiral Brock was probably alone in the belief that in view of 'what the Canadians did in the last war, if their backs are in it they ought to be able to hold the banks of the St. Lawrence. If their backs are not in it, then I quite allow that Canada will fall.' NSC 5th Mtg, 11 January 1921, CAB 16/37/1.

20 Admiralty memorandum, 'Imperial Naval Defence,' October 1919, ADM 167/56.

21 Ibid.

22 Ibid. Similar views were expressed in Wemyss' memorandum, 'Future Naval Programme,' 24 March 1919, ADM 167/58.

23 The USN's 'War Plan Red' did not envisage the despatch of a fleet across the Atlantic. See Christopher Bell, 'Thinking the Unthinkable: American and British Naval Strategies for an Anglo-American War, 1918–31,' *International History Review*, XIX (November 1997) 789–808.

24 NSC 3rd Mtg, 5 January 1921, CAB 16/37/1.

25 See in particular the testimony of Brock and Admiral Charles de Bartolomé to the Capital Ship Committee, CAB 16/37/1.

3 Far Eastern War Plans and the Myth of the Singapore Strategy

1 For the conventional view of the Singapore Strategy see Malcolm H. Murfett, '"Living in the Past": A Critical Re-examination of the Singapore Naval Strategy, 1918–1941,' *War and Society* 11, 1 (May 1993); Paul Haggie, *Britannia At Bay* (Oxford, 1981); Arthur J. Marder, *Old Friends, New Enemies* (Oxford, 1981); Ian Hamill, *The Strategic Illusion* (Singapore, 1981). The history of the Singapore Naval Base has been fully treated in James Neidpath, *The Singapore Naval Base and the Defense of Britain's Eastern Empire, 1919–1941* (Oxford, 1981) and W. David McIntyre, *The Rise and Fall of the Singapore Naval Base, 1919–1942* (London, 1979).

2 Haggie, *Britannia*, is a partial exception.

3 CP 2957, 'Anglo-Japanese Alliance,' memorandum by the First Lord, 21 May 1921, CAB 24/123.

4 CP 139(25), 'Political Outlook in the Far East,' Naval Staff memorandum, 5 March 1925, CAB 24/172.

5 Minute by the DNI, 27 March 1934, ADM 116/3116.

6 CID 165th Mtg, 30 November 1922, CAB 2/4. Beatty expressed similar views in his memorandum of 28 April 1924, ADM 1/8666/151.

7 Keyes to Churchill, 21 March 1925, *Keyes Papers*, II, p. 110.

8 CP 139 (25), 'Political Outlook in the Far East,' 5 March 1925, CAB 24/172.

9 War Memorandum (Eastern), July 1931, ADM 116/3118.

10 On this point see in particular the Naval Staff memorandum, 'The Naval Situation of the British Empire in the event of war between Japan and the U.S. of America,' June 1921, ADM 1/8948.

11 Keyes to Churchill, 24 March 1925, *Keyes Papers*, II, p. 112.

12 See also Christopher Bell, 'The Royal Navy, War Planning and Intelligence Assessments of Japan between the Wars,' paper presented to a Symposium on Intelligence and International Relations, Yale University, 3 May 1996.

13 'Report No. 12 of 1922' by Captain Colvin, 19 May 1922, FO 371/8051; also 'Japan, Annual Report, 1922,' 26 March 1923, FO 371/9233.

14 CID 193rd Meeting, 5 January 1925, CAB 2/4.

15 See Marder, *Old Friends*; Wesley Wark, 'In Search of a Suitable Japan: British Naval Intelligence in the Pacific before the Second World War,' *Intelligence and National Security*, I (May 1986), 189–211; Geoffrey Till, 'Perceptions of Naval Power Between the Wars: The British Case,' *Estimating Foreign Military Power*, ed. Peter Towle (London, 1982).

16 See especially Till, 'Perceptions' and Marder, *Old Friends*, chapter XII.

17 Wark, 'Suitable Japan,' pp. 206–7. Force Z was the code-name given to the *Prince of Wales*, *Repulse*, and their destroyer escort when they left Singapore on 8 December 1941.

18 ADM 116/4393.

19 CID 348th Mtg, 24 February 1939, CAB 2/8.

20 War Memorandum (Eastern), Section XVI, August 1939, ADM 1/9767; COS 931, 'Situation in the Far East,' CAB 53/50. It is worth noting that when the 80 per cent rating first appeared it was applied not to the IJN's fighting efficiency, but only to its maintenance efficiency. See COS 303rd Mtg, 19 June 1939, CAB 53/11.

21 The Admiralty's first Eastern War Memorandum was prepared by the Plans Division in 1920 (ADM 116/3124); new editions were issued in 1923 (ADM 116/3124), 1924 (ADM 116/3125), 1931 (ADM 116/3118), 1933 (ADM 116/3475) and 1937 (ADM 116/4393). Each of these underwent numerous revisions during its lifetime.

22 ADM 116/3124.

23 COS 27th Mtg, 11 March 1926, CAB 53/1.

24 War Memorandum (Eastern), 29 July 1924, ADM 116/3125. In the 1931 Memorandum, Phase I was defined as the period before the relief of Hong Kong. In 1933 this was changed to the relief of Singapore, and Phase II became the relief of Hong Kong. In 1938 the three phases were reduced to two: the 'period before relief' and the 'period subsequent to the relief of Singapore.' Naval War Memorandum (Eastern), Section IX, December 1937, ADM 116/4393.

25 NSC 5th Mtg, 11 January 1921, CAB 16/37/1.

26 War Memorandum (Eastern), February 1923, ADM 116/3124.

27 Memoranda covering the 'Passage of the Fleet to the Far East,' can be found in ADM 116/3125 (17 March 1925), and in ADM 116/3123 (June 1925, revised May 1927). Beginning in 1933 this information was incorporated directly into the Eastern War Memoranda. See the minutes by the D of P and the DCNS in ADM 116/3475.

28 War Memorandum (Eastern), February 1923, ADM 116/3124.

29 'Memorandum on Naval Dispositions in the Far East in Emergency,' Admiralty to C-in-C China, 26 April 1933, ADM 116/3472. For a more detailed discussion of Hong Kong's role in British strategy during this period see Christopher Bell, '"Our Most Exposed Outpost": Hong Kong and British Far Eastern Strategy, 1921–1941,' *Journal of Military History*, 60 (January, 1996), 61–88.

30 War Memorandum (Eastern), July 1931, ADM 116/3118.

31 These were comprised principally of the forces assigned to the China Station and the East Indies Squadron, supplemented by the navies of Australia and New Zealand.

32 War Memorandum (Eastern), February 1923, ADM 116/3124.

33 Ibid.

34 Ibid.

35 War Memorandum (Eastern), 29 July 1924, ADM 116/3125.

36 Requests were made by eastern Cs-in-C to increase the priority assigned to Hong Kong on three separate occasions between 1924 and 1928. See C-in-C China to Admiralty, 24 April 1924, ADM 116/3124; memorandum by R. Y. Tyrwhitt, 11 January 1928, ADM 116/3126; and Richmond to Admiralty, 13 April 1925, ADM 116/3125.

37 ADM 116/3126.

38 Minute by Madden, 12 April 1928, ADM 116/3126.

39 Admiralty to C-in-C China Station, 3 May 1928, ADM 116/3126.

40 Bell, 'Exposed Outpost.'

41 War Memorandum 1923, February 1923, ADM 116/3124.

42 Richmond to Haldane, 16 April 1924, Haldane Papers, Volume 5916, National Library of Scotland. For a more detailed discussion of Richmond's criticisms and his subsequent role in the historiography of the navy's Far Eastern strategy see Christopher Bell, '"How Are We Going to Make

War?'': Admiral Sir Herbert Richmond and British Far Eastern War Plans,' *Journal of Strategic Studies*, 20 (September 1997), 123–41.

43   War Memorandum (Eastern), 29 July 1924, ADM 116/3125.

44   Richmond to Admiralty, 13 April 1925, ADM 116/3125.

45   Ibid.

46   Richmond's views on the application of economic pressure are developed in several of the essays in his *National Policy and Naval Strength*.

47   Richmond to Admiralty, 13 April 1925, ADM 116/3125.

48   Ibid.

49   Ibid.; Haggie, *Britannia*, p. 11; McIntyre, *Rise and Fall of the Singapore Naval Base*, pp. 114–15; Neidpath, *Singapore Naval Base*, pp. 90–1; Murfett, 'Living in the Past,' p. 83.

50   Richmond to Admiralty, 13 April 1925, ADM 116/3125.

51   Ibid.

52   Richmond to Haldane, 24 June 1924, Haldane Papers, Volume 5916.

53   'Precis of C-in-C East Indies Memorandum and Notes by Plans Division,' undated, ADM 116/3125.

54   Pound to Richmond, 13 August 1924, RIC/7/4.

55   Minute by the D of P, 16 June 1925, ADM 116/3125.

56   'Precis of C-in-C East Indies Memorandum and Notes by Plans Division,' undated, ADM 116/3125.

57   Egerton to Richmond, 8 October 1925, RIC/7/3.

58   War Memorandum (Eastern), July 1931, ADM 116/3118.

59   Ibid.

60   Ibid.

61   ATB 89, 'Dependence on Overseas Trade and the Possibilities of the Exercise of Naval Pressure on such trade,' CAB 47/4; War Memorandum (Eastern), July 1931, Appendix 5, ADM 116/3118.

62   ATB 89, CAB 47/4.

63   Ibid.

64   War Memorandum (Eastern), July 1931, ADM 116/3118.

65   Ibid.

66   See Bell, 'Exposed Outpost.'

67   COS 234th, 4 April 1938, CAB 53/9.

68   The suggestion that Hong Kong would be a valuable base for defensive operations appears to have first been made in COS 405, 'Strategical Situation in the Far East with Particular Reference to Hong Kong,' CAB 53/25. This was later included in numerous COS and JPC documents, including the 1937 Far Eastern Appreciation, COS 579 (JP), CAB 53/31.

69   COS 725, 'The Policy for the Defence of Hong Kong,' memorandum by the CIGS, May 1938, CAB 53/38. COS 731, 'The Policy for the Defence of Hong Kong,' memorandum by the CAS, CAB 53/39; also COS 234th Mtg, 4 April 1938 and 240th Mtg, 13 June 1938, CAB 53/9.

70   COS 740, 'The Policy for the Defence of Hong Kong', 15 July 1938, CAB 53/39.

71   Bell, 'Exposed Outpost.'

72   COS 132nd Mtg, 24 July 1934, CAB 53/5. COS 347, 'Strategic Position in the Far East with Particular Reference to Hong Kong and Air Requirements for the Far East,' 29 October 1934, CAB 53/24.

73 Chatfield to Dreyer, 7 August 1934, Chatfield Papers, CHT/4/4.
74 On the progress of this committee see Dreyer's telegrams to the Admiralty of 18 July 1933, 4 May 1934 (ADM 116/3471) and 14 November 1934 (ADM 116/3338).
75 Dreyer to Admiralty, 11 August 1934, ADM 116/3471.
76 Ibid.
77 Ibid.
78 Dreyer, 14 November 1934, ADM 116/3338.
79 See the minutes by the D of P and DCNS on Dreyer's memorandum of 14 November 1934 , and 'Notes on M00582/35 Prepared Jointly by D. of P. and DNI for Discussion with Admiral Sir Frederic Dreyer,' 31 March 1936, ADM 116/3338.
80 Naval War Memorandum (Eastern), ADM 116/4393. The first sections were issued in December 1937 and new sections were added regularly until February 1939. Subsequent revisions can be found in ADM 116/3863 and ADM 1/9897.
81 The 1933 War Memorandum covered only Phase I of an Eastern war. Notwithstanding this, it appears to have superseded the entire 1931 Memo, including those sections dealing with phases II and III. See Dreyer to Admiralty, 11 August 1934, ADM 116/3471.
82 Naval War Memorandum (Eastern), Section IX, December 1937, ADM 116/4393.
83 Ibid.
84 Ibid., Section XI, October 1938. ADM 116/4393
85 Ibid. On this question see also Ian Cowman, 'An Admiralty 'Myth': The Search for an Advanced Far Eastern Fleet Base before the Second World War', *Journal of Strategic Studies*, 8 (September 1985), 317–26.
86 COS 579 (JP), 7 May 1937. CAB 53/31.
87 See IIC Paper ICF/448, 'Japan: General Survey of Material Resources & Industry in their Bearing Upon National War Potential,' 2 November 1936. AWM 124 (3/139). On the IIC see Robert Young, 'Spokesmen for Economic Warfare: The Industrial Intelligence Centre in the 1930s,' *European Studies Review*, 6 (1976), 473–86; W. N. Medlicott, *The Economic Blockade* (London, 1952), I, pp. 13–24; F. H. Hinsley et al., *British Intelligence in the Second World War* (London, 1979), I, chapter 1; Wesley Wark, *The Ultimate Enemy* (London, 1985), chapter 7.
88 IIC Paper ICF/448, AWM 124 [3/139].
89 Materials for which Japan would probably have to rely on imports included iron and ferro-alloys, non-ferrous metals, textile raw materials, petroleum, rubber, coking coal, salt, and certain varieties of timber. COS (JP) 579, CAB 53/31.
90 Ibid.
91 Ibid. On the methods which planners intended to adopt in a future war, and on the lessons they derived from Britain's experiences with economic warfare in the First World War, see Medlicott, *Economic Blockade*, vol. I, Introduction.
92 For example, Murfett, 'Living in the Past'; Russell Grenfell, *Main Fleet to Singapore* (London, 1951).
93 For example, Roskill, *Naval Policy*; Neidpath, *Singapore Naval Base*, Peter Lowe, 'Great Britain's Assessment of Japan before the Outbreak of the

Pacific War,' *Knowing One's Enemies*, ed. Ernest R. May (Princeton, NJ, 1986); Marder, *Old Friends*, pp. 62–5.

94 For example, Wark, 'Suitable Japan'; Haggie, *Britannia*.
95 Haggie, *Britannia*, pp. 108–9, 117–20; Wark, 'Suitable Japan,' pp. 198–9.
96 COS 596, CAB 53/32.
97 T. C. Hampton, 'Naval Problems in an Eastern War,' F10819/10819/61, FO 371/22176. See also R. J. Pritchard, *Far Eastern Influence upon British Strategy Towards the Great Powers, 1937–39* (New York, 1987), pp. 174–5. Pritchard wrongly suggests that Hampton's views were 'unorthodox.'
98 SAC 4, Note by the First Sea Lord, 28 February 1939, CAB 16/209.
99 Ibid. See also Backhouse's minute of 24 March 1939, ADM 1/9909.
100 Drax also recommended an additional force of 8 cruisers, 17 destroyers, 15 submarines, 2 minelayers, and 12 MTBs for trade defense. Paper OPC 11, 'Composition of the Far Eastern Fleet in War,' 15 March 1939, Drax Papers, DRAX 2/9.
101 Ibid.
102 Ibid.
103 Drax memorandum, 'Disposition for three eventualities,' 16 March 1939, ADM 1/9897.
104 For the former view see Haggie, *Britannia*, pp. 137–41; for the latter see Murfett, 'Living in the Past.'
105 SAC (Strategic Appreciation Committee) 6th Mtg, 17 April 1939, CAB 16/209.
106 See SAC 2nd Mtg, 13 March 1939, CAB 16/209.
107 CID 348th Mtg, 24 February 1939, CAB 2/8. In June 1939 Chatfield informed the Cabinet Foreign Policy Committee that the largest force that could be made available for the Far East by abandoning the Mediterranean would be seven capital ships, FP (36) the 52nd Mtg, CAB 27/625.
108 CID 348th Mtg, 24 February 1939, CAB 2/8. See also Chatfield's comments to the First meeting of the SAC, 1 March 1939: 'He considered that the British Fleet in the Far East would have to adopt the normal strategy of the weaker fleet, a strategy which was well defined in history and which had been employed by the German Fleet in the last war.'
109 FP (36) 52nd Mtg, 19 June 1939, CAB 27/625.
110 COS 928, 'The Situation in the Far East,' 18 June 1939, CAB 53/50.
111 See COS 303rd Mtg, 19 June 1939, CAB 53/11; FP (36) 53rd Mtg, 20 June 1939, CAB 27/625; COS 930, 'The Situation in the Far East,' Admiralty memorandum, 20 June 1939; and COS 931, 'The Situation in the Far East,' CAB 53/50.
112 Minute by Phillips, 5 July 1939, ADM 1/9767.
113 These revisions are dated 16 May 1939, ADM 116/3863.
114 War Memorandum (Eastern), Section XVI, July 1939. These changes were approved by both Pound and Phillips.
115 See COS 928, 'The Situation in the Far East,' 18 June 1939, CAB 53/50.
116 See the COS's Far East Appreciation, COS (40) 592 (Revise), 15 August 1940, CAB 80/15.
117 Pound to Churchill, 28 July 1941, Winston S. Churchill, *The Second World War* (London, 1950), III, pp. 769–73; Marder, *Old Friends*, p. 220.
118 Admiralty to C-in-C China, 15 October 1940, ADM 1/11183.

119 The text of the ADB agreement may be found in AWM 113 (1/97). For the context of the April 1941 Singapore Conference see Marder, *Old Friends*, chapter VII.

120 Marder, *Old Friends*, p. 209–10; Cowman, 'Main Fleet,' 84.

121 Ian Cowman, *Dominion or Decline* (Oxford, 1996).

122 'Record of a Meeting Held in V.C.N.S' Room: 30th September, 1941'; Aide-Mémoire for use by the British Representatives at Naval Planning Conference Singapore, n.d., revised draft by D of P, ADM 116/4877.

123 Ibid.

124 Pound to Admiral Stark, US Chief of Naval Operations, 5 November 1941, ADM 116/4877. The Americans remained dubious, however, about Manila's facilities being up to the task. Stark to British Admiralty Delegation, Washington, 11 November 1941, *Strategic Planning in the U.S. Navy*, roll 6.

125 For example, Murfett, 'Living in the Past'; Cowman, *Dominion or Decline*; Haggie, *Britannia*, p. 211; Hamill, *Strategic Illusion*, pp. 309–11; Marder, p. 241. Another school of thought blames Churchill for this decision and holds the Admiralty up as the purveyors of common sense in this instance. See for example Stephen Roskill, *Churchill and the Admirals* (London, 1977) and S. Woodburn Kirby, *Singapore: Chain of Disaster* (New York, 1971).

126 Ian Cowman has added a new twist to the debate over the navy's role in the despatch of the *Prince of Wales* and *Repulse* by suggesting that, contrary to accepted views, the Admiralty actually outmaneuvered Churchill on this occasion (*Dominion or Decline*; 'Main Fleet to Singapore?: Churchill, the Admiralty, and Force Z,' *Journal of Strategic Studies* (March 1995), pp. 79–83). Pound's objective in late 1941, Cowman claims, was to cement Anglo-American cooperation in the Far East by building up a British fleet at Manila which could operate north of the Malay barrier against Japan's lines of communications. In order to divert the Prime Minister's attention from the Admiralty's plans, Cowman asserts that Pound deliberately provoked Churchill by opposing the despatch of the *Prince of Wales*, a matter of great interest to him but purportedly 'an issue of only conditional concern to the Admiralty.' Distracted by the Admiralty's smokescreen, Churchill failed to realize the deception until it was too late to stop it. Although Cowman is correct about the Admiralty's hopes for eventually operating British forces from Manila, his argument as a whole does not stand up to scrutiny. He fails to provide a single piece of real evidence to support his charges, and the circumstantial case he builds is exceedingly weak.

127 See especially Hamill, *Strategic Illusion*, pp. 3, 310; Murfett, 'Living in the Past,' pp. 77–8.

128 Hamill, *Strategic Illusion*, p. 310.

129 Till, *Air Power*.

130 On the evolution and execution of American war plans, see Edward S. Miller, *War Plan Orange* (Annapolis, MD, 1997).

131 Steven Ross (ed.), *American War Plans: 1919–1941* (New York, 1992), II, p. 146; Miller, *War Plan Orange*, chapter 14.

132 Ibid., pp. 162–4.

133 Correlli Barnett, *Engage the Enemy More Closely* (New York, 1991), p. 11.

4 'The Ultimate Potential Enemy': Nazi Germany and British Defense Dilemmas

1 COS 296, 'The Situation in the Far East,' 3 March 1932, CAB 53/22; Roskill, *Naval Policy*, II, p. 145; Michael Howard, *The Continental Commitment* (Harmondsworth, 1974), p. 99.

2 DRC 14, 'Report of the DRC,' 28 January 1934, CAB 16/109.

3 For example, Wark, 'Suitable Japan,' pp. 190–1; Howard, *Continental Commitment*, p. 106; Peter Bell, *Chamberlain, Germany and Japan, 1933–4* (London, 1996).

4 Note by Fisher, 29 January 1934, Enclosure I to DRC 12, CAB 16/109.

5 DRC 14, 28 January 1934, CAB 16/109.

6 DRC 19, 'Note by Fisher as an Addendum to the DRC Report,' 17 February 1934, CAB 16/109.

7 Note by Fisher, 29 January 1934, Enclosure I to DRC 12, CAB 16/109. For Fisher's views on the United States see also DRC 16 and DRC 19.

8 At this time Pownall records that Hankey believed Fisher to be 'rather mad. Apparently he has some mysterious nerve disorder and his judgement is affected thereby. The papers he occasionally puts in are astonishing, long tirades far removed from the point and irrelevant to the Committee's terms of reference.' *Chief of Staff: The Diaries of Lieutenant-General Sir Henry Pownall*, ed. Brian Bond (London, 1972), I, p. 36. See also Ferris, *Men, Money and Diplomacy*, pp. 4–5.

9 DRC 2nd Mtg, 27 November 1933, CAB 16/109.

10 Chatfield to Dreyer, 2 February 1934, CHT/4/4.

11 DC(M)(32) 120, 'Note by the Chancellor of the Exchequer on the Report of the D.R.C.,' 20 June 1934, CAB 16/111. In terms of priority, Chamberlain ranked the expansion of the Army a far-distant second.

12 Ibid.

13 Minutes by DCNS and Chatfield, 21 June 1934, ADM 116/3436.

14 DC(M)(32) 125, 'Naval Defence Requirements,' memorandum by the First Lord, 18 July 1934, CAB 16/111.

15 Uri Bialer, *The Shadow of the Bomber* (London, 1980).

16 Wark, *Ultimate Enemy*, chapter 6; Paul Kennedy, 'British "Net Assessment" and the Coming of the Second World War,' *Calculations: Net Assessments and the Coming of World War II*, eds A. R. Millett and W. Murray (New York, 1992); Till, 'Perceptions'.

17 Wark, *Ultimate Enemy*, pp. 151–2. Wark implicitly criticizes the navy for assuming 'that the Nazi's ideological quarrel was with Bolshevik Russia,' 'that Nazi land hunger was directed eastward,' and that Hitler's naval program was designed to avoid antagonizing Britain. However, these assessments were essentially correct. Nazi territorial ambitions *were* oriented eastward, Hitler did *not* initially expect to go to war with Britain, and the German navy was not at first being built for the purpose of challenging Britain's maritime position. It was only when Hitler realized that Britain might, despite his best efforts, become involved in a European war against him that he finally decided on building up a navy capable of contesting Britain's position at sea.

18 Chatfield to the First Lord, 10 November 1937, ADM 205/80.
19 Chatfield, 'Notes by the First Sea Lord on Sir Robert Vansittart's Memo on the World Situation and Re-armament, and on the comments thereon by Sir Maurice Hankey,' 5 January 1937, CHT/3/1.
20 Wark, *Ultimate Enemy*, chapter 6; Kennedy, 'Net Assessment.'
21 Naval Intelligence Report: Germany, 14 October 1936, ADM 178/137.
22 On the AGNA see Scammell, 'Royal Navy'; Maiolo, *Royal Navy*.
23 PD memorandum, 'Notes on German Naval Strength', 27 May 1935, ADM 116/3373.
24 Maiolo, *Royal Navy*, pp. 66–73.
25 According to Peter Bell, for example, the Admiralty's opposition to Chamberlain's proposals stemmed from 'resentment at seeing denied its primary *raison d'être*, preparations for war with Japan.' He also argues that Chatfield's views were 'blinkered,' 'short-sighted,' and clouded by 'Service loyalty.' *Chamberlain*, pp. 49–52, 138.
26 'Additional Needs of the Navy (June 1939),' draft memorandum by the First Lord, 15 June 1939, ADM 167/104.
27 Chatfield to Warren Fisher, 4 June 1934, CHT/3/1.
28 Undated PD memorandum, 'Relation between the Bomber Force and our future Naval strength,' ADM 205/80.
29 Chatfield memorandum, 5 January 1937, CHT/3/1.
30 DCNS minute to CNS, 6 July 1938, ADM 205/80.
31 Undated PD memorandum, 'Relation between the Bomber Force and our future Naval strength,' ADM 205/80.
32 Ibid.
33 Chatfield, 'Notes by the First Sea Lord', 5 January 1937, CHT/3/1.
34 Ibid.
35 Chatfield to Inskip, 25 January 1938, CHT/3/1.
36 Chatfield, 'Notes by the First Sea Lord', 5 January 1937, CHT/3/1.
37 Phillips, 'Notes on Defence Expenditure Papers,' 10 November 1937, ADM 116/3631.
38 Lambert, 'Seapower 1939–1940'; H. P. Willmott, 'The Organizations: The Admiralty and the Western Approaches,' *The Battle of the Atlantic 1939–1945*, eds Stephen Howarth and Derek Law (London, 1994); Maiolo, *Royal Navy*.
39 Lambert, 'Seapower 1939–1940'; Willmott, 'The Organizations,' p. 182.
40 COS 747 (JP), 'Appreciation of the Situation in the Event of War Against Germany in April, 1939,' 15 July 1938, CAB 53/40.
41 See, for example, 'Naval Appreciation (1937) of War with Germany, 1939,' ADM 199/2365. Naval planning against Germany is well covered in Maiolo, *Royal Navy*, chapters 5 and 7.
42 COS 549, 'Planning for War with Germany,' CAB 53/30.
43 On the Admiralty's appreciation of German naval strategy and the possibility of a German knockout blow against shipping see Maiolo, chapter 3.
44 C-in-C Plymouth Station to Admiralty, 3 September 1937, DRAX 2/10.
45 Ibid.
46 Compare Drax's comments with Churchill's minute of 11 December 1939 to Pound, Phillips and Sir Archibald Carter: 'I could never become responsible [Churchill wrote] for a naval strategy which excluded the offensive

principle and relegated us to keeping open the lines of communications and maintaining the blockade.' *The Churchill War Papers*, ed. Martin Gilbert (New York, 1993), I, p. 498.

47 Chatfield to Drax, 5 November 1937, CHT/4/11.
48 Ibid.

5 The Search for the 'Knock-Out Blow': War Plans against Italy

1 Chatfield to Admiral Fisher, 25 August 1935, CHT/4/5; Steven Morewood, 'The Chiefs of Staff, the 'Men on the Spot' and the Italo-Abyssinian Emergency, 1935–36', *Decisions and Diplomacy*, eds Dick Richardson and Glyn Stone (London, 1885), pp. 83–107.
2 Robert Mallett, *The Italian Navy and Fascist Expansionism 1935–40* (London, 1998), pp. 213–4.
3 PD memorandum 'The Possibilities of the Exercise of Maritime Economic Pressure upon Italy', March 1931, ADM 1/8739/47.
4 Ibid.
5 DPR 15, 'Italo-Abyssinian Dispute', memorandum by the First Sea Lord, 3 September 1935, CAB 16/138.
6 On the Royal Navy and the Abyssinia crisis see Arthur Marder, *From the Dardanelles to Oran* (London, 1974), chapter 3; Roskill, *Naval Policy* (London, 1976), II, chapter 9. The Mediterranean in British defense planning during this period is covered in Lawrence R. Pratt, *East of Malta, West of Suez: Britain's Mediterranean Crisis, 1936–1939* (Cambridge, 1975).
7 Backhouse to Chatfield, 19 September 1935, CHT/4/1; *Portrait of an Admiral*, ed. Arthur J. Marder (London, 1952), p. 192.
8 DPR 19, 'Joint Admiralty and Board of Trade Memorandum on Effects on overseas trade of Great Britain, normally using the Mediterranean, in event of war against Italy', 10 September 1935, CAB 16/138.
9 DPR 15, 'Italo-Abyssinian Dispute,' memorandum by the First Sea Lord, 3 September 1935, CAB 16/138.
10 Chatfield to Pound, 5 August 1937, CHT/4/10.
11 Chatfield to Dreyer, 16 September 1935, CHT/4/4.
12 Pound to Admiralty, 'The Strategical aspect of the Situation in the Mediterranean on 1st October 1938' and 'Situation in the Mediterranean – 1st October, 1938,' both dated 14 November 1938, ADM 116/3900.
13 Pound to Admiralty, 'The Strategical aspect of the Situation in the Mediterranean on 1st October 1938,' 14 November 1938, ADM 116/3900.
14 Pound to Admiralty, 'Strategy in the Mediterranean,' 10 May 1939, ADM 116/3900.
15 Minute by D of P, 13 June 1939; Admiralty to Pound, 6 July 1939, ADM 116/3900.
16 Stanhope minute to DCNS, 2 April 1939, ADM 1/9897.
17 Drax, 'Major Strategy,' 1 February 1939, DRAX 2/11.
18 Pratt, *East of Malta, West of Suez*, chapters 6 and 7. On French attitudes at this time see Reynolds Salerno, 'The French Navy and the Appeasement of Italy, 1937–9,' *English Historical Review* (1997), 66–104.

19 Pound to Cunningham, 24 July 1939, Cunningham Papers, Add. 52560.
20 DTSD (Director of Training and Staff Duties) Minute, 8 June 1939, ADM 1/10076. A study by the Tactical School, Portsmouth, in April 1939 also concluded that 'immediate offensive action against the Italians was imperative, not only for the actual material results obtainable, but also on account of the effect such operations would undoubtedly have on the enemy's morale.' ADM 1/10076.
21 On offensive operations against Italy see also Pound to Admiralty, 15 May 1939, 1/9946; Cunningham to Pound, 26 July 1939, Cunningham Papers, Add. 52560; Pratt, *East of Malta, West of Suez*, p. 186.
22 Report by the Tactical School, HM Dockyard, Portsmouth, 21 April 1939, ADM 1/10076.

6   Neither Corbett nor Mahan: British Naval Strategy and War Planning

1 Chatfield to Warren Fisher, 4 June 1934, CHT/3/1.
2 CID 131–C, Admiralty memorandum, 'Empire Naval Policy and Cooperation,' February 1921, CAB 5/4.
3 Beatty to his wife, 5 August 1920, *Beatty Papers*, II, p. 97.
4 Beatty to his wife, 4 August 1920, ibid., p. 96.
5 Keyes' plan for war with Turkey, dated 6 February 1926, is published in *Keyes Papers*, II, pp. 166–76. See also CID 512-B, 'Military situation in Iraq,' Report by COS, 4 November 1924, CAB 4/11.
6 Captain B.H. Liddell Hart, 'Economic Pressures or Continental Victories,' *Journal of the Royal United Services Institute*, 76 (1931), 486–510; on the relevance of this theory to British practice since the seventeenth century, see David French, *The British Way in Warfare 1688–2000* (London, 1990). John Mearsheimer notes that Liddell Hart abandoned this theory around 1933: *Liddell Hart and the Weight of History* (Ithaca, NY, 1989), p. 93.
7 See in particular Richmond's *National Policy and Naval Strength*. Andrew Lambert's preface to the Gregg edition notes Richmond's central role in the development of the idea of a 'British way in warfare.'
8 On British war planning before the First World War see Paul Haggie, 'The Royal Navy and War Planning in the Fisher Era', *The War Plans of the Great Powers 1880–1914*, ed. Paul Kennedy (Boston, 1979); and *The Fisher Papers*, ed. P. K. Kemp (London, 1964), Vol. II.
9 Marder, *Dardanelles*, p. 52; David MacGregor, 'The Use, Misuse, and Non-Use of History: The Royal Navy and the Operational Lessons of the First World War', *Journal of Military History*, 56 (October 1992), 603–15; Allan Millett, 'Assault from the Sea,' *Military Innovation in the Interwar Period*, eds Williamson Murray and Arthur Millett (Cambridge, 1996), pp. 50–95.
10 Admiral Sir John Fisher to King Edward VII, 4 October 1907, *Fear God and Dread Nought*, ed. Arthur J. Marder (London, 1956), II, p. 143.
11 CID 131–C, 'Empire Naval Policy and Co-operation,' February 1921, CAB 5/4.

12 PD Memorandum, 'The Possibilities of the Exercise of Maritime Economic Pressure upon Italy,' March 1931, ADM 1/8739/47.

13 CID 845-B, 'Economic Pressure on Soviet Russia: Report of the Advisory Committee on Trading and Blockade in Time of War,' 28 November 1927, CAB 4/17.

14 'War with Russia: Naval Appreciation,' August 1932, ADM 116/3480.

15 Wemyss memorandum, 'Future Naval Programme,' 24 March 1919, ADM 167/58.

16 PD memorandum, 'The Possibilities of the Exercise of Maritime Economic Pressure on France,' August 1930, ADM 1/8739/45.

17 Ibid.

18 COS 209th Mtg, 1 June 1937, CAB 53/7.

19 Bryan Ranft, 'The Protection of British Seaborne Trade and the Development of Systematic Planning for War, 1860–1906,' *Technical Change and British Naval Policy, 1860–1939*, ed. Bryan Ranft (London, 1977).

20 Corbett, *Some Principles*. On the resistance within naval circles to Corbett's ideas, see Donald Schurman, *Julian S. Corbett, 1854–1922* (London, 1981).

21 *Beatty Papers*, II, p. 176.

22 'Naval Staff Appreciation of Requirements for the 1935 Naval Conference,' April 1934, ADM 1/8802.

23 Roskill, *Naval Policy*, I, pp. 534–5; Marder, *Dardanelles*, pp. 48–9; Barnett, *Engage the Enemy*, p. 44.

24 On British battle-fleet tactics during the interwar period see Sumida, 'Best Laid Plans' and Till, *Air Power*, chapter 6.

25 Geoffrey Till, 'Adopting the Aircraft Carrier: The British, American, and Japanese Case Studies,' *Military Innovation in the Interwar Period*, eds Williamson Murray and Alan Millett, (Cambridge, 1996).

26 Herbert Richmond, *National Policy and Naval Strength* (Aldershot, 1993), p. 219.

27 Corbett, *Some Principles*, p. 16.

28 Backhouse to Admiral Sir Ragnar Colvin, 9 January 1939, ADM 205/3.

29 Lord Chatfield, *The Navy and Defence* (London, 1942), p. 219.

30 CID 134th Mtg, 14 December 1920, CAB 2/3.

31 Pound to Cunningham, 1 December 1940, Cunningham papers, Add. 52561. The loss of the *Prince of Wales* and *Repulse* was one such occasion. Robert Bruce Lockhart describes the scene in his club the day after their loss: 'Going into the smoking-room, crowded with high-ranking naval and military officers, was like entering a Scottish house in which the will is being read after a funeral. There were drinks on the table, but gloom on every face. Officers spoke in low tones. The atmosphere was heavy with the dead weight of tradition. Military defeats are the initial fate of the English in almost every war and can be borne with stoical courage. A disaster to the navy is unthinkable and unbearable.' R. H. Bruce Lockhart, *Comes the Reckoning* (New York, 1972), p. 146.

32 DNI to FO, 17 October 1935, FO 371/19619.

33 CID 134th Mtg, 14 December 1920, CAB 2/3; see also Beatty's letter to Long, 15 December 1920, *Beatty Papers*, II, p. 126.

7   'Showing the Flag': Deterrence, and the Naval Armaments Industry

1   'Notes by the First Sea Lord,' 5 July 1929, PRO 30/69/267.
2   Chatfield memorandum, 11 September 1937, ADM 1/9909.
3   Crosby to FO, 7 November 1938 and 17 February 1939, FO 371/23544; Head of M minute,16 December 1938, ADM 1/9909.
4   Craigie to FO, 23 March 1939, ADM 116/4087.
5   Craigie to FO, 15 December 1938, FO 371/23544; Craigie's proposal was endorsed by Sir Archibald Clark Kerr, the ambassador to China.
6   Nicholls minute, 23 January 1939, FO 371/23544.
7   'Memorandum Respecting the Proposal to Station a British Battle Squadron Permanently at Singapore,' 27 January 1939, FO 371/23544; *Documents on British Foreign Policy* (London) Series III, Vol. VIII, Appendix 1; Pritchard, *Far Eastern Influence upon British Strategy*, pp. 133–7; Haggie, *Britannia*, pp. 130–2.
8   Backhouse minute, 24 March 1939, ADM 1/9909.
9   Backhouse minutes, 16 February, 1 March and 24 March 1939, ADM 1/9909.
10   FE (40) 65, R. A. Butler memorandum, 'Far Eastern Situation,' 23 November 1940, CAB 96/1.
11   David Day, *The Great Betrayal* (New York, 1988), *passim*; Marder, *Old Friends*, p. 215; COS (41)80(O), 'Despatch of a Fleet to the Far East,' 18 May 1941, CAB 80/57; Menzies to Churchill, 11 August 1941, PREM 3/156/1.
12   Churchill to the First Lord and First Sea Lord, 25 August 1941, in Churchill, *Second World War*, III, appendix K; also PREM 3/156/1.
13   Pound to Churchill, 28 August 1941, ibid.
14   Churchill to Pound, 25 and 29 August 1941, ibid.
15   Eden to Churchill, 12 September 1941, FO 371/27981; Antony Best, *Britain, Japan and Pearl Harbor: Avoiding War in East Asia, 1936–41* (London 1995), p. 172.
16   JP(41)816, 'Japan: Our Future Policy', 7 October 1941, Annex I, CAB 84/35.
17   Eden to Churchill, 16 October 1941, DO(41)21, CAB 69/3.
18   DO (41) 65th Meeting, 17 October 1941, CAB 69/2; DO(41) 66th Meeting, 20 October 1941, CAB 69/8.
19   On the Admiralty's opposition to the movement of these vessels see Marder, *Old Friends*, chapter VIII, and Roskill, *The War at Sea* (London, 1954), I, pp. 553–9.
20   Phillips to Pound, 17 October 1941, ADM 178/322. This letter was written to fill Pound in on the 17 October Defence Committee meeting, which he was unable to attend.
21   Best, *Britain, Japan and Pearl Harbor*, chapter 8; Bell, 'Our Most Exposed Outpost', pp. 84–7.
22   Best, *Britain, Japan, and Pearl Harbor*, chapter 8; Christopher Thorne, *Allies of a Kind* (London, 1978), pp. 71–4.
23   Admiralty memorandum, 'Admiralty Proposals for Reduction in Expenditure,' ADM 167/66.
24   Foreign Office Letter A431-431-51, 24 January 1921, quoted by the DOD in his minute of 4 December 1922, ADM 116/2129.
25   DNI minute, 28 May 1921, ADM 116/2129.

26 DNI minute, 30 November 1922, ADM 116/2129.
27 Ibid.
28 DOD minute, 4 December 1922, ADM 116/2129.
29 Keyes minute, 1 January 1923, ADM 116/2129.
30 Keyes minute, 18 January 1923, ADM 116/2129.
31 Board of Admiralty minute 1984, 4 December 1924, ADM 167/69.
32 Undated BOT memorandum, ADM 167/72.
33 P. Cunliffe-Lister to Bridgeman, 22 December 1924, ADM 167/72.
34 Austen Chamberlain to Bridgeman, 18 December 1924, ADM 167/72.
35 Board of Admiralty minute 1995, 1 January 1925, ADM 167/71.
36 On the Admiralty's relationship with the British naval armaments industry
    during the interwar period see in particular Gordon, *Seapower*, and Ferris,
    'Last Decade'.
37 Fisher minute, 29 October 1926, ADM 116/2568.
38 Fisher minute, 29 October 1926, ADM 116/2568.
39 Cunningham of Hyndhope, *A Sailor's Odyssey* (London, 1951), pp. 132–3.
40 Malcolm A. Robertson to Beatty, 1 August 1927, ADM 167/76.
41 D of P minute, 2 September 1927, ADM 116/2568.
42 DNI minute, 16 September 1927, ADM 116/2568.
43 Board of Admiralty minute 2388, 3 November 1927, ADM 167/75.
44 Board of Admiralty minute 2813, 31 March 1931, ADM 167/83.
45 Admiralty to Treasury, 3 July 1928, ADM 1/8728/173.
46 Treasury to Admiralty, 31 August 1928, ADM 1/8728/173.
47 DNI minute, 12 October 1928, ADM 1/8728/173.
48 Treasury to Admiralty, 20 December 1928, ADM 1/8728/173.
49 Drax to Admiralty, 4 July 1932, ADM 116/3061.
50 Head of M Branch minute, 25 July 1932, ADM 116/3061.
51 Drax to Little, 1 April 1933, ADM 116/3061.
52 Wemyss minute, 1 July 1919, ADM 1/8603/57.
53 Commander Diggle to HM Chargé d'affaires, Bucharest, 9 September 1919,
    ADM 116/1899.
54 Ottley to Sinclair, 20 September 1919, ADM 116/1899. Ottley, a former DNI,
    was in Romania as a representative of Vickers.
55 DNI minute, 1 October 1919, ADM 116/1899.
56 DNI minute, 8 June 1921, ADM 116/1899.
57 Wemyss to Admiral John Kelly, 17 February 1919, Kelly Papers, KEL/28.
58 DNI minute, 25 March 1925, ADM 116/2298.
59 Treasury to the Undersecretary of State, FO, 4 February 1925, ADM 116/2298.
60 DNI minute, 11 May 1925, ADM 116/2298.
61 DNC minute, 16 May 1925, ADM 116/2298.
62 Treasury to Admiralty, 26 October 1925, ADM 116/2298.
63 Murray minute, 24 April 1926 and Chatfield minute, 27 April 1926, ADM
    116/2298.
64 Bridgeman minute, 29 April 1926, ADM 116/2298.
65 Minute by head of military branch, 1 February 1933, ADM 116/3251.
66 Unidentified minute of 16 May 1933, ADM 116/3251.
67 Baillie-Grohman, 'Report on British Naval Mission in Nanking,' 11 February
    1932, Baillie-Grohman Papers, GRO/5.
68 ACNS minute, 10 June 1933, ADM 116/3251.

69 For an outline of the training provided to foreign officers prior to the First World War see the undated CW memorandum in ADM 1/9167.
70 Board of Admiralty minute 2070, 21 July 1925, ADM 167/71.
71 Board of Admiralty minute 2180, 8 March 1926, ADM 167/73.
72 CW memorandum, 'Foreign Officers – Training Afloat,' 5 March 1926, ADM 167/74.
73 Board of Admiralty minute 2180, 8 March 1926, ADM 167/73.
74 Appendix to Board of Admiralty minute 2418, 20 December 1927, ADM 167/75.
75 Undated memorandum by Murray, 'Training of Foreign Officers in the Royal Navy: Future Policy,' ADM 167/87.
76 Board of Admiralty minute 3004, 20 October 1932, ADM 167/85.
77 DNI minute, 14 May 1937, ADM 1/9167.
78 Chatfield minute, 4 November 1926, ADM 1/8696/57.
79 Ibid.
80 DNI minute, 19 October 1925, ADM 1/8695/35.
81 Memorandum by Dreyer and Chatfield, 9 February 1926, ADM 1/8695/35.
82 Ibid.
83 Minute by Henderson to the First Sea Lord, 21 September 1937, ADM 116/3921.
84 DNO minute, 27 July 1937, ADM 116/4394.
85 Controller minute, 13 March 1939, ADM 116/3921.
86 Backhouse minute, 15 March 1939, ADM 116/3921.

8 'Something Very Sordid': Naval Propaganda and the British Public

1 'Address to Men of the Combined Home and Mediterranean Fleets,' 19 March 1938, CHT/3/4.
2 Hardinge to Hankey, 21 June 1934, CAB 21/388.
3 For example, John MacKenzie, *Propaganda and Empire* (Manchester, 1984); John MacKenzie (ed.), *Popular Imperialism and the Military, 1850–1950* (Manchester, 1992).
4 Rear Admiral Sir Douglas Brownrigg, *Indiscretions of the Naval Censor* (London, 1920), pp. 37–9, 70, 152; Gary Messinger, *British Propaganda and the State in the First World War* (Manchester, 1992), pp. 48, 115–18.
5 Keyes to Lt-Colonel Norman Thwaites, 18 March 1919, *Keyes Papers*, II, pp. 20–3.
6 ADM 167/57.
7 W. Rudolph Bentinck minute, 2 June 1919, ADM 1/8559/149.
8 H. Manisty minute to First Sea Lord, 10 June 1919, ADM 1/8559/149; CMD 451, *Statement of the First Lord Explanatory of Navy Estimates 1919–20.*
9 Beatty to de Robeck, 30 November 1919, de Robeck Papers, DRBK 5/13.
10 [Lt T. Davys Manning], 'The Silent Service,' *Naval Review*, XV (1927), 614.
11 Burnham to Hurd, 11 October 1926, HURD 1/12.
12 Hurd to Burnham, 12 October 1926, HURD 1/12.
13 Hector Bywater, *A Searchlight on the Navy* (London, 1935), p. 50. See also William Honan, *Bywater* (London, 1990) for Bywater's career and relationship with the Admiralty during this period.

14 *The Navy*, February 1920, p. 28.

15 Beatty to Long, 20 June 1922, Beatty Papers, BTY/13/28/58.

16 *The Navy*, November 1928, p. 326.

17 Callender, 'The Navy League,' *The Navy*, July 1926, p. 206.

18 A public meeting at Winchester House on 28 March 1924 to protest the decision to cancel work on the Singapore base included as speakers Lord Carson (in the chair), Lord Curzon, Leopold Amery, and Winston Churchill. A similar meeting at the Cannon Street Hotel on 26 February 1930 to denounce the London Naval Treaty featured Winston Churchill as the principal speaker. *The Navy*, May 1924, pp. 132–9 and April 1930, pp. 101–4.

19 See in particular Nicholas Reeves, *Official British Film Propaganda During the First World War* (London, 1986); Brownrigg, *Indiscretions, passim*.

20 Ibid., p. 152.

21 Geddes to Beatty, undated, ADM 116/1805.

22 DPTS minute, December 1925, ADM 116/2490.

23 Ibid.

24 Memorandum by Murray, 'Naval Facilities for the Production of Films,' 31 October 1927, ADM 167/76.

25 Ibid.

26 Board of Admiralty minute 2389, 3 November 1927, ADM 167/75.

27 Fisher minute, 2 January 1929, ADM 116/2669.

28 Report of the Naval Cinematograph Films Committee, undated, ADM 116/2669.

29 Fisher to Chatfield, 21 July 1933, CHT/4/5.

30 Mr Justice Charles, 'Notes of Judgement,' 18 January 1932, ADM 116/2490.

31 Board of Admiralty minute 2952, 2 June 1932, ADM 167/85.

32 Memorandum by Murray, 'Admiralty Policy in regard to Naval Facilities for the Production of Films,' 15 November 1933, ADM 167/89. The USN did indeed enjoy a close relationship with the American film industry during these years, although not to the extent implied here. See Lawrence Suid, *Sailing on the Silver Screen: Hollywood and the U.S. Navy* (Annapolis, MD, 1996), chapters 1–2.

33 Lee of Fareham, 'The British Film Industry and the Question of Naval Facilities,' 10 November 1933, ADM 167/89.

34 Board of Admiralty minute 3139, 30 November 1933, ADM 167/88.

35 Board of Admiralty minute 3146, 7 December 1933, ADM 167/88.

36 Rachael Low, *Documentary and Educational Films of the 1930s* (London, 1979), p. 58.

37 C-in-C Portsmouth to Admiralty, 7 February 1927, ADM 116/2478.

38 Memorandum by Charles Walker, 'Proposed "Naval Charities Week" at Portsmouth,' 10 March 1927, ADM 167/76.

39 Board of Admiralty minute 2314, 23 March 1927, ADM 167/75.

40 C-in-C Portsmouth to Admiralty, 14 September 1927, 'Report on "Naval Charities Week" – Portsmouth,' ADM 116/2478.

41 C-in-C Plymouth to Admiralty, 'Trafalgar Day Orphan Fund – New Method of Collection,' 3 July 1927, ADM 116/2478. Admiral Goodenough, C-in-C the Nore, also believed that the 'spectacle of the Navy annually appealing for funds by pageants, etc., for orphanages, which in some cases really do not require the money, is becoming increasingly distasteful to all those who know the facts.' Goodenough to Admiralty, 12 May 1927, ADM 116/2478.

42 Board of Admiralty minute 2452, 13 March 1928, ADM 167/77.
43 C-in-C Portsmouth to Admiralty, 12 November 1928, ADM 116/2478.
44 *The Times*, 8 August 1938, p. 17.
45 Memorandum by Commander C. W. Round-Turner, 1928, ADM 116/2478.
46 Board of Admiralty minute 3279, 14 February 1935, ADM 167/92.
47 Memorandum by Murray, 'Navy Week,' 12 February 1935, ADM 167/93.
48 Draft Souvenir Programme, ADM 116/2478.
49 *The Navy*, September 1933; *The Times*, 7 August 1933, p. 7; 3 August 1936, p. 7.
50 *The Times*, 2 August 1938, p. 7.
51 For descriptions of the full programs for individual Navy Weeks see 'Navy Week,' *Naval Review*, 1935, pp. 726–34, and Nauticus, 'The Pleasure of Your Company,' *The Navy*, July 1938.
52 *The Navy*, September 1933.
53 C-in-C Portsmouth to the Second Sea Lord, 12 February 1935, ADM 167/93.
54 Simon minute, 7 June 1934, W5693/1/98, FO 371/18527.
55 Trenchard to Churchill, 6 April 1937, Churchill papers, CHAR 2/305.
56 Chatfield, *It Might Happen Again*, p. 163.
57 Peden, *British Rearmament*, p. 205.
58 According to David French, Britain's ratio of spending on its land, sea and air forces during the Second World War was 38 : 36 : 26, indicating a substantial improvement in the navy's overall relative position during the course of the war. According to figures provided by Peden, this ratio in 1939 was approximately 38:23:39. French, *The British Way*, p. 227; Peden, *British Rearmament*, p. 205.

Conclusion

1 CID 158th Mtg, 5 July 1922, CAB 2/3.
2 Andrew Lambert dates the 'liberal illusion' of the navy as a purely defensive force from the mid-Victorian period. 'The Royal Navy, 1856–1914', *Navies and Global Defense*, eds Keith Neilson and Elizabeth Jane Errington (Westport, CT, 1995), p. 18.
3 *The Navy*, February 1930, p. 50.
4 Chatfield, *It Might Happen Again*, pp. 12, 114.
5 NP (27) 2nd Conclusions, 18 November 1927, CAB 27/355.
6 *The Navy*, February 1922, p. 23.
7 Richmond to Keyes, 29 June 1942, *Keyes Papers*, ed. Paul Halpern (London, 1981), III, p. 251.

Bibliography

Primary sources

Unpublished documents
Public Record Office, London

ADM 1	Admiralty and Secretariat Papers
ADM 116	Admiralty and Secretariat Cases
ADM 167	Board of Admiralty Minutes and Memoranda
ADM 178	Admiralty Papers and Cases, Supplementary Series
ADM 205	First Sea Lord Papers
CAB 2	Committee of Imperial Defence Minutes
CAB 4	Committee of Imperial Defence, Imperial Defence Memoranda
CAB 5	Committee of Imperial Defence, Colonial Defence Memoranda
CAB 16	Committee of Imperial Defence *Ad Hoc* Sub-Committees
CAB 21	Cabinet Office Registered Files
CAB 23	Cabinet Minutes
CAB 24	Cabinet Memoranda
CAB 27	Cabinet Committees, General Series
CAB 29	International Conferences
CAB 47	Advisory Committee on Trade Questions in Time of War
CAB 53	Chiefs of Staff Committee
CAB 54	Deputy Chiefs of Staff Committee
CAB 55	Joint Planning Committee
FO 371	Foreign Office, General Correspondence, Political
PREM 1	Prime Minister's Office
PRO 30/69	Ramsay MacDonald Papers
T 161	Supply Files
T172	Chancellor of the Exchequer's Office, Miscellaneous Papers
T175	Sir Richard V. N. Hopkins Papers

Private papers

British Museum:

Viscount Cunningham of Hyndhope
Admiral of the Fleet Lord Keyes
Walter Long, First Viscount Long

Churchill College Archives Centre, Cambridge:

1st Earl Alexander of Hillsborough
Sir Winston S. Churchill
Admiral Sir John M. de Robeck
Admiral Sir Reginald Plunkett-Ernle-Erle Drax
Admiral Sir Frederic Charles Dreyer
1st Baron Hankey
Sir Archibald Hurd
Admiral of the Fleet Sir Alfred Dudley Pound
Captain Stephen S. Roskill
Admiral of the Fleet Rosslyn Erskine-Wemyss, 1st Baron Wester
  Wemyss of Wemyss

Liddell Hart Centre for Military Archives, King's College, London:

Sir Basil Liddell Hart

National Maritime Museum, Greenwich:

Vice-Admiral Harold Tom Baillie-Grohman
Admiral of the Fleet Earl Beatty
Admiral of the Fleet Baron Chatfield
Sir Julian Corbett
Admiral Sir Walter Henry Cowan
Admiral Sir W. A. Howard Kelly
Admiral Sir Herbert Richmond

Wiltshire Record Office:

Walter Long, First Viscount Long

Published sources

Periodicals

The Journal of the Royal United Services Institute
Naval Review
The Navy
The Times

Published primary sources

Documents on British Foreign Policy 1919–1939, 4th Series, London, 1946–77.
House of Commons Debates [Hansard], Series 3–5.

Bond, Brian (ed.). *Chief of Staff: The Diaries of Lieutenant-General Sir Henry Pownall*, vol. I. London, 1972.
Clarke, Alan (ed.). *'A Good Innings': The Private Papers of Viscount Lee of Fareham*. London, 1974.
Halpern, Paul G. (ed.). *The Keyes Papers*, 3 vols. London, 1979–81.
Hattendorf, John B. et al. (eds). *British Naval Documents 1204–1960*. Aldershot, 1993.
Marder, Arthur J. (ed.). *Portrait of an Admiral*. London, 1952.
Marder, Arthur J. (ed.). *Fear God and Dread Nought*, 3 vols. London, 1952–9.
Patterson, A. Temple (ed.). *The Jellicoe Papers*, 2 vols. London, 1966–8.
Ranft, B. McL. (ed.). *The Beatty Papers*, 2 vols. Aldershot, 1989–93.
Simpson, Michael (ed.). *Anglo-American Naval Relations 1917–1919*. Aldershot, 1991.
Tracy, Nicholas (ed.). *The Collective Naval Defence of the Empire, 1900–1940*. Aldershot, 1997.

Secondary sources

Monographs

Barnett, Correlli. *Engage the Enemy More Closely*. New York, 1991.
Beesly, Patrick. *Very Special Intelligence*. London, 1977.
——. *Very Special Admiral*. London, 1980.
Bell, Peter. *Chamberlain, Germany and Japan, 1933–4*. London, 1996.
Best, Antony. *Britain, Japan and Pearl Harbor: Avoiding War in East Asia, 1936–41*. London, 1995.
Bialer, Uri. *The Shadow of the Bomber*. London, 1980.
Brownrigg, Rear Admiral Sir Douglas. *Indiscretions of the Naval Censor*. London, 1920.
Bywater, Hector. *A Searchlight on the Navy*. London, 1935.
Chatfield, Lord. *The Navy and Defence*. London, 1942.
——. *It Might Happen Again*. London, 1947.
Churchill, Winston. *The World Crisis*, 5 vols. London, 1923–31.
——. *The Second World War*, vols 1–3, London, 1948–50.
Corbett, Julian S. *Some Principles of Maritime Strategy*. London, 1988.
Cowman, Ian. *Dominion or Decline*. Oxford, 1996.
Cunningham of Hyndhope, *A Sailor's Odyssey*. London, 1951.
Day, David. *The Great Betrayal*. New York, 1989.
Dewar, Vice-Admiral K. G. B. *The Navy From Within*. London, 1939.
Domvile, Admiral Sir Barry. *By and Large*. London, 1936.
Dreyer, Admiral Sir Frederic. *The Sea Heritage*. London, 1955.
Ferris, John. *Men, Money, and Diplomacy*. Ithaca, NY, 1989.
Freedman, Lawrence, Paul Hayes, and Robert O'Neill. *War, Strategy and International Politics*. Oxford, 1992.

French, David. *The British Way in Warfare 1688–2000*. London, 1990.

Gibbs, N. H. *Grand Strategy*, vol. I. London, 1976.

Gilbert, Martin. *Winston S. Churchill*, vols III–VI. London, 1971–95.

Goldrick, James and John B. Hattendorf (eds). *Mahan Is Not Enough*. Newport, RI, 1993.

Gordon, G. A. H. *British Seapower and Procurement Between the Wars*. Annapolis, MD, 1988.

Gray, Colin. *The Leverage of Seapower*. New York, 1992.

——. and Roger W. Barnett (eds). *Seapower and Strategy*. Annapolis, MD, 1989.

Grenfell, Russell. *Main Fleet to Singapore*. London, 1951.

Gretton, Vice-Admiral Sir Peter. *Former Naval Person*. London, 1968.

Haggie, Paul. *Britannia At Bay*. Oxford, 1981.

Hall, Christopher. *Britain, America and Arms Control, 1921–37*. New York, 1987.

Hamill, Ian. *The Strategic Illusion*. Singapore, 1981.

Hattendorf, John and Robert Jordan (eds). *Maritime Strategy and the Balance of Power*. London, 1989.

Hill, J. R. *The Oxford Illustrated History of the Royal Navy*. Oxford, 1995.

Hinsley, F. H. et al. *British Intelligence in the Second World War*, vol. I. London, 1979.

Honan, William. *Bywater*. London, 1990.

Howard, Michael. *The Continental Commitment*. Harmondsworth, 1974.

Hunt, Barry. *Sailor–Scholar: Admiral Sir Herbert Richmond, 1871–1946*. Waterloo, Ontario, 1982.

Jordan, Gerald. *Naval Warfare in the Twentieth Century*. London, 1977.

Kennedy, Paul. *The Rise and Fall of British Naval Mastery*. London, 1976.

——. *The Realities Behind Diplomacy*. London, 1981.

Kirby, S. Woodburn. *Singapore: Chain of Disaster*. New York, 1971.

Leutze, James. *Bargaining for Supremacy: Anglo-American Naval Collaboration, 1937–1941*. Chapel Hill, NC, 1977.

Louis, Wm Roger. *British Strategy in the Far East 1919–1939*. Oxford, 1971.

Low, Rachael. *The History of the British Film*, vols 3–7. London, 1971–85.

McIntyre, W. David. *The Rise and Fall of the Singapore Naval Base, 1919–1942*. London, 1979.

MacKenzie, John M. *Propaganda and Empire*. Manchester, 1984.

—— (ed.). *Imperialism and Popular Culture*. Manchester, 1986.

—— (ed.). *Popular Imperialism and the Military, 1850–1950*. Manchester, 1992.

McKercher, B. J. C. *The Second Baldwin Government and the United States, 1924–1929*. Cambridge, 1984.

—— (ed.). *Arms Limitation and Disarmament: Restraints on War, 1899–1939*. Westport, CT 1992.

Mahan, Captain A. T. *The Influence of Sea Power upon the French Revolution and Empire 1793–1812*, 4th edn. Boston, 1894.

——. *The Influence of Sea Power upon History, 1660–1783*. Williamstown, KY, 1978.

Maiolo, Joseph. *The Royal Navy and Nazi Germany, 1933–39*. London, 1998.

Mallett, Robert. *The Italian Navy and Fascist Expansionism 1935–40*. London, 1998.

Marder, Arthur. *From the Dreadnought to Scapa Flow*, 5 vols. Oxford, 1961–71.

——. *From the Dardanelles to Oran*. London, 1974.

——. *Old Friends, New Enemies*, vol. I. Oxford, 1981.

May, Ernest (ed.). *Knowing One's Enemies*. Princeton, NJ, 1986.

Medlicott, W. N. *The Economic Blockade*, 2 vols. London, 1952 and 1959.

Messinger, Gary. *British Propaganda and the State in the First World War*. Manchester, 1992.

Miller, Edward S. *War Plan Orange*. Annapolis, MD, 1997.

Murfett, Malcolm H. *Fool-Proof Relations*. Singapore, 1984.

—— (ed.). *The First Sea Lords: From Fisher to Mountbatten*. Westport, CT, 1995.

Murray, Williamson and Alan Millett (eds). *Military Innovation in the Interwar Period*. Cambridge, 1996.

Neidpath, James. *The Singapore Naval Base and the Defence of Britain's Eastern Empire, 1919–1941*. Oxford, 1981.

Neilson, Keith and Elizabeth Jane Errington (eds). *Navies and Global Defense*. Westport, CT, 1995.

Neilson, Keith and Greg Kennedy (eds). *Far Flung Lines*. London, 1996.

Nish, Ian (ed.). *Anglo-Japanese Naval Relations*. London, 1985.

Ong Chit Chung, *Operation Matador: Britain's War Plans Against the Japanese 1918–1941*. Singapore, 1997.

Paret, Peter (ed.). *Makers of Modern Strategy from Machiavelli to the Nuclear Age*. Oxford, 1990.

Parker, R. A. C. *Winston Churchill: Studies in Statesmanship*. London, 1995.

Patterson, A. Temple. *Tyrwhitt of the Harwich Force*. London, 1973.

Peden, G. C. *British Rearmament and the Treasury: 1932–1939*. Edinburgh, 1979.

Postan, M. M. *British War Production*. London, 1952.

Pratt, Lawrence R. *East of Malta, West of Suez: Britain's Mediterranean Crisis, 1936–1939*. Cambridge, 1975.

Pritchard, R. J. *Far Eastern Influence upon British Strategy Towards the Great Powers, 1937–39*. New York, 1987.

Ranft, Bryan (ed.). *Technical Change and British Naval Policy, 1860–1939*. London, 1977.

Richmond, Admiral Sir Herbert. *Sea Power in the Modern World*. London, 1934.

——. *The Navy*. London, 1937.

——. *Statesmen and Sea Power*. Oxford, 1947.

——. *National Policy and Naval Strength*. Aldershot, 1993.

Roskill, Stephen. *The War at Sea*, vol. I. London, 1954.

——. *Naval Policy Between the Wars*, 2 vols. London, 1968 and 1976.

——. *Hankey: Man of Secrets*, 3 vols. London, 1970–4.

——. *Churchill and the Admirals*. London, 1977.

——. *Admiral of the Fleet Earl Beatty*. New York, 1981.

——. *The Strategy of Sea Power*. Aylesbury, 1986.

Schurman, Donald M. *The Education of a Navy*. London, 1965.

——. *Julian S. Corbett, 1854–1922*. London, 1981.

Shay, Robert Paul, Jr. *British Rearmament in the Thirties*. Princeton, NJ, 1977.

Till, Geoffrey. *Air Power and the Royal Navy*. London, 1979.

——. *Maritime Strategy and the Nuclear Age*. London, 1982.

Tracy, Nicholas. *Attack on Maritime Trade*. Toronto, 1991.

Wark, Wesley. *The Ultimate Enemy*. London, 1985.

Watt, D. C. *Too Serious A Business*. London, 1975.

Wolff, Michael (ed.). *Winston S. Churchill: The Collected Essays*, 4 vols. London, 1976.

Articles

Babij, Orest. 'The Second Labour Government and British Maritime Security, 1929–1931', *Diplomacy and Statecraft*, 6 (November 1995), 645–71.

——. 'Advisory Committee on Trade and Blockade in Time of War, 1920–1934', *The Northern Mariner*, VII (July 1997), 1–10.

Bell, Christopher M. '"Our Most Exposed Outpost": Hong Kong and British Far Eastern Strategy, 1921–1941.' *Journal of Military History*, 60 (January, 1996), 61–88.

——. 'The Royal Navy, War Planning and Intelligence Assessments of Japan between the Wars,' Paper presented to a Symposium on Intelligence and International Relations, Yale University, 3 May 1996.

——. '"How are we going to make war?": Admiral Sir Herbert Richmond and British Far Eastern War Plans,' *Journal of Strategic Studies*, 20 (September 1997), 123–41.

——. 'Thinking the Unthinkable: American and British Naval Strategies for an Anglo-American War, 1918–31', *International History Review*, XIX (November 1997), 789–808.

Best, Antony. 'Constructing an Image: British Intelligence and Whitehalls Perception of Japan, 1931–1939,' *Intelligence and National Security*, 11 (July 1996), 403–23.

——. '"This Probably Over-Valued Military Power": British Intelligence and Whitehall's Perception of Japan, 1939–41,' *Intelligence and National Security*, 12 (July 1997), 67–94.

Brown, David K. 'Naval Rearmament, 1930–1941: The Royal Navy', *Revue Internationale d'Histoire Militaire*, 73 (1991), 11–29.

Cowman, Ian. 'An Admiralty "Myth": The Search for an Advanced Far Eastern Fleet Base before the Second World War,' *Journal of Strategic Studies*, 8 (September 1985), 317–26.

——. 'Main Fleet to Singapore? Churchill, the Admiralty, and Force Z,' *Journal of Strategic Studies*, 18 (March 1995), 79–93.

Dunbabin, J. P. D. 'British Rearmament in the 1930s: a Chronology and Review,' *Historical Journal*, XVIII (1975), 587–609.

Ferris, John R. 'A British "Unofficial" Aviation Mission and Japanese Naval Developments, 1919–29', *Journal of Strategic Studies*, 5 (1982), 416–39.

——. 'The Symbol and Substance of Seapower: Britain, the United States and the One-Power Standard, 1919–1921,' in B. J. C. McKercher (ed.), *Anglo-American Relations in the 1920s*. Edmonton, 1990, 55–80.

——. '"The Greatest Power on Earth": Great Britain in the 1920s,' *International History Review*, XIII (November 1991), 726–50.

——. '"Worthy of Some Better Enemy?": The British Estimate of the Imperial Japanese Army 1919–41, and the Fall of Singapore,' *Canadian Journal of History* XXVIII (August 1993), 223–56.

Gordon, Andrew. 'The Admiralty and Imperial Overstretch, 1902–41', *Journal of Strategic Studies*, 17 (March 1994), 63–85.

Haggie, Paul. 'The Royal Navy and War Planning in the Fisher Era', *The War Plans of the Great Powers 1880–1914*, ed. Paul Kennedy. Boston, 1979.

Hamill, Ian. 'Winston Churchill and the Singapore Naval Base, 1924–1929,' *Journal of Southeast Asian Studies*, 11 (September 1980), 277–86.

Hunt, Barry D. 'British Policy on the Issue of Belligerent and Neutral Rights, 1919–1939,' *New Aspects of Naval History*, ed. Craig L. Symonds. Annapolis, MD, 1981.

Kennedy, Greg C. 'Great Britain's Maritime Strength and the British Merchant Marine, 1922-1935, *The Mariner's Mirror* (February 1994), 66–76.

Kennedy, Paul. 'The Influence and Limitations of Seapower', *International History Review*, X (February 1988), 2–17.

———. 'British "Net Assessment" and the Coming of the Second World War', *Calculations: Net Assessments and the Coming of World War II*. eds. A. R. Millett and W. Murray. New York, 1992.

Lambert, Andrew. 'Seapower 1939–1940: Churchill and the Strategic Origins of the Battle of the Atlantic', *Journal of Strategic Studies*, 17 (March 1994), 86–108.

Liddell Hart, Captain B. H. 'Economic Pressures or Continental Victories', *Journal of the Royal United Services Institute* 76 (1931), 486–510.

McDonald, J. Kenneth. 'Lloyd George and the Search for a Postwar Naval Policy, 1919,' *Lloyd George: Twelve Essays*, ed. A. J. P Taylor. New York, 1971, 191–222.

MacGregor, David. 'The Use, Misuse, and Non-Use of History: The Royal Navy and the Operational Lessons of the First World War,' *Journal of Military History*, 56 (October 1992), 603–15.

———. 'Former Naval Cheapskate: Chancellor of the Exchequer Winston Churchill and the Royal Navy, 1924–29,' *Armed Forces and Society* (Spring 1993), 319–33.

McKercher, B. J. C. 'A Sane and Sensible Diplomacy: Austen Chamberlain, Japan and the Naval Balance of Power in the Pacific Ocean, 1924–1929,' *Canadian Journal of History*, XXI (1986), 187–213.

———. ' "Our Most Dangerous Enemy": Great Britain Pre-Eminent in the 1930s,' *International History Review*, XIII (November 1991), 751–83.

Morewood, Steven. 'The Chiefs of Staff, the "Men on the Spot" and the Italo-Abyssinian Emergency, 1935–36', *Decisions and Diplomacy*, eds. Dick Richardson and Glyn Stone. London, 1885.

Murfett, Malcolm H. '"Living in the Past": A Critical Re-examination of the Singapore Naval Strategy, 1918–1941, *War and Society*, XI (May 1993), 73–103.

Neilson, Keith. '"Greatly Exaggerated": The Myth of the Decline and Fall of Great Britain', *International History Review*, XIII (November 1991), 695–725.

Peden, George. 'Winston Churchill, Neville Chamberlain and the Defence of Empire,' *The Limitations Of Military Power*, eds John B. Hattendorf and Malcom H. Murfett. London, 1990.

Post, Jr., Gaines. 'Mad Dogs and Englishmen: British Rearmament, Deterrence and Appeasement, 1934–35,' *Armed Forces and Society*, 14 (Spring 1988), 329–57.

Pritchard, John. 'Winston Churchill, the Military, and Imperial Defence in East Asia,' *From Pearl Harbor to Hiroshima*, ed. Saki Dockrill. New York, 1994.

Richmond, Admiral Sir Herbert, 'Singapore,' *Fortnightly Review* (March 1942), 240–43.

Salerno, Reynolds M. 'The French Navy and the Appeasement of Italy, 1937–9,' *English Historical Review* 112 (1997), 66–104.

Scammell, Clare. 'The Royal Navy and the Strategic Origins of the Anglo-German Naval Agreement of 1935,' *Journal of Strategic Studies*, 20 (June 1997), 92–118.

Sumida, Jon. '"The Best Laid Plans": The Development of British Battle-Fleet Tactics, 1919–42', *International History Review*, XIV (November 1992).

Till, Geoffrey, 'Perceptions of Naval Power Between the Wars: The British Case,' *Estimating Foreign Military Power*, ed. Peter Towle. London, 1982.

Wark, Wesley. 'In Search of a Suitable Japan: British Naval Intelligence in the Pacific before the Second World War,' *Intelligence and National Security*, I (May 1986) 189–211.

Willmott, H. P. 'The Organizations: The Admiralty and the Western Approaches,' *The Battle of the Atlantic 1939–1945*, eds Stephen Howarth and Derek Law. London, 1994.

Young, Robert J. 'Spokesmen for Economic Warfare: The Industrial Intelligence Centre in the 1930s', *European Studies Review*, 6 (1976), 473–87.

Index